REASONING WITH LAW

Reasoning with Law

ANDREW HALPIN

·HART·
PUBLISHING

OXFORD – PORTLAND OREGON
2001

2001
Hart Publishing
Oxford and Portland, Oregon

Published in North America (US and Canada) by
Hart Publishing c/o
International Specialized Book Services
5804 NE Hassalo Street
Portland, Oregon
97213-3644
USA

Distributed in the Netherlands, Belgium and Luxembourg by
Intersentia, Churchillaan 108
B2900 Schoten
Antwerpen
Belgium

Hart Publishing is a specialist legal publisher based in Oxford, England.
To order further copies of this book or to request a list of other
publications please write to:

Hart Publishing, Salter's Boatyard, Folly Bridge,
Abingdon Road, Oxford OX1 4LB
Telephone: +44 (0)1865 245533 or Fax: +44 (0)1865 794882
e-mail: mail@hartpub.co.uk
WEBSITE: http//www.hartpub.co.uk

British Library Cataloguing in Publication Data
Data Available
ISBN 1–84113–070–2 (hardback)
1–84113–244–6 (paperback)

Typeset by Hope Services (Abingdon) Ltd.
Printed and bound in Great Britain on acid-free paper by
Bell & Bain Ltd., Glasgow

Preface

This book attempts to engage in legal theory without losing touch with the practice of law, and without losing sight of the place legal theory occupies in the wider reflective efforts undertaken across other disciplines concerned with the human situation. I hope that it will be of interest to a variety of readers with differing concerns about the theory and practice of law, and even to some with concerns beyond the law. Those seeking more details of the contents will find them in the brief introduction provided in chapter 1. My own interests in writing the book have been broadened and assisted by a number of people.

I am grateful to the City Solicitors' Educational Trust and the encouragement of Richard Youard for a grant to support a research project on legal reasoning and theory in the core subjects from which chapter 2 draws, and to Richard Southwell of Serle Court chambers for further support for the project. The project culminated in a symposium at Southampton University in April 1997 and I am indebted to the participants, Kit Barker, Tony Bradney, Fiona Cownie, Stephen Gough, Tim Jewell, John Machell, Katherine O'Donovan, Philip Palmer, Richard Southwell, Jenny Steele, William Twining, and Richard Youard, for specific material arising out of the symposium which is used towards the end of that chapter. None of the participants necessarily agrees with the final form of that material, and the use to which I have put it. I am also grateful to a number of practitioners who contributed their views to the project, some of which I have cited. Since anonymity was offered as an inducement to frankness, I refrain from offering thanks or making attribution on an individual basis.

The broader themes of chapter 2 were presented in a paper at the second colloquium on Theory in Legal Education at the Institute of Advanced Legal Studies, University of London, in January 1998; and some of the key themes of chapter 9 were presented in a paper at the third colloquium in January 1999. I am grateful to Avrom Sherr and David Sugarman, organisers of the colloquia, and to the participants at the colloquia for stimulating discussion; and also to colleagues and research students who participated in a seminar at the Law Faculty in Southampton in March 1998 which addressed the themes of chapter 2.

I am grateful to Neil MacCormick and Oren Ben-Dor who commented on earlier drafts of chapter 3, to Richard Bronaugh whose insightful editorial advice at the stage the material was being worked into an article proved helpful in many ways, and to David Lewis for discussion of how dentists reason.

I am grateful to Liz Fisher for helpful discussions of judicial review when working on chapter 4, to Dawn Oliver for her detailed comments on a finished draft, and to Neil Duxbury for assisting in his editorial capacity with some helpful suggestions when the material was being turned into a briefer review article.

Colleagues at Southampton who assisted me in discussing their more substantive legal interests include Kit Barker, Peter Sparkes, Natalie Lee, Nick Wikeley, Jenny Steele, Jonathan Montgomery and Alasdair Maclean—and for discussion of even wider interests I am also grateful to Andrew Mason.

I am grateful to the Arts and Humanities Research Board for an award which supported a year of sabbatical leave in 1999/2000, which enabled me to make significant progress towards completing this book. For general support and encouragement I am particularly grateful to David Feldman and Neil MacCormick.

Particular thanks are also due to Oren Ben-Dor who has benefited me with his discussions more than can be called for from a colleague, and to Richard Hart whose incisive comments have assisted me more than can be expected from a publisher. I am also grateful to Hannah Young of Hart Publishing for guiding the book through the production process.

I remain grateful to Dorit for providing her valuable sense of balance on things both inside and outside this book; to Rafael, Daniel and Avital for importantly tipping the balance in all sorts of ways; and to Bill, Audrey, Chanan and Alisa for providing crucial support for the scales.

*

An earlier version of chapter 2 has been previously published in (2000) 7 *International Journal of the Legal Profession* 205. The material used in chapter 3 was previously published in (2000) 13 *Canadian Journal of Law and Jurisprudence* 75. A briefer version of chapter 4 was published as "The Theoretical Controversy Concerning Judicial Review" (2001) 64 *Modern Law Review* 500.

Readers unfamiliar with English law might like to know that the Human Rights Act 1998 came into effect in October 2000. Those inhibited by the sight of logical symbols are encouraged to consult the clear brief appendix to Simon Blackburn's *Oxford Dictionary of Philosophy*, or else to read "not" when confronted by "~", "or" for "∨", "and" for "∧"—and to carry on regardless.

Contents

1

Introduction

THE CAPACITY OF law to provide authoritative resolution of disputes (or of the appropriate means for securing some mutual benefit) often seems to be matched by the openings law provides to controversy. It has often been thought that ironing out the controversy is the way to improve the law's performance of its role in determining the outcome of disputes. With this in mind legal theorists have set about two related tasks, classifying legal materials and clarifying the nature of legal reasoning, striving to reach the position where there remains no controversy over the legal determination of any case.

Morris Cohen reported that in 1910 the American Association of Law Schools gave official recognition to the need for "a conscious philosophy of law as a way out of the *impasse* into which we have got by pseudo-intellectualism and the empirical manipulation of cases".[1] Cohen proceeded to endorse the Association's modification of the Platonic dictum: "philosophers must become lawyers or lawyers philosophers, if our law is ever to be advanced into its perfect workings."[2] Approaching one hundred years later perfection is no longer sought with such enthusiastic idealism, but the two causes of the *impasse* noted by the Association are evidently still with us.

The idea that philosophers should become lawyers, or even baseball players, is anathema to Stanley Fish. A response to Fish's views on theory and practice forms a major part of the first of the preliminary studies found in Part I of this book. Since I endeavour in this book to join the concerns of the theory and practice of law, my response to Fish is a critical one. Chapter 2 endeavours to explore the extent to which conflicting perspectives on the nature of law as practised and as an academic subject are inevitable. Whilst recognising the possibility of conflicting perspectives within and between practitioner and academic outlooks, it seeks to consider whether there exists any common ground among the potential plurality of practitioner and theoretical perspectives. The underlying objective is to provide a broader picture in which the place of theory can be considered.

The aim of this chapter is not to advance any particular theoretical, or atheoretical, perspective. Nevertheless, it is argued that the broader picture does provide an important place for theory in the practice (and teaching) of law, and

---

[1] Morris Cohen, "Jurisprudence as a Philosophical Discipline" (1913) 10 *Journal of Philosophy Psychology and Scientific Methods* 225 at 231.

[2] *Ibid.* Cohen's remarks were made in an address to a meeting of the American Philosophical Association, in which he suggested that philosophers have something to learn from the law—a sentiment that finds an echo in ch. 6 below. The AALS's aspiration is to be found in the General Introduction to the Modern Legal Philosophy Series which it commissioned.

issue is taken with Stanley Fish's assertion that theory can be "made to disappear in the solvent of an enriched notion of practice". The chapter draws on
material collected during a research project at Southampton University on differing perspectives of academics and practitioners towards the role of reasoning
in law, as well as making some reference to disagreements on the role of theory
in the literature. In proposing the general view that a richer notion of practice
depends on a restorative theoretical cleanser, the need to be aware of the existence of different proprietary brands of cleanser is stressed, and a warning is
sounded on the dangers of brand loyalty when it comes to theory.

The nature and scope of legal reasoning has been subjected to an extraordi-
nary amount of deliberation in recent years, and yet its practice continues to be
often accompanied by an unreflective assurance about what is going on. The
enactment in the UK of the Human Rights Act 1998 has been the catalyst for far
more reflection on the practice of legal reasoning, at least among certain sections
of the judiciary. Writing to the Heads of University Law Schools in 1999, Lord
Justice Sedley expressed the concern that "the judiciary will be looking to the
[practising] profession to continue the process of judicial education in what is a
new mindset", and that this in turn depended on the profession obtaining from
the law schools "the injection they need of new and creative thinking."[3]
Endorsing this letter in his Lord Upjohn Lecture in June 2000, Lord Woolf contrasts the "spectrum of relatively sharply defined concepts" in the substantive
law prior to the 1998 Act with the complex value judgements that the Act would
require. However, Lord Woolf then acknowledges that the "new approach" is
not confined to human rights, and has already been found in the law.[4]

The contrast between "sharply defined concept" and "complex value judge-
ment" characterises two aspects of legal reasoning, but does so in a way that jux-
taposes them—here as the old and the new. As Lord Woolf's further reflection
brings out, they are not so simply divided. One consequence of allowing the evaluative into the clearly legal is that it appears to undermine any distinctively legal
territory. Joseph Raz's attempt to rebut this suggestion by allowing a moral evaluative element into legal reasoning while maintaining the autonomy of law
forms the subject of the second preliminary study undertaken in chapter 3.

This chapter focuses on Joseph Raz's notion of legal reasoning and attempts
to further the discussion on some of the issues arising in an exchange between
Joseph Raz and Gerald Postema. The analysis proposed here indicates certain
deficiencies in Raz's theoretical model of law, to which a number of modifications are suggested. More generally, it is argued that the ideas of legal reasoning
and the autonomy of law cannot survive as accurate depictions of the legal practices they have been related to, and some of the implications of a more detailed

---

[3] Letter from Lord Justice Sedley (as Chairman of the Human Rights Working Group of the
Judicial Studies Board) to Professor Alan Paterson (as Chair of the Committee of Heads of
University Law Schools), 25 March 1999.
[4] Lord Woolf CJ, "The Legal Education the Justice System Requires Today" (2000) 34 *The Law
Teacher* 263 at 266.

analysis of the underlying phenomena are considered. The chapter concludes with some observations on the role of law in social interaction, the judicial role, and law's instability.

The judicial role is considered more fully in chapter 4 through a study of the theoretical basis for judicial review, as debated between supporters of the *ultra vires* and common law models. Recent contributions to this debate have brought both parties to acknowledge significant common ground, yet the difference between them has still been fiercely contested. Both sides invoke logic to support their distinctive positions over the respective roles of Parliament and the courts in providing authority for the principles of judicial review. It is suggested here that the reliance on logic is unfounded or confused, and an attempt is made to clarify the logical parameters of the debate. Within this setting the features of both models are examined further. It is suggested that the continuing debate rests not so much on the merits of the arguments employed on either side but on a shared perception that the solution to the problem has to be a legal one. This assumption is questioned.

The logical law of the excluded middle, which enters the discussion in chapter 4, is considered further in chapter 5, providing the final preliminary study. One of Ronald Dworkin's major contributions to legal theory has been his persistent and imaginative defiance of the conventional jurisprudential wisdom which holds that in certain cases of a particularly complex or novel character the law does not provide a definite answer. It is suggested here that Dworkin's argument for his right answer thesis rests on a flawed application of the law of the excluded middle. Dworkin's other principal support for his position is the assertion of a common sense view of the law. The latter has attracted more critical response than his logical argument, without resolving the dispute between Dworkin and his critics. However, it is argued that a rigorous analysis of the points raised in Dworkin's purported application of the law of the excluded middle actually supports the possibility of a no-right-answer thesis, and moreover that it does so in a way that embraces the common sense positions that Dworkin has misappropriated to lend credibility to his own view of the law.

The application of the law of the excluded middle is then considered further, and it is suggested that the analysis underlying the discussion of judicial review in the previous chapter, as well as Dworkin's right answer thesis, is of wider significance. In particular, it is shown how the analysis could provide a way of dealing with the problem of vagueness in the law.

These preliminary studies serve the twin purposes of clearing away certain obstacles to the approach to legal reasoning taken in Part II of this book, and also introducing some of the themes that are developed there in further detail. Those readers who are less troubled by the relationship between theory and practice, who have no need to maintain an autonomous legal territory, or to find sufficient explanation for the judicial role in legal terms, or to establish the right answer thesis for law, and who remain unperplexed by the problem of vagueness in the law, may, if they so wish, commence at chapter 6.

Part II of the book seeks to demonstrate, in chapters 6 to 9, how the problems of understanding legal reasoning replicate difficulties encountered in the philosophy of language, but challenges the attempts that have been made to harness approaches from within that discipline to illuminate legal reasoning. Instead it is suggested that the practice at the heart of legal reasoning itself manifests the way in which the limitations of language and the incompleteness of human experience allow the opportunity for coherent development of the law and at the same time produce an inherent incoherence within the law.

The approach to reasoning with law that is expounded in part II relies upon an analysis of our uses of words, undertaken in chapter 6, which is developed further in a detailed analysis of the nature of legal concepts, undertaken in chapter 9. These two chapters form the analytical basis of the book. The chapters between them, chapter 7 on Wittgenstein and chapter 8 on Realism, seek to illuminate the approach being developed by contrasting it (and in the former case, in important respects, comparing it) with these two significant influences on studies of language and the law.

The final chapter, 10, briefly considers some of the implications of the proposed approach for the practice and theory of law, commenting on an institutional approach to law, the legitimacy of law, legal definitions, different approaches to legal reasoning, the role of appellate courts, the general possibility of providing a theoretical model of law, the use of legal rules, and the nature of law's critical aperture. I would hope that the general impact of this book would be to encourage in both theoretical and practical perspectives on law a clearer awareness of the opportunities for legal certainty *and* legal instability; and to emphasise the essentially human limitations of the legal enterprise. If this means abandoning claims to a discrete legal territory, it may nevertheless involve securing law as a distinctive and valuable discipline.

Part I
Preliminary Studies

2

Law, Theory and Practice: Conflicting Perspectives?

NO CONFLICT—NO THEORY

THE FIRST OF our preliminary studies seeks to consider those views which take a sceptical position on the relationship between theory and practice in one form or another. A particularly illuminating starting point for this chapter is Stanley Fish's view that theory can be "made to disappear in the solvent of an enriched notion of practice".[1] Fish's view, which is expounded in a number of essays in his book *Doing What Comes Naturally*, compresses the fundamental issues with which we shall be dealing: the nature of practice, the nature of theory, and the relationship between the two. It is a view that is argued for with great subtlety and flair. Challenging its underlying elements will, I think, not simply undo the Fish view, but also release greater understanding on these fundamental issues. There are other reasons for considering the Fish view in detail at this preliminary stage. In an almost caricatured manner Fish provides an animated and more accessible introduction to some of the perplexing features of language that we shall be examining at a deeper level in Part II of this book. In particular, two points can be noted for future reference. Fish's notions of "interpretive construct" and "interpretive community" replicate some of the key features of Wittgenstein's notions of "language game" and "form of life", which we shall encounter in chapter 7. Secondly, our observation on the use made by Fish of his device of an interpretive construct so as to avoid confronting ignorance will prefigure a major theme of this book developed throughout Part II. I shall attempt there to explore more fully the implications of ignorance for the theory and practice of law.

With characteristic directness Fish illustrates his view by telling the tale of the taciturn baseball player, Dennis Martinez.[2] Martinez rebukes the eager journalist sensing a scoop when spotting an exchange between Martinez and his coach before a game. To the journalist's request for details of the exchange, Martinez simply informs him: "He said, 'Throw strikes and keep 'em off the bases', . . . and I said, 'O.K.' What else could I say? What else could he say?"[3]

[1] Stanley Fish, *Doing What Comes Naturally: Change, Rhetoric, and the Practice of Theory in Literary and Legal Studies* (Oxford, Clarendon Press, 1989), hereinafter, DWCN, at ix.
[2] "Dennis Martinez and the Uses of Theory", DWCN ch. 17, previously published in (1987) 96 *Yale Law Journal* 1773.
[3] DWCN 372.

Simply put, Fish's position is that all he wants from his baseball players is to know how to do it and to get on with it: "Throw strikes and keep 'em off the bases". And there is nothing more that anyone can say. By the end of the chapter in which Martinez appears Fish is making the same point for statesmen and judges. Promoting the philosopher-king, the philosopher-judge, or the philosopher-baseball player, is all put down to the territorial ambition of philosophers, and it does not help one bit.

So what we want is people with the right practical skills. Yet within this enriched notion of practice there is room for "theory-talk":[4]

> ". . . one expression of the skill is knowing when theory-talk will or will not be useful. While it is certainly the case that the successful performance of a skill will sometimes require the invocation of theory—even of a theory of that particular skill—it is never the case that the theory thus invoked is acting as a blueprint or set of directions according to which the performance is unfolding."

The relationship between theory and practice is quite clear for Fish. Practical skills can make use of theory so as to give those practical skills better expression in appropriate contexts, but theory does nothing to shape the practical skills. The point is reiterated in a critique of Dworkin:[5]

> ". . . if Dworkin's claim is to be giving direction to judicial decisionmaking, the claim fails, and the best that *he* can be is a cheer-leader. (C'mon, fellows, do your best.) . . . Now Dworkin has a real project: to give you examples of how that story has been constructed in the past and to provide you with rules of thumb that might be of help when you are asked to construct such a story in the future. It is not the project he announces; it is not the building of a grand theory. It is just a rhetoric, a manual of practical know-how; but precisely because it is a rhetoric and not a theory it might even be something you could actually use."

Seen in this relationship to practice, theory assumes the role of mere rhetoric. This point is made by Fish elsewhere in his book, with Catherine MacKinnon as the target theoretician:[6]

> "That is power greater than any theory, and it is the power MacKinnon at once taps and extends in her essays. The fact that in these same essays she attributes that power to a theory (of male and female epistemologies) that is at most a component (a 'bit player') in her rhetorical program is a tribute to the hold theory continues to have on the academic mentality; but while that hold is not a negligible fact and can itself be the basis of effective political action, it can never be strong enough to validate theory's strongest claim, the claim to be a special kind of activity in relation to which practice is, or should be, derivative and as a consequence of which practice can be transformed."

Underlying Fish's position are three elements: a particular role for theory, a particular understanding of language, and a particular view as to how people

---

[4] DWCN 378.
[5] DWCN 392.
[6] DWCN 25.

behave. First, Fish by his own admission limits theory to "an abstract or algorithmic formulation that guides or governs practice from a position outside any particular conception of practice." The practitioner consults theory so as to obtain understanding of how to perform correctly, "independently of his preconceptions, biases, or personal preferences."[7] Secondly, for Fish meaning depends on contextual interpretation rather than a property of language, and so no sentence has a fixed meaning but is open to an indeterminate number of meanings depending on the contextual interpretations made of it.[8] Thirdly, the indeterminacy associated with language runs into an indeterminacy for human life generally,[9] and so when it comes to our attempts to construct a theory by which to explain something, the meaning delivered by our "theory" is nothing more than the product of an interpretive construct we have been influenced by. Moreover, we have nothing apart from other interpretive constructs to check our interpretive construct with.[10] People behave not in accordance with the guidance that theory provides but in accordance with their beliefs. People open doors because they believe in the solidity of matter.[11]

Although beliefs, and associated interpretive constructs, may change, this change for Fish cannot be attributed to theoretical insight because there is no such thing—only a different interpretive construct. Theory-talk acts as a rhetorical enticement to go along with one way of doing things, as seen and practised to be the way of doing things in the outworking of an interpretive construct.[12]

Each of the elements underlying Fish's position is open to challenge. First, theory can be regarded differently from Fish's narrow rendering of it.[13] The idea that theory offers an antidote to the preconceptions, biases, or personal preferences of the practitioner, which the practitioner can self-administer whilst

---

[7] DWCN 378.

[8] DWCN 2.

[9] DWCN 5.

[10] DWCN 394–6.

[11] DWCN 328.

[12] DWCN 10–13, 15, 17, 24–5. There are more complex issues lurking here. First, it is not always clear whether Fish is referring to change to an interpretive construct, or change from one interpretive construct to another (e.g., compare DWCN 15 ("if you are persuaded by Specter you will still be in the same relation to intention as you always were") with DWCN 17 ("the worldview, and therefore the world, of many persons will have been changed")). However in his major treatment of change in ch. 7 Fish clearly relies on change within an interpretive community, and the nature of an interpretive community as "an engine of change", in order to provide an account of change. This leaves unanswered the question of how to account for change from one interpretive community to another, and fails to address the problem of one community splitting into different schisms. This gap in Fish's account of change has a number of repercussions for the subject of our subsequent discussion. Critically, change *from* an interpretive community allows for the recognition that the interpretive community abandoned was incomplete in some respect, which brings in the significance of ignorance and the need for an instrument of challenge to that ignorance.

[13] Also differently from the alternative Fish rejects. I do not dispute that regarding theory simply in terms of a "high-level generalization or heuristic" (DWCN 14, 325–6, 378) fails to provide a distinct role for theory. (That is not to say that such techniques may not operate as instruments of theory properly conceived—a possibility Fish would allow for (DWCN 326) if he allowed for a proper conception of theory, on which, see further Steven Winter, "Bull Durham and the Uses of Theory" (1990) 42 *Stanford Law Review* 639 at 645–8).

suffering from those preconceptions etc., is odd in the extreme. Try to imagine the practitioner set upon a course of action motivated by some preconception, and then withdrawing on the basis that theory tells him otherwise whilst still entertaining that preconception. It is absurdly impossible to do. If theory (whatever theory is) convinces the practitioner ~x whereas he entertained the preconception x, he will simply abandon his preconception. If on the other hand, his preconception is so strong as to blind him to the information that theory would impart, then he will not accept the theory. At least he will not accept that theory, though he may find another theory more supportive of his preconception. In neither case does theory offer a correct course of action that conflicts with an incorrect course of action offered by preconception. There is one course of action, condoned by whatever preconception and theory he happens to accept.

Similarly with bias or personal preference, his bias or personal preference will either be changed by the information theory imparts, or will obstruct the acceptance of one theory but perhaps endorse the adoption of another. Fish gets the relationships between theory, personal preconception etc, and practice, wrong. Our preconception, bias and preference are not in antipathy to our theory, but influence which theory we are prepared to adopt; or, are influenced by our adoption of a theory that seems otherwise irresistible to the point that our preconception, bias and preference change. We act in accordance with both theory and preconception or bias or preference when we decide what to do in practice.[14]

It is worth pausing to note the error that Fish enters at this point. Fish would agree with the point that preconception, bias and preference are not in antipathy to our theory, subject only to the modification that theory is nothing more than the rhetorical aspect of practice.[15] It is the alternative possibility of adopting a theory that seems otherwise irresistible to the point that our preconception, bias and preference change that Fish will not swallow. This is not simply because of his view of theory, although it underlies that. It is principally due to his view of interpretive constructs or interpretive communities as being the agents of change rather than the subjects of change.[16] This is reinforced by a dualist notion of interpretive construct or community, at once "totalizing"[17] or "fully articulated"[18] and yet "heterogeneous"[19] or "entirely flexible".[20] Fish uses the totalizing side to leave no room for theory and then resorts to the flexible side to accommodate change.[21] This dualism conceals the scope theory has to operate on our preconceptions (interpretive construct, interpretive

---

[14] That is to say, when theory has a possible impact on our actions it will be a theory that is compatible with our preconceptions etc. I do not intend to suggest that theory always has an impact on our actions, as I make clear below.

[15] DWCN 149, 157, 522.

[16] Noted above, n. 12.

[17] DWCN 16.

[18] DWCN 151.

[19] DWCN 149.

[20] DWCN 151.

[21] Cp Winter, above n. 13, at 668.

community) so as to change them, even if by so doing it is relying recognition accorded to it by other preconceptions (part of our package of interpretive constructs, an element of our interpretive community). The key issue avoided by Fish is what accounts for the change which leaves at least part of our former preconceptions (interpretive construct, interpretive community) abandoned.[22]

Although these comments leave Fish's position vulnerable, the argument so far knocks down not Fish's position but the position that Fish set up to knock down himself. To mount a serious challenge to Fish's position, we have to do more than dispose of the view that theory is wrapped up with providing a correct view of practice. We have to demonstrate that there is something distinct about theory as opposed to practice.

The key to providing this part of the first challenge lies in acknowledging that there is some force in Fish's point that an enriched notion of practice is sufficient. It is sufficient when our practice is rich enough to provide us with all that is required from our practice. Doubtless in certain contexts this can be the case. Moving the sporting imagery across the Atlantic to the 1998 World Cup finals in France, when Dennis Bergkamp took a long pass under control with one touch of his foot, positioned the ball to find space around a defender, and then struck the ball with the outside edge of his right boot so as to guide it through a tight angle towards the Argentinian goal and win the match for Holland, theoretical considerations of velocity, material science, and the calculation of forces were irrelevant. Bergkamp just knew how to do it, and he did it.

The point is that even if we do possess the practical skill or know-how to deal with the situation in one context, we do not possess the practical skill or know-how to deal with the situation in another context; or we can deal practically with the immediate situation but cannot deal with further ramifications of what we have done. Theory finds a role precisely where our practice is not rich enough.

Take apples falling from trees. The practice of apple picking was doubtless rich enough and in no need of improvement from a theory of gravity, but theoretical reflection on falling apples led to insights being gathered where practice was far from rich, like the exploration of space. Or take judges delivering judgment, and allow for the sake of argument that each judge is good at being a judge.[23] Even if the right judgment is delivered, we may want to ask other questions about the process of judgment which we cannot readily answer, and so resort to theory to give us a broader picture bringing in a possible explanation of, say, democratic implications of the process of judgment. Or less optimistically, we may not be sure that the judgment is right, and will then resort to theory to help us to find the criteria which will determine a good judgment.

---

[22] This does not demonstrate the existence of theory but it does leave space for it.
[23] Cp DWCN 398.

The general point to be made here is that there is room for a distinct role for theory precisely where our practical skill or know-how runs out. Theory provides a possible way of explaining things when our practical experience is not sufficiently rich to provide us with all the answers we need or ask for. Put bluntly, theory is built on ignorance. Ignorance is perhaps the single most important thing that Fish overlooks. Although he recognises error and its correction,[24] the acquisition of greater understanding in a situation not previously encountered[25] and the possibility of there being a limit to what we know,[26] he does not appear to allow for a simple state of ignorance (we do not know things that we can know).[27] In part this may be attributed to the totalising side of his thinking: "a world without gaps or spots of unintelligibility,[28] which only has room for the "puzzling and mysterious" but not sheer ignorance.

As a corollary of the link between theory and ignorance it follows that, if our practical experience becomes enriched due to adopting a theoretical solution, testing it, and finding it works, we no longer call the explanation theoretical but accept it as fact.[29] We can refer to the Copernican theory of the solar system historically, but now we no longer regard the proposition that the planets circle the sun as theoretical but as fact.

The second challenge is to Fish's understanding of language. I do not propose to offer here any contribution to a deep understanding of the nature of language.[30] However, even if we adopt Fish's perspective on the nature of language, the inferences he draws do not necessarily follow. Let us travel with Fish down the anti-formalist road.[31] This involves accepting that meaning cannot be found in a formal connection between words and what words are taken to refer to, but must be found in the interpretation of what is meant in the particular context of that speaker speaking those words on that occasion. The second point on the anti-formalist road is recognising that since words can be used by innumerable speakers on innumerable occasions, there are an indeterminate number of interpretations possible for any given group of words.[32] Fish then takes us on to the next point in concluding that all meaning is subject to the interpretive construct used, and hence relative to the employment of one interpretive construct as opposed to another.

---

[24] DWCN 15.

[25] DWCN 150–1.

[26] DWCN 153.

[27] It does not make any difference to the point that all of these states are regarded as relative to a particular interpretive community.

[28] DWCN 16.

[29] It also follows that there may be some intellectual enterprises where due to the lack of prospects for testing to the point where propositions fall within the conventions for acceptance as fact, or due to the generation of issues that will always exceed those issues that have already been resolved into fact, there is acknowledgment that the enterprise is essentially theoretical.

[30] For some illuminating comments on the problems of linguistic indeterminacy and law, see Timothy Endicott, "Linguistic Indeterminacy" (1996) 16 *Oxford Journal of Legal Studies* 667 (now incorporated in his *Vagueness in Law* (Oxford, OUP, 2000)).

[31] DWCN 2.

[32] For present purposes I take a group of words as covering one or more words.

The objection to the route down the anti-formalist road that Fish so speedily follows,[33] is that the road has a fork at the second point, which Fish fails to recognise. Turning off at this fork in the road leads to some quite different conclusions. Accepting that words can be used by innumerable speakers on innumerable occasions, it does indeed follow that there are an indeterminate number of interpretations *possible* for any given group of words, but this is a contingency and therein lies the fork. It is contingent upon different speakers on different occasions actually using the words to convey different things, and/or different hearers taking the words to convey different things. For convenience, I shall treat hearers as imagining themselves using the words spoken when interpreting what the words should convey, and talk collectively of speakers and hearers as speakers using words.[34]

The contingency of different speakers on different occasions actually using the words to convey different things is itself dependent upon those different speakers experiencing[35] different things on the different occasions, which they then convey by the same words. The fork in the road is apparent if we take the counter contingencies. Suppose that on every occasion that anyone uses these words, he has experienced the same thing and is using those words to convey what he has experienced.

This possibility itself depends on our capacity for common experience, and on a known practice of denoting that common experience by a particular group of words. In fact the requirement is somewhat less than that, for we could allow that one group of words is used by convention to convey different meanings but that all our speakers can detect from the context which meaning is being employed.[36] Moreover, the requirement can be lessened in another respect, in that the full details of each speaker's experience do not have to be common, so long as there is sufficient in common for there to be an identifiable constant referred to by each of them.

The possibility of turning off at Fish's unnoticed fork is not at all fanciful. Every reader of this book may do so by turning to the Contents and finding the page on which chapter 5 starts. In fact, despite his hurry, it appears that Fish himself may have noticed the fork in passing. Fish refers to some meanings that

---

[33] As Fish puts it, "once you start . . . there is no place to stop" (DWCN 2).

[34] I accept that this ignores further complications arising out of a situation where A recognises that he regularly uses the words with meaning$_a$ but also that B in this context is using the words with meaning$_b$, but would argue that this is not germane to the point at issue. We could talk of A imagining himself in B's shoes using the words.

[35] I amplify the meaning of this term in the following section.

[36] So, all speakers of English reading this book are capable of distinguishing in the same way the separate senses of "bank" in the following: (1) "Excuse me, can you tell me where there is a bank that I can exchange travellers cheques at?" and (2) "The river flooded so much that it burst its bank on one side." Even the requirement of conventional practice can be loosened where such is the commonality of experience that the audience is capable of inferring from the context what the speaker means without prior use of the words with that meaning. A well chosen metaphor to an empathetic audience illustrates the point—as does a rather more bizarre exchange in which Fish himself was a participant, discussed in n. 38 below.

"seem perspicuous and literal". However Fish puts these down to "forceful interpretive acts and not . . . the properties of language."[37] But in this way Fish poses a false issue. Abandon any formal properties of language, still it is not the force of our interpretive acts that renders perspicuous and literal meanings, but our capacity for common experience and our need to denote that common experience to each other that restrict our interpretive possibilities.[38]

The challenge to Fish's third underlying element follows on from the challenges already mounted. The possibility of a distinctive role for theory in dealing with areas of practical ignorance, and the possibility of some determinacy in our use of language derived from common experience, taken together open up the possibility of people changing their conduct not because they are enticed by rhetoric but because they change their beliefs and their practice due to the impact theoretical insights have in actually enriching practical possibilities that previously lay hidden. One can continue to see the need for opening doors without a theory of matter, but a theory of matter capable of being expressed in a language that relates to some degree of common experience, may just provide the practical know-how to ensure that the room we walk into is heated by sources of power derived from nuclear fusion.

PRELIMINARY OBSERVATIONS

In this section I hope to develop the criticisms made of Fish's position into some preliminary observations on the nature of theory and its relationship to practice. The view that theory does have a role in dealing with areas of practical

---

[37] DWCN 9.

[38] The tenacity with which Fish clings to an interpretive construct as the necessary device for providing meaning can be examined further by considering two incidents. First, there is the recognition by Fish of considerable determinacy that use of an interpretive construct within a particular interpretive community can bring, to the point that Timothy Endicott has raised doubts over whether it is possible to "attribute any sort of indeterminacy claim to Stanley Fish"—in his book, above n. 30, at 12, citing Stanley Fish, "How Come You Do Me Like You Do? A Reply to Dennis Patterson" (1993) 72 *Texas Law Review* 57, at 61–2. Fish attributes to use of an interpretive construct limitations on meaning that take us "about as far as one could get (short of an out-and-out determinism) from a condition in which 'everything is permitted' ". Secondly, there is the anecdote provided by Michael Moore, *Educating Oneself in Public: Critical Essays in Jurisprudence* (New York, NY, OUP, 2000) 55–6, of an exchange between himself and Fish in a seminar at the University of Pennsylvania in 1989 which commenced with (Moore) "gleeg, gleeg, gleeg" and (Fish) "glug, glug, glug". The point that Fish actually cottoned on to what Moore meant was subsequently put down by Fish to hearing the words "with ears informed of the present context—focus, emphasis, concerns, strategies, desires, etc"; to being the product of "the interpretive conditions within which [the words] are heard." Yet if Fish and Moore are able to understand each other they must share an interpretive construct, while at the same time they must operate from different interpretive constructs in order to disagree. (Cp Dennis Patterson, "You Made Me Do It: My Reply to Stanley Fish" (1993) 72 *Texas Law Review* 67 at 72–7.) The medium by which the extent of determinacy within an interpretive community can be measured, as Fish would put it, and also through which speakers are able to move from one community to another, is nothing other than common experience.

ignorance has a number of implications. These implications can be drawn out by adopting a simple model of theorising composed of three stages:

EXPERIENCE
giving rise to
REFLECTION
provides
UNDERSTANDING

Each of the three stages requires some explanation. Experience should be understood loosely, not simply covering direct sensuous experience, but also covering indirect experience arising out of observation[39] or being informed of the experience[40] of other persons, and even taking in experience that is imagined or constructed in a hypothetical.

Reflection should be understood as involving a process of thinking beyond the actual experience, so as to offer explanations, draw out implications, make connections with other actual or potential experiences.

Understanding should be understood in a tentative and contingent sense. These qualities possess two dimensions. First, in relation to the experience, the understanding is contingent upon that experience and is tentative in depending upon the as yet untested adequacy of the reflection that has taken place upon that experience. Secondly, in relation to offering a wider understanding of other actual or potential experiences, the contingency spreads across an area of experiences, and the tentativeness similarly extends through all the points of connection that reflection might make within this area of experiences. In short, theoretical understanding is not absolute—it is exploratory.

At an extreme point it follows that if one were capable of experiencing everything and at the same time were conscious of all possible connections that could be made among all that one had experienced, there would be no scope for further reflection or theoretical understanding. One would simply know everything that one was capable of knowing.[41] At a less extreme point it may be possible to specify a limited area of experience and say that one had acquired all the knowledge[42] that one could need in that limited area and had no need of theory. The goal scoring skills of Dennis Bergkamp are sufficient.

---

[39] Including observations made with the aid of scientific instruments.

[40] Direct or indirect.

[41] Such knowledge would of course be limited by the human capacity to experience and make connections between experiences, so we are talking about reaching the limits of human knowledge. But the point is that human theorising is limited by the same constraints, so that it is still the case that at the extreme point of human knowledge there is no room left for theory.

[42] Based on past experience and, where necessary, reflection. I doubt whether any practical knowledge is possible without some low level theorising at some point, even if only in the form of "this doesn't work here, it may be because of *a*, let's see if it works without *a*". The point is that the skilled person has no need for further theory, any such low level theorising has already been tested out in further experience and he can simply rely upon the practice of the skills he has acquired.

However, the very act of specifying a limited area suggests related areas where ultimately we may find the need for theory. Whilst Bergkamp was employing his skills, it was reported that his club manager, Arsène Wenger, was attending the World Cup amongst other things to keep a watch on developments in tactical strategy.[43] This opens up the significant possibility of recognising a specified area of practice where theory is redundant whilst at the same time recognising that theory may be required for related areas.

Elements in the three stages of our model of theorising can be brought together in two other important ways. First we can take our output of theoretical understanding and subject it to the test of further experience. If this confirms our understanding it can be a way of strengthening or developing our theory. (Given sufficient confirmatory experience it will lead to the transmutation of the theoretical understanding into accepted fact.) This process is evident when scientists seek to falsify a hypothesis.

The second relationship also occurs between understanding and experience, but in this case the relationship is inverted. That is to say that we confront a further experience with the theoretical understanding obtained through reflection on our first experience but instead of seeking to put the theoretical understanding to the test, we use that understanding to explain the experience. This is a possibility that again arises from the fact that our experience is less than total, so that we can be selective about which elements of the experience we will acknowledge, or even what we are prepared to let in to our experience. Crucially, for this inverted relationship between experience and understanding to succeed, we have to be prepared to close down our faculty of reflection.

We may now portray together the three relationships among the elements in the stages of our model of theorising as follows.

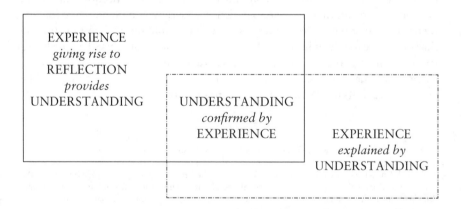

EXPERIENCE
giving rise to
REFLECTION
provides
UNDERSTANDING

UNDERSTANDING
confirmed by
EXPERIENCE

EXPERIENCE
explained by
UNDERSTANDING

---

[43] Ironically, it would seem that Dennis Martinez's skills might have benefited from a further dose of theory. Fish rates him as "a pitcher who is unlikely ever to make it into the baseball Hall of Fame, if only because he seems to experience every pitch as a discrete event" (DWCN 372).

The line around the first two columns represents the development of theory. The broken line around the last two columns represents the degeneration of theory into rhetoric. The exploratory character of theory depending upon an openness to reflection has been stunted by the partisan aim of accounting for all further experience in terms of the theory already adopted. The degeneration may involve a subtle slide from a willingness to test theoretical understanding by experience to an imposition of theoretical understanding on experience.

To a limited extent Fish's portrayal of theory as rhetoric has been vindicated, but only to the extent that we are dealing with degenerate theory. The prospect for finding a positive role for theory still beckons.

CONFLICTS

If we are endorsing the virtue of open reflection on experience, then part of our search for a positive role for theory must deal with the manifest conflict that exists, not only between theorists and practitioners but also among theorists themselves. I shall deal first with the theorists.

One example of conflict between theorists is to be found in two articles in the *Oxford Journal of Legal Studies* discussing the role of theory in the criminal law. The setting for the dispute is a review article that has been coauthored by John Gardner of a book by Antony Duff. JA Laing responds to this review article,[44] and Gardner makes reply to Laing.[45] The point at issue is to what level of generality criminal theory should aspire.

Laing expresses her concern that Duff (and his coauthor Heike Jung) have put forward a view of the heterogeneity of culpable states of mind required for different criminal offences in criticising Duff's attempt to provide a general theory of *mens rea*. On this point she comes to Duff's rescue:[46]

> ". . . we *must* assume that the classification of offences together with some kind of paradigm is possible at the broadest levels of theory if an analysis is not to degenerate into thoroughgoing incoherence. It is important to see just how threatening is the heterogeneity claim to the very possibility of theory in order to appreciate the manner in which Duff (and theorists like him) may save himself from the charge of embarking on a theoretically insignificant programme; one which accounts for liability for homicide, for example, but not for criminal liability generally or paradigmatically conceived."

In taking exception to Laing's view, Gardner does more than reiterate his scepticism that Duff "was too optimistic about the chances of providing a comprehensive theory of *mens rea*."[47] He suggests that there is an improper recourse

---

[44] JA Laing, "The Prospects of a Theory of Criminal Culpability: Mens Rea and Methodological Doubt" (1994) 14 *Oxford Journal of Legal Studies* 57.

[45] John Gardner, "Criminal Law and the Uses of Theory: A Reply to Laing" (1994) 14 *Oxford Journal of Legal Studies* 217.

[46] Laing, above n. 44, at 60.

[47] Gardner, above n. 45, at 217.

to theory by those who are unsettled by a "vast plurality of valid moral concerns" and who "take refuge in moral 'systems' and 'theories'."[48] And in words that taken out of context[49] could be mistaken for echoing the Fish view of theory, Gardner states:[50]

> "[This] still gives us no reason to hope, as Laing seems to hope, that a general theory of *mens rea* will charge in to save the day. More likely it would corroborate our original suspicion that many of the major battles now raging between and among criminal lawyers and their moral and political critics will not be won or lost on the playing fields of theory. They will be settled, if at all, in the muddy trenches of substantive moral and legal argument. . . . We thought that Duff, like many other contemporary writers on important and controversial issues in the criminal law and beyond, was too ready to diagnose theoretical problems where only ordinary moral and legal problems exist."

The concern expressed by Gardner is not in fact an antipathy to theory as such but a concern that theory of an inappropriately general form may be used to obfuscate rather than clarify matters. The real difficulties in dealing with the particular aspects of culpability associated with different offences will be wrapped up in a comprehensive "system" or "theory".

Concern with the totalitarian character of all embracing theory has been expressed by other theorists. In her collection of feminist essays in social and legal theory, Nicola Lacey castigates grand theory:[51]

> "There are at least three elements to the idea of 'grand' theory as a pejorative. The first objection is to theories which have pretensions to assert Truth (with a capital T!). . . . The second theme which can be identified in the debate about 'grand' theory is an objection to theories which are monolithic in the sense that they seek to reduce all aspects of women's oppression to one or two basic factors such as sexuality or, as in the case of early marxist feminism, a particular conception of class. . . . Finally, a third objection is to the (high) degree of abstraction of 'grand' theories. Again this seems to me to be an important objection given that the move from concrete to abstract can indeed serve as a cover for the marginalisation or suppression of varying perspectives: abstraction can indeed serve totalisation."

A final example of one theorist expressing reservation about excesses in the use of theory by others is provided by John Griffith in his comment on the extra-judicial theorising of two High Court judges:[52]

> Another High Court judge, Sir Stephen Sedley, has written about the shape of human rights in the next century . . . . He comes close to Sir John Laws's metaphysic when he

---

[48] Gardner, above n. 45, 219.

[49] Elsewhere in his article Gardner affirms his status as a practising theorist.

[50] *Ibid.* at 223, 228.

[51] Nicola Lacey, *Unspeakable Subjects* (Oxford, Hart Publishing, 1998) 176–8.

[52] John Griffith, "Judges and the Constitution" in Richard Rawlings (ed.), *Law, Society, and Economy* (Oxford, Clarendon Press, 1997) at 308–9, referring to Sir John Laws, "Law and Democracy" [1995] *Public Law* 72, and Sir Stephen Sedley, "Human Rights: a Twenty-First Century Agenda" [1995] *Public Law* 386.

speaks of a 'bi-polar sovereignty of the Crown in Parliament and the Crown in its courts, to each of which the Crown's Ministers are answerable—politically to Parliament, legally to the courts'. In this paradigm, he says, the government of the day has no separate sovereignty.

I believe this kind of language lifts our feet off the ground and endangers more than our sense of balance. . . . Sedley comes round at last to reliance on 'our present epoch's consensus about society's ground rules' which at least frees him from both judicial supremacism and higher-order everything."

There exists a legitimate concern that theory might incarcerate our understanding in darkness instead of bringing enlightenment: by overriding significant particulars (Gardner's concern), by marginalising or even bypassing the significant interests of particular individuals (Lacey's concern), or by spuriously attributing significance to vested interests that they do not merit (Griffith's concern). However, this concern needs to be balanced by a recognition that theory can have a proper role at a more general level than particular events or specific individual interests.

This point is recognised by Lacey in the text immediately following the excerpt above. She notes that the question whether abstraction does actually serve totalisation "must be a question of degree", and acknowledges that, "*Any* use of theoretical terms inevitably involves conceptualisation and hence a degree of abstraction".[53]

In this light the dispute between Gardner and Laing cannot be regarded as profitable if it simply polarises the approach to criminal law theory in terms of decreeing either heterogeneity or paradigm based coherence. The real issue is which approach provides understanding to the subject that is being studied. If there is diversity and even incoherence in the subject, our theory should increase our understanding of that.[54] On the other hand, if there are connections to be made between the apparently disparate elements of the criminal law, so as to provide an underlying coherence which can increase our understanding of the surface phenomena, then our theory should not be precluded from offering that.

Neil MacCormick and William Twining have argued for the value of theory in the subject context that Laing is considering, but also for a role for theory at a higher level:[55]

"One role of 'theory' within a course on contract or torts or constitutional law is to provide a coherent view of the subject as a whole. . . . Whatever other educational objectives are served by separate theory courses, perhaps their most important function is to provide an opportunity to students to stand back from the detailed study of particular topics and to look at their subject as a whole at a higher level of generality

[53] Above n. 51, at 178.
[54] For an attempt to provide some understanding on one incoherent area of the criminal law, see Andrew Halpin, "Definitions and directions: recklessness unheeded" (1998) 18 *Legal Studies* 294.
[55] Neil MacCormick and William Twining, "Theory in the Law Curriculum" in William Twining, *Law in Context: Enlarging a Discipline* (Oxford, Clarendon Press, 1997) at 144, previously published in William Twining (ed.), *Legal Theory and Common Law* (Oxford, Blackwell, 1986).

and from a variety of perspectives. Such a course . . . helps to provide the basis for an integrated educational experience . . ."

This role for theory does not necessarily take us back to the totalitarianism of grand theory. These authors recognise coherence, or "integration" at the higher level whilst acknowledging "a variety of perspectives". The stigma attached to grand theory in the critical views collected above seems to be linked to an exclusive sway that a comprehensive theory purports to hold over a subject area. Such a grand theory is eschewed by MacCormick and Twining, but in commending the study of a variety of theoretical perspectives in order to bring about "an integrated educational experience", it would seem that the theoretical quest for a form of higher level coherence has not been abandoned.

Whether we are dealing with theory within particular legal subjects or general theory of law, the question of the legitimacy of theory has to be addressed. In terms of the model proposed above, we have to be sensitive to the point at which theory proper degenerates into rhetoric, and the distinguishing mark of the former is that it retains its exploratory character: a willingness to recognise existing ignorance and to confront possibilities for increasing our understanding.

The instances we have surveyed of conflict between theorists do at least maintain a concern for the proper role of theory rather than dismissing theory completely. A more dismissive attitude to theory can be discerned in the conflict that can arise between practitioners and theorists.

It is possible to identify three strands of practitioner scepticism towards theory: (1) practice has no need of theory; (2) practice has only a limited need for theory; (3) theory is diammetrically opposed to practice. These can be related to our observations on theory in the preceding section. In (1) practice is regarded as sufficiently rich as to make theory redundant: the practitioner as skilled player. In (2) although a limited area of practical skill is specified it is acknowledged that theory can provide an ancillary role: the theorist is admitted to manage the long term strategy without detracting from the opportunities for the practitioner to shine in performing at his skill. In (3) theory has overstepped the mark. In relation to the practice it is supposed to represent, it takes the form of an alien rhetoric, closed to the values of what the practitioner holds dear and espousing the cause of insurgency: the theorist has joined the unenlightened mob who are calling for a ban on the game.

The actual composition of practitioner scepticism varies with the practitioner and the theory being targeted. An illustration of (1) is provided by the judicial opposition to the attempted reforms of the English criminal law in the nineteenth century, which has been recorded by Keith Smith.[56] Although Smith hails Lord Goff's willingness to acknowledge a partnership with academic theorists as an enlightened contrast,[57] Lord Goff still exhibits a scepticism composed of

---

[56] Keith Smith, *Lawyers, Legislators and Theorists* (Oxford, Clarendon Press, 1998) 138, 147, 171–2, 368.
[57] *Ibid.* at 369.

strand (2) in setting boundaries to the proper contribution of academics.[58] An outright example of strand (3) figures in the scepticism Weber considers (but does not endorse) directed at the idea of appointing an anarchist as a law lecturer.[59] A more recent illustration, combining (2) with (3) is found in the words of Judge Harry Edwards complaining in the *Michigan Law Review* about the "growing disjunction" between academics and practitioners: "The 'impractical' scholar . . . produces abstract scholarship that has little relevance to concrete issues, or addresses concrete issues in a wholly theoretical manner."[60]

The problems in tackling such scepticism are worsened by the fact that what appears to be rich practice to one is impoverished to another, precisely because it fails to address matters that are cut off by specifying a limited area of practice. And at a higher level, one man's theory is another man's rhetoric, because it takes in what is of value to the one but shuts out what is of value to the other. Faced with these problems, one might reasonably resort to deep scepticism on the value of theory, but in the following section I want to see whether some degree of resolution of the conflict and the scepticism is possible, by emphasising the exploratory character of theory noted above and also clarifying what it is we are prepared to explore.

TAKING THEORY OUT OF CONFLICT

Let us start with some simple and, I hope, uncontroversial propositions. (i) Law performs roles in society of coordinating harmonious interests and resolving competing interests. (ii) It is possible to find a number of outlooks or beliefs that can provide the basis for performing these roles in different ways, which may or may not be incorporated in the way that the law does perform these roles. (iii) There will always be a way to perform these roles on any given occasion different to the way actually adopted by the law (whether a minor modification or a radical alternative). (iv) When asked for advice about the law the practitioner is required to indicate how the law will perform its role, not how the law should perform its role in accordance with one of the available alternatives. (v) Working out how the law will perform its role requires considering legal materials and also how these legal materials may (or may not) affect those authorised to judge the law's response to a particular case. (vi) However, it may be possible to argue for two different potential legal responses to a particular case given the current state of legal materials and/or predictability of judicial responses to

---

[58] Robert Goff, "The Maccabean Lecture: The Search for Principle" (1983) 69 *Proceedings of the British Academy* 169 at 185; "The Mental Element in the Crime of Murder" (1988) 104 *Law Quarterly Review* 30 at 31. How the boundaries work was indicated by Lord Goff in the subsequent case of *Hunter* v. *Canary Wharf Ltd* [1997] 2 WLR 684 at 697.

[59] Max Weber, "Value-judgments in Social Science" in WG Runciman (ed.), *Max Weber* (Cambridge, Cambridge University Press, 1978) at 75.

[60] Harry Edwards, "The Growing Disjunction between Legal Education and the Legal Profession" (1992) 91 *Michigan Law Review* 34 at 35.

them. (vii) It may separately be possible to argue for change to the law on the basis of an outlook or belief that would suggest a way of performing the legal role in a manner that is not at present within the range of potential legal responses.

The relationship between theory and practice may obviously vary considerably. A practitioner who works within (iv) and (v) and avoids the occasion of (vi) will be uninterested in theory and rely on rich technical skills. Such skills will be untouched by considerations of conflicting values that the law might otherwise incorporate, found in (ii) and (iii). This profile fits the way a mergers and acquisitions partner of a leading City of London law firm described[61] his work: politically disinterested, employing keen technical skills, and avoiding areas of uncertain law due to the large sums of money at stake.[62]

The profile also fits a QC who regarded a barrister's job as primarily involving the skill of marshalling the facts to fit the law rather than adapting the law to fit the facts:

> "Practising law involves shaping the issue in such a way that the legal solution favours the result contended for. You tailor the problem to condition the answer. In one sense none of them have an ethical dimension, what one is looking for is a 'result'."

Such technical skill is acquired by a barrister "through his cases. He learns almost nothing from articles and periodicals, comfortable though they are to have as bathroom reading."[63]

A contrasting view is provided by a barrister practising at the Personal Injuries Bar who writes:

> "A broader vision and ability to think on a wider level, including lateral thinking, is required for practice. The common law in particular, as well as statutory interpretation, is an evolving process and one which does not remain static. At a very minimum the lawyer has got to appreciate that the law is a living breathing mass, ever-changing.

---

[61] Information on the work of practitioners comes from respondents to the project acknowledged in the Preface. Responses were in the form of written or oral responses to loosely structured thematic questions.

[62] This last sentiment was echoed at a lower level of financial risk by a provincial solicitor who indicated that he would always avoid areas of uncertain law, unless the client absolutely insisted on taking the risk.

[63] On the subsidiary point concerning the value of academic legal material to the practitioner, a contrasting experience is found in the opinion expressed by Richard Southwell QC: ". . . there should be no divide between academic lawyers and practising lawyers. Both should be talking the same language. Both should be seeking the right solution to difficult legal problems. Naturally the practitioner will be arguing the case for his client, but on one side or the other the right way forward founded on the best academic research should be presented. I have recently argued mistake of law (*Bilbie* v. *Lumley*) in the House of Lords and virtually the entire hearing of 4 days was taken up with presentation of the various solutions which have been propounded by Professor Birks, Professor Burrows and others. In the medical profession dons, researchers and practising physicians and surgeons are pursuing the same ends of perfecting preventative measures and cures. I see no reason to have the present unfortunate divide between the academic and the practising which has done so much to damage the development of the law, both case law and statutory." (Letter to author, 17 September 1998.)

That change is brought about to address particular social or economic problems, real or perceived."

Endorsement for this view came from a City tax partner, who stressed the importance of seeking the underlying social purpose in approaching the interpretation of statutes.

The danger of assuming that when we do reach (vi) we are necessarily dealing with theory is rebuffed by an anecdote related by a QC at the Patent Bar:

> "I remember very clearly having a pupil some years ago who was very successful academically both scientifically and legally. . . . Having researched a problem for me he produced a solution which was, from a theoretical legal standpoint, undoubtedly justified. I knew that the judge in question would never accept it and that he would reach his conclusions in such a way that the Court of Appeal would not interfere. This is something which can never be taught."

A positive view of theory emerged from discussions with two City solicitors experienced in international banking law who felt that their grasp of the technical possibilities of the law was expanded by theoretical insights relating to its general structure or ethical foundations. One of them attributed his ability to analyse the complex features of an international transaction to what he had learned from Hart's lectures on jurisprudence.

This sample of practical experience suggests opportunities for theory in relation to the practice of law: providing a more coherent view of legal materials (even though some practitoners will await the transformation to accepted law before relying on it, this does not detract from the initial work theory has to do);[64] providing a greater general understanding of the law so as to use it better in particular circumstances; and more adventurously, working out how the existing state of the law might be transformed to accommodate cases not yet entertained as possible.

There remains, however, a residual tension between practice and theory due to the contrast between proposition (iv) and (vii).[65] The dynamic nature of this tension can be brought out by considering different manifestations of what might loosely be described as legal reasoning,[66] in the sense of reasoning towards a legal response to a particular case. It would be possible to arrange different manifestations of legal reasoning in the form of a continuum, ranging from mundane uncontroversial applications of the law to radically critical

---

[64] On this see Peter Birks, "Historical Context" in Peter Birks (ed.), *Reviewing Legal Education* (Oxford, OUP, 1994) at 2–4; Editor's Preface in *Pressing Problems in the Law, vol. 2, What are Law Schools for?* (Oxford, OUP, 1996) at vi–vii; "The Academic and the Practitioner" (1998) 18 *Legal Studies* 397 at 398–400. The point is made more generally against Fish's failure to recognize such a relationship between theory and practice in Winter, above n. 13, at 648. For broader discussion, see Neil Duxbury, *Jurists and Judges: An Essay on Influence* (Oxford, Hart Publishing, 2001).

[65] The importance of this distinction was made by a number of respondents. As one of them put it, "teaching how to distinguish between interpreting the law as it stands and identifying the inadequacies of the law is vital."

[66] For a more detailed analysis of legal reasoning, see ch. 3.

positions that exist in a hypothetical realm which goes beyond anything that fits within the scope of present plausible legal positions:

a   SIMPLE INFERENCE FROM CLEAR LEGAL MATERIALS
                                    |
b   CREATIVE INFERENCE FROM CLEAR BUT NOT OBVIOUS LM
                                    |
c   ARGUING FOR APPLICATION OF VALUES FOUND IN LM
                   (WITHIN RANGE OF PLAUSIBLY ACCEPTABLE)
                                    |
d   ARGUING FOR APPLICATION OF VALUES FOUND IN NOT
                              OBVIOUS LM
                   (WITHIN RANGE OF PLAUSIBLY ACCEPTABLE)
                                    |
e   ARGUING FOR APPLICATION OF VALUES FOUND IN LM
                  (OUTSIDE RANGE OF PLAUSIBLY ACCEPTABLE)
                                    |
f   ARGUING FOR APPLICATION OF VALUES NOT FOUND IN LM
                   (WITHIN RANGE OF PLAUSIBLY ACCEPTABLE)
                                    |
g   ARGUING FOR APPLICATION OF VALUES NOT FOUND IN LM
                  (OUTSIDE RANGE OF PLAUSIBLY ACCEPTABLE)

Stereotypically, the work of the practitioner is concerned with *a–d*, with the volume diminishing as we progress alphabetically. Nevertheless, due to the dynamic nature of law, the work that is done at the cutting edge of *b,c,d* today may become the *a* of tomorrow. More rarely will the practitioner be concerned with *f*, yet this possibility must be recognised as interrupting the smooth interchange between the interests of practitioners and academics, and has become something of a topic for reflection by the appellate judges themselves.[67]

If this covers the range of interests of practitioners and theorists, it also acknowledges the possibility of a conflict between their respective interests. Nor have we yet shed the prospects of internal strife between theorists. In particular, the recognition of the force of preconceptions in influencing our theoretical predispositions[68] weakens the distinction between adopting theory to provide coherence within legal doctrine and adopting a particular theoretical perspective on law.

To see whether the resolution of conflict and the role of theory can be taken any further, let us finally consider two points. In relation to the conflict between practice and theory, Weber's answer to the scepticism over appointing an anarchist as a law lecturer is pertinent:[69]

[67] See Lord Lowry's discussion in *C (A Minor)* v. *DPP* [1996] 1 AC 1 at 28.
[68] This factor is openly confronted in Lacey, above n. 51, e.g., at 174–5, 181–2, 185.
[69] Above n. 59, at 75.

"An anarchist can certainly be a good legal scholar. And if he is, then it may be precisely that Archimedean point, as it were, outside the conventions and assumptions which seem to us so self-evident . . . which equips him to recognise, in the axioms of conventional legal theory, certain fundamental problems which escape the notice of those who take them all too easily for granted."

Whether it is comfortable or not, theory can provide a broader understanding to those elements of our practice that we may choose to remain ignorant about.[70]

This further relates theory and practice but does little to reduce the conflict, and there still remains the conflict between theorists. Is there any basis for viewing our disparate attempts to carve out limited areas of practice, or keep grasp of our limited theoretical understanding, as in some way subject to a uniform demand upon us all? This question may be related to some of the points noted above. The indeterminacy of our meaning, practice, or theory, is potentially countered by the contingency of common experience. Our ability to explore the possibility of having a common experience is dependent on our current recognition of ignorance. The usefulness of theory is ultimately a matter of what we are prepared to experience, or indeed are capable of experiencing, in common.

ENDNOTE

For further discussion of the value of legal theory, see Neil MacCormick, "The Democratic Intellect and the law" (1985) 5 *Legal Studies* 172; Alan Hunt, "Jurisprudence, philosophy and legal education—against foundationalism" (1986) 6 *Legal Studies* 292; William Twining (ed.), *Legal Theory and Common Law* (Oxford, Basil Blackwell, 1986); Charles Sampford and David Wood, " 'Theoretical Dimensions' of Legal Education—A Response to the Pearce Report" (1988) 62 *Australian Law Journal* 32; Charles Sampford, "Rethinking the Core Curiculum" (1989) 12 *Adelaide Law Review* 38; William Twining, *Blackstone's Tower* (London, Sweet & Maxwell, 1994); Philip Thomas (ed.), *Legal Frontiers* (Aldershot, Dartmouth, 1996); William Twining, *Law in Context: Enlarging a Discipline* (Oxford, Clarendon Press, 1997) and *Globalisation and Legal Theory* (London, Butterworths, 2000); Roger Cotterrell, "Pandora's box: jurisprudence in legal education" (2000) 7 *International Journal of the Legal Profession* 179; Roscoe Pound, "Do We Need a Philosophy of Law?" (1905) 5 *Columbia Law Review* 339.

For discussion of the nature of legal theory, see Joseph Raz, *The Authority of Law* (Oxford, Clarendon Press, 1979) 84, 103–4, 132; John Finnis, *Natural Law and Natural Rights* (Oxford, Clarendon Press, 1980) ch. I; Joseph Raz, *The Morality of Freedom* (Oxford, Clarendon Press, 1986) 63–6, 149–50, 288–9, 344; Michael Moore, *Placing Blame: A General Theory of the Criminal Law* (Oxford, Clarendon Press, 1997) 4–23;

---

[70] For a modern attempt at just this, see Arthur Applbaum, "Are Lawyers Liars?" (1998) 4 *Legal Theory* 63. The complacency may exist as much in the academy as amongst practitioners, and "interdisciplinary borrowing" may provide the goad here: Winter, above n. 13, at 681. See also Twining, above n. 55, *Law in Context* at 348–51, and Anthony Bradney, "An educational ambition for 'law and literature' " (2000) 7 *International Journal of the Legal Profession* 343.

Joseph Raz, "Two Views of the Nature of the Theory of Law: A Partial Comparison" (1998) 4 *Legal Theory* 249.

Discussion of the role of conceptual analysis within legal theory can be found in Brian Bix, "Conceptual Questions and Jurisprudence" (1995) 1 *Legal Theory* 465; Andrew Halpin, "Concepts, Terms, and Fields of Enquiry" (1998) 4 *Legal Theory* 187; Joseph Raz "Two Views" above. Bix's view is developed futher in his discussion of Brian Tamanaha's *Realistic Socio-Legal Theory* (Oxford, Clarendon Press, 1997), "Conceptual Jurisprudence and Socio-Legal Studies" (2000) 32 *Rutgers Law Journal* 227, which is responded to in Part I of Brian Tamanaha, "Conceptual Analysis, Continental Social Theory, and CLS: A Response to Bix, Rubin and Livingston" (2000) 32 *Rutgers Law Journal* 281. This exchange, which at one level exhibits a local dispute between two refined emanations of analytical positivism and socio-legal studies, manifests one of the deep problems facing legal theory in general: finding the basis for an analytical perspective. Significantly, both authors have recourse to the device of "an interpretive community". In Part II of Tamanaha's article the community is extended to embrace "the broadest community of inquirers over the long run". One of the central concerns of the present book is to challenge the device of an interpretive community for concealing (or insulating) areas of ignorance and disagreement, whether in general discussion of the role of theory or in carrying out the analysis of particular phenomena. In the latter respect, it is employed (e.g., in his book at 234–5) to undergird Tamanaha's notion of legal determinacy.

Wider reading on conceptual analysis reveals a lack of agreement on what the technique (or art) of conceptual analysis amounts to. See for examples of the wider debate: Alfred Schutz, "Concept and Theory Formation in the Social Sciences" (1954) 51 *Journal of Philosophy* 257; Donald Davidson, "On the Very Idea of a Conceptual Scheme" (1974) 47 *Proceedings and Addresses of the American Philosophical Association* 5; Christopher Peacocke, *A Study of Concepts* (Cambridge, MA, MIT Press, 1992); Frank Jackson, *From Metaphysics to Ethics: A Defence of Conceptual Analysis* (Oxford, Clarendon Press, 1998); Harold Brown, "Why Do Conceptual Analysts Disagree?" (1999) 30 *Metaphilosophy* 33. The definition of terms is often regarded as the other side of the coin to conceptual analysis (for some discussion of the relationship between concepts and terms, see Halpin, "Concepts, Terms" above). The controversial nature of definition is surveyed in Richard Robinson, *Definition* (Oxford, Clarendon Press, 1954), and for further discussion see, David Lewis, "How to Define Theoretical Terms" (1970) 67 *Journal of Philosophy* 427.

For further discussion of the theory of criminal law, see Moore, *Placing Blame* above, and Nicola Lacey's review (2000) 63 *Modern Law Review* 141; George Fletcher, "The Fall and Rise of Criminal Theory" (1998) 1 *Buffalo Criminal Law Review* 275; Nicola Lacey, "Philosophy, History and Criminal Law Theory" (1998) 1 *Buffalo Criminal Law Review* 295; Antony Duff (ed.), *Philosophy and the Criminal Law* (Cambridge, Cambridge University Press, 1998); Alan Norrie, *Punishment, Responsibility, and Justice: A Relational Critique* (Oxford, OUP, 2000).

For reaction to Edwards' "growing disjunction", see Symposium: Legal Education (1993) 91(8) *Michigan Law Review* concluding with Harry Edwards, "The Growing Disjunction between Legal Education and the Legal Profession: A Postscript" at 2191; Richard Posner, *Overcoming Law* (Cambridge, MA, Harvard University Press, 1995) 91–102; Twining *Law in Context* above, ch. 16.

For a broad and provocative survey of grand theory in the work of recent past and contemporary theorists, see Quentin Skinner, "Introduction" in *The Return of Grand*

Theory in the Human Sciences (Cambridge, Cambridge University Press, 1985); and for an expressed preference for middle range theory, see Robert Merton, *Social Theory and Social Structure* (New York, NY, The Free Press, 1968) ch. II. Finally, some of the broader theoretical issues related to indeterminacy are surveyed in reasonably accessible forms in Hilary Putnam, *Renewing Philosophy* (Cambridge, MA, Harvard University Press, 1992); David Lyon, *Postmodernity* 2nd edn. (Buckingham, Open University Press, 1999).

3

Law, Autonomy, and Reason

INTRODUCTION

THE SIGNIFICANCE OF our experience as human beings, and the implications of its limitations, will be considered more fully in Part II. In each of the remaining chapters of Part I we shall be more concerned with what has been portrayed as the experience of lawyers. The theme connecting these chapters is legal reasoning, but the particular focus varies from one study to another. In this chapter I shall be concerned to examine the idea that there is something distinctive about the reasoning employed by lawyers which enables us to identify a form of *legal* reasoning. To consider the nature of legal reasoning in this way necessarily draws us into the broader enterprise of constructing a theoretical model of law. Whatever we find distinctive about legal reasoning will influence the shape of our general model of law, and conversely the absence of a distinctive character for legal reasoning will require us to modify our model of law to accommodate the more open character of legal reasoning.

Although the construction of a detailed theoretical model of law is not a principal concern of this book, it is both a working assumption and a concluding reflection of this work that clearer understanding of the nature of legal reasoning has direct implications for our broader understanding of law. The current chapter provides the opportunity to explore the nature of legal reasoning within this wider theoretical setting. The direction of my argument is towards recognition of a more general arena of reasoning in which a more complex and diverse character for legal reasoning can be discerned. In the final section of this chapter I shall offer some suggestions on a theoretical model of law but, in relation to the main objective of the book, in stressing the complexity and diversity of legal reasoning this chapter seeks to provide a surface map of characteristics of legal reasoning that will be explored more deeply in Part II.

A promising point of engagement for this study is Joseph Raz's discussion of law's autonomy and public practical reasons,[1] in response to an essay by Gerald Postema.[2] Raz's article provides further illumination of his own view of the nature of law; it forcefully challenges Postema's purported identification of the defining task of law; and it clarifies the relationships between a number of

---

[1] "Postema on Law's Autonomy and Public Practical Reasons: A Critical Comment" (1998) 4 *Legal Theory* 1.

[2] "Law's Autonomy and Public Practical Reason" in Robert George (ed.), *The Autonomy of Law* (Oxford, Clarendon Press, 1996) 79.

strands, or theses, that enter the debate over an appropriate theoretical model for law. It is not necessary to locate this discussion within the more general setting of the conflict between Natural Law and Positivism—nor is it in any case clear that that sharp contrast is sustainable.[3] Within the traditionally accentuated divide between Natural Law and Positivism, to talk of the autonomy of law would be taken as a simple positivist proclamation against the subjugation of law to moral standards. What emerges from Raz's article is a subtle interplay between different characteristics and expressions of the law, which is capable of entertaining moral influence and social objective whilst retaining clear theses that seek to capture the distinctively legal nature of the phenomenon under investigation.

In Raz's article, the distinctive nature of law is still linked to an idea of autonomy expounded in terms of the sources thesis and the pre-emption thesis[4]. The former identifies legal materials with legal sources free from the constraints of a further evaluative check, and the latter provides legal reasons to act for those subject to the law free from the consideration of further extra-legal factors. The greater sophistication of this concept of autonomy rests on the allowance Raz gives to the impact of moral factors and issues of social cooperation[5] on *legal reasoning*,[6] and his acknowledgment that legal reasoning itself is not autonomous.

This theoretical model is both elegant and attractive. One retains a distinctive sense of law as operating through its sources and upon those subject to it in a peculiarly legal (autonomous) manner; one does this while accepting the evident influence that moral factors and issues of social cooperation have in shaping the law within the process of legal reasoning. The parentage of moral and social evaluative factors may have played its part, but the law is capable of deciding for itself. The picture is of the law coming of age.

Raz's notion of *legal reasoning* is a crucial element of this theoretical model of law. Its importance lies in opening up Raz's model to those factors which, in a less sophisticated model, would defeat law's autonomy, but whose complete omission would deny credibility to the model. The moral and social evaluative factors enter legal reasoning so that legal reasoning is not autonomous, whilst being denied a place in identifying the content of law so that law is autonomous.[7] Here the notion of legal reasoning must be seen to be separate from any process of identifying the content of law. To express this point in a manner

---

[3] See e.g., Joseph Raz, *The Authority of Law* (Oxford, Clarendon Press, 1979) 157–9.

[4] Raz denies the link between the pre-emption thesis and the autonomy of legal reasoning, but not the link between the pre-emption thesis and the autonomy of law as expressed in the sources thesis, above n. 1, at 8 n20.

[5] Or coordination, *ibid.* at 9 n24.

[6] Legal reasoning as ordinary evaluative reasoning is taken by Raz to cover moral and other evaluative factors, *ibid.* at 4–6. I take "other" to refer to broad values of living together in society, other than those regarded as moral. In a different context, Raz expresses the view that it is "fairly obvious that the law plays an important role in securing some forms of social cooperation", *ibid.* at 10.

[7] *Ibid.* at 4.

consistent with the way in which Raz himself portrays his theoretical model of law, we can say that Raz has provided us with a distinctive thesis regarding legal reasoning, as a way of supplementing his well known sources thesis.

We shall consider Raz's legal reasoning thesis in some detail shortly, but there is another important role that his notion of legal reasoning plays. This arises from emphasising the *legal* attribute of the reasoning process found in Raz's model. If the reasoning in which moral and social evaluative factors play a part were not regarded as *legal*, then this part of Raz's model could be characterised as a non-legal element, and it would in turn be possible to argue for dominance of the non-legal element over the legal, so as to defeat the autonomy of law. Although Raz allows that this part of his model is not itself autonomous, by characterising it as legal he avoids the issue of whether this part could subvert the claim that law is autonomous as a whole.

Clearly law that is regarded as autonomous in relation to its operations could not have its autonomy threatened by the recognition that the *legal* territory extends to another operation. The threat would be real, however, if the operations of the law were seen to depend upon a further operation that was not properly legal. The legal operations captured in the sources thesis and pre-emption thesis, relating to the identification of legal materials and the performance of conduct in accordance with the law, will not suffer a diminution in their distinctively legal character by noting that a related operation of legal reasoning exists. Our understanding of their legal character would, however, be affected if they were dependent on an operation that was not legal. The issue at stake is the autonomy of *law*. If the operation of legal reasoning is not autonomous, it is not possible to maintain a stand on the autonomy of law without considering further just how the non-autonomous aspect of legal reasoning impinges on its legal character, and beyond that how the operation of legal reasoning relates to the other two operations found in the sources and pre-emption theses, that are regarded as autonomous.

A rather crude analogy may help to indicate the way these issues interact. If the proclamations of the royal herald are identified strictly with the herald performing a formal introduction to the proclamation he announces, and the people have reason to comply with the proclamations without consideration of any other factors, we may speak of a sources thesis and a pre-emption thesis relating to the identification of proclamations and the performance of conduct in accordance with them. Yet the herald only issues proclamations that he is given from the determinations of the king. It would be false to speak of the autonomy of the herald. In fact, there would be no practical point in discussing the autonomy of the herald, or the instrumentality of the herald to the will of the king—we only need to identify the proclamations and behave accordingly.

Suppose, however, someone suspects that we have a rogue herald, who is taking bribes to make proclamations that favour the special interests of the local baron or who simply decides for himself what to put in the proclamation. It now becomes pertinent to question the autonomy or instrumentality of the herald, and if we decide on an instrumental role for the herald subservient to the king, we can question the validity of a putative proclamation and decline to follow a proclamation we consider does not derive from the determination of the king. In doing so we upset the simple appearance of autonomy that we previously enjoyed in the practices of identifying proclamations and behaving in accordance with them. This analogy serves to make the point that we cannot talk of the autonomy of the whole social practice without addressing the nature of the autonomy of the constituent operations and how they relate to each other.

There are then two ways in which it is important to consider further Raz's use of legal reasoning in his theoretical model of law. First, there is the preliminary matter of clarifying his legal reasoning thesis: one must question how exactly Raz's notion of legal reasoning merits the legal epithet he gives it, and how this attribute of legality fits with the lack of autonomy Raz suggests for legal reasoning. Secondly, it is important to explore how the legal reasoning thesis relates to Raz's sources thesis and pre-emption thesis—and what implications follow for the autonomy of law.

I want to suggest that consideration of these matters will reinforce the position that Raz takes against Postema. Nonetheless, I shall seek to cast doubt over the position that Raz himself maintains, causing us to reconsider the nature of both the reasoning and the autonomy that is associated with law.

In the second section of this chapter I shall seek to identify a legal reasoning thesis drawn from Raz's remarks, and relate this thesis to his sources thesis. I shall suggest that my investigation throws up a conundrum about the legal reasoning thesis. I will question in the third section what is distinctively *legal* about the reasoning in Raz's legal reasoning thesis. Having concluded that Raz fails to provide a distinctively legal character to any of the forms of reasoning found within his legal reasoning thesis, I shall examine in the fourth section Raz's treatment of legal reasoning (together with his sources and pre-emption theses) in relation to the position he maintains on the autonomy of law. I shall argue that Raz's approach fails to account for a complex variety of forms of legal reasoning. In the fifth and final section I shall seek to sketch the different forms of legal reasoning revealed in the previous discussion, and suggest how their recognition has consequences for the construction of a theoretical model of law. Ultimately, I shall deny that we can identify legal reasoning as a distinctively legal form of reasoning, and deny that the autonomy of law exists as a meaningful doctrine, but not before suggesting that in order to construct an adequate theoretical model of law we need a richer analysis of what these expressions may be taken to convey.

RAZ'S LEGAL REASONING THESIS

It is perhaps doing Raz an injustice to speak of a single legal reasoning thesis, for he has many things to say about legal reasoning in the article I am discussing.

But just as one may have much to say on sources of law and still capture a fundamental point in a sources thesis, so it seems reasonable to note any fundamental point occurring in his observations about legal reasoning and characterise this as a *legal reasoning thesis*. Further support for elevating a portion of his observations on legal reasoning in this article to a legal reasoning thesis comes from the fact that this portion is made in direct contrast to the observations on legal sources found in the sources thesis so as to qualify the impact of that thesis, and thus merits a similar status as a legal reasoning thesis.

Accordingly, reminding ourselves of the sources thesis seems a good point at which to commence our efforts to identify his legal reasoning thesis:[8]

> "*Sources thesis*: membership in law's limited domain [of practical reasons or norms] is determined by criteria which are defined exclusively in terms of non-evaluative matters of social fact (about their sources), such that the existence and content of member norms can be determined entirely without appeal to moral or evaluative argument."

Raz speaks of a thesis concerning the autonomy of law as being expressed within this sources thesis: "i.e., that it is possible to identify the content of the law without recourse to moral reasoning."[9] He then rejects "any thesis of the autonomy of legal reasoning".[10]

However, in rejecting the autonomy of legal reasoning Raz is careful to clarify exactly what he means by legal reasoning. Legal reasoning in a narrow sense, which is limited purely to reasoning to the conclusion that the law has a particular content, may be autonomous.[11] This is hardly surprising; it is merely another way of expressing that part of what is found within the sources thesis which Raz has identified with the autonomy of law.[12] Reasoning to the conclusion that the law has a particular content amounts to the process of identifying the content of law, which can always be undertaken without recourse to moral argument.

Legal reasoning is regarded as not being autonomous only in a broader sense. This sense of legal reasoning may include legal reasoning in the narrow sense but encompasses "any reasoning to conclusions which entail that, according to law, if a matter were before a court the court should decide thus and so".[13]

Raz informs us of a number of features of this broader form of legal reasoning:

(a) it may be interpretive;[14]
(b) it is "ordinary evaluative reasoning";[15]

---

[8] *Ibid.* at 7. Raz follows the formulation used by Postema, which Postema attributes to Raz: Postema, above n. 2, at 113 n11.

[9] Raz, above n. 1, at 4.

[10] *Ibid.*

[11] *Ibid.* at 4–6.

[12] As Raz himself points out in his discussion of what Postema might mean by legal reasoning, *ibid.* at 4.

[13] *Ibid.*

[14] *Ibid.*

[15] *Ibid.* at 5.

(c) it may include reasoning to the conclusion that the law has a particular content;[16]

(d) it is not a matter of simple deduction from legal rules and standards but allows these to "compete with other reasons"—it "imports moral and other premises";[17]

(e) it is "according to law".[18]

This final characteristic is particularly important for Raz. He tells us that he "will use legal reasoning to refer only to reasoning according to law."[19] Based upon these remarks of Raz, we may venture to advance a legal reasoning thesis:

> *Legal reasoning thesis*: any reasoning to conclusions which entail that, according to law, if a matter were before a court the court should decide thus and so, amounts to legal reasoning, and is a form of ordinary evaluative reasoning which may make appeal to moral or other evaluative argument.

The contrast with the sources thesis above is evident. Moreover, the legal reasoning thesis operates as a qualification on the sources thesis or, at least, on how one might interpret the sources thesis. For now that we have the explicit statement that legal reasoning may have recourse to moral or other evaluative argument, it is not possible to interpret the sources thesis as cutting off this prospect for legal reasoning in general. Or, to put it another way, the form of legal reasoning implicit in the sources thesis (described as reasoning as to the content of legal norms) is not the only form of legal reasoning as Raz has been at pains to point out to us.[20]

There is a final inference to draw. It must follow that the legal norms whose existence and content is mentioned in the sources thesis as not depending upon moral or other evaluative argument are in fact insufficient to provide us with every answer required for legal problems. This is true because the legal reasoning thesis informs us that certain conclusions embodying the answer to a problem before a court may be the outcome of reasoning that does depend on moral or other evaluative argument. In other words, *the legal sources referred to in the*

---

[16] Joseph Raz, *The Authority of Law* (Oxford, Clarendon Press, 1979) at 6.

[17] *Ibid*. at 5–6.

[18] *Ibid*.

[19] *Ibid*. at 6. The precise relationship between the law and this form of ordinary evaluative reasoning that is undertaken "according to" it will be examined further below, text at n. 29 and following.

[20] Raz distinguishes an autonomous form of legal reasoning restricted to reasoning as to the content of legal norms, from a non-autonomous form of legal reasoning, *ibid*. at 4. Raz also refers to reasoning *to* and *from* the content of law, *ibid*. at 6. The same position is maintained by Raz in *Ethics in the Public Domain* (Oxford, Clarendon Press, 1994) 316–17. There is ample evidence that some form of legal reasoning thesis has been assumed alongside Raz's sources thesis in his earlier writing without perhaps receiving so much attention, see above n. 1, at 5 n10. Whether Raz has always regarded legal reasoning as embracing the two forms of (autonomous and non-autonomous) legal reasoning is questionable, see above n. 3, at 48–50, which contrasts functions of a judge relying respectively on legal ability and moral character.

sources thesis are not the source of every answer provided by the law to the problems requiring legal resolution.

A conundrum arises from considering the sources and legal reasoning theses together. If from the sources thesis we observe that the existence and content of a legal norm can be determined entirely without appeal to moral or other evaluative argument, and then from the legal reasoning thesis we observe that the decision reached by a court in a particular case may be determined by reasoning that makes appeal to moral or other evaluative argument, how can these two observations both be true without reaching the unacceptable conclusion that the judgment of the court is not a legal norm?

I want to dig deeper into this conundrum. In general, the situation is confused by the fact that a judgment of a court can be regarded as a norm not simply in disposing of the case being adjudicated, but also as a norm to be applied to similar cases in the future. It is relatively easy to argue that the sources thesis is upheld in the latter case, in determining the existence and content of the norm derived from the judgment that *has been given*; obviously one is relying exclusively on matters of non-evaluative social fact. The same cannot be done for the judgment that is given in the instant case itself. If this is a legal norm, it is a norm whose content has been determined by the evaluative matters relied upon by the judge in exercising ordinary evaluative reasoning to determine the content of his judgment.

In considering the views of Raz in particular, further confusion is caused by a failure to bring an explicit statement of the legal reasoning thesis alongside the sources thesis, and also by the compressed nature of his notion of legal reasoning. The following sections will attempt to look more fully at Raz's idea of legal reasoning, before considering to what extent he deals with the conundrum.

THE LEGAL EPITHET

I have already remarked on the significance of Raz's characterising as *legal* the process of reasoning in which moral and social evaluative factors appear. This legal epithet sustains a dominant legal character for an operation which might otherwise pose a threat to the autonomy of law. Accordingly, it becomes pertinent to investigate the basis for conferring the legal epithet on this process of reasoning. Raz allows this epithet to be applied to two forms of reasoning he identifies as legal: the narrow one, which sits within his sources thesis and his view of law as autonomous, and the broader one, which sits within his legal reasoning thesis. This latter form may include the narrower form but is open to moral and other evaluative argument. A full investigation of Raz's use of the legal epithet should consider both of these forms of legal reasoning.

We may remind ourselves that Raz's narrow legal reasoning, which may be regarded as autonomous, is limited to reasoning to the conclusion that the law has a particular content, and amounts to a way of expressing part of his sources thesis. So, we could reason to the conclusion that a contract for the sale of land (in English law) has to be in writing by reference to section 2 of the Law of Property (Miscellaneous Provisions) Act 1989. This reasoning provides a conclusion about the content of a particular part of English law, which is conducted purely by reference to legal materials, identified "exclusively in terms of non-evaluative matters of social fact"—the Law of Property (Miscellaneous Provisions) Act 1989 is an Act of Parliament, which is a recognised source of English law, which no higher source has overturned.

This illustrates the principal case of Raz's narrow legal reasoning, but there is also a secondary case alluded to in his discussion of what Postema might mean by legal reasoning. Raz considers that hypothetically there could be a case of reasoning solely from the premise that the law has a particular content, whose conclusion would "merely state the content of existing law".[21] Raz denies that this is a practical possibility, at least in common-law countries, on the grounds that judges must also take into account a further premise "that there is nothing in the situation that would justify modifying the law".[22] However, what is under consideration here is that a factual situation might come before the courts for a decision which would follow solely from the recognition that the law had a particular content, and so the disposition of that case would in itself simply confirm the content of the law we had recognised. In essence, the secondary case of narrow legal reasoning presupposes the principal case, by which the content of the law has been identified, and takes it a step further by applying that content to a specific factual situation.

It is far from obvious that such a case *never* arises, even in a common-law jurisdiction. What it amounts to is a factual situation that clearly falls within the law whose content we have recognised, and whose circumstances make it unquestionable that there is anything in that situation that could justify modifying the law. In terms of the illustration provided, it would be a case of an unwritten agreement to sell land which could be disposed of purely on the basis of recognising as the content of the law that a contract for the sale of land has to be in writing, so as to hold that the agreement is not a contract (for example, a verbal agreement over a pint of beer in a pub concluded with a handshake and nothing more).

Although Raz in his response to Postema would have us note only the hypothetical possibility of this secondary case of narrow legal reasoning, and would dismiss it altogether for English common law, there are a number of grounds for disagreeing with him and reinstating it as a practical case of legal reasoning in common-law jurisdictions.

First, cases of clear law (i.e., where, if the facts are undisputed, the law is sufficiently straightforward to make the disposition of the case unquestionable to

---

[21] Raz, above n. 1, at 4.

[22] *Ibid*. Raz's rejection of this possibility is also found boldly stated in "Facing Up" (1989) 62 *Southern California Law Review* 1153 at 1204.

the extent that it is not open to argue for a modification of the law) are recognised within the courts themselves. This is evident from the provision in the Rules of the Supreme Court which deals with a point of law being raised in answer to an application for summary judgment under Order 14. This states, "if the point [of law] is clear and the Court is satisfied that it is really unarguable, leave to defend will be refused". The paragraph provides a number of examples of such clear law.[23]

Secondly, outside court, lawyers and laymen regularly recognise that clear legal rules apply to the situation before them, without giving a second thought to whether anything would justify modifying the law. Every year thousands of written contracts to sell houses are drafted by solicitors, and thousands of wills signed by clients in the presence of witnesses, in the confident assurance that nothing will be contemplated to threaten the legal effectiveness of these documents in so far as the legal formalities have been complied with.[24] And this is to say nothing of the millions of instances of complying with the mundane requirements of road traffic law without a thought that we might wish to consider modifying, say, the legal significance of a red traffic light.

Thirdly, it is recognised widely, and by Raz himself elsewhere, as a general characteristic of law, that there can be clear cases where the decision in one case is determined by it factually falling within a class of cases governed by a general legal proposition.[25]

Fourthly, Raz implicitly relies on the existence of such a clear case in his response to Postema, when towards the end of his article he admits that, "[t]he limits on the intelligibility of the claim that a norm exists are transgressed when every occasion for its application is also an occasion for its modification or repeal."[26] Despite Raz's dilution of this admission by the subsequent suggestion that what effectively prevents occasions for modification or repeal are the obstacles to litigation, and the "variety of strategies" employed by the courts to make it difficult to get the law changed,[27] there nevertheless remain cases where the law that will not be challenged (or is seen to be unchallengeable due to our being informed about the "strategies" of the courts) is clearly applied and followed.

---

[23] RSC para 14/3–4/11 (*The Supreme Court Practice 1997* 1:161).

[24] Allegations such as fraud or undue influence may of course be raised in some cases, so as to render the compliance with legal formalities redundant. However, such cases do not question the rules as to what legal formalities are required.

[25] I rely upon Raz's discussion in above n. 20, at 229–32. Acknowledgment of particular cases falling within a general class is found at 229, and acknowledgment that it is possible to derive a true legal statement from a statement of law found in a legal source together with another true factual premise is found at 232. This is sufficient to provide a clear legal answer to a case whose accepted facts fall within a general category found stated within a legal statement found within a source of law. Raz is unconcerned with this conclusion, being occupied with denying that such a clear case exists where a moral (rather than factual) premise is involved (on that point, see further the discussion at n. 42 below). For further discussion of the law's use of general classes to provide clear guidance for particular cases, see John Finnis, *Natural Law and Natural Rights* (Oxford, Clarendon Press, 1980) at 269.

[26] Above n. 1, at 19.

[27] *Ibid.* at 20.

I shall refer to the primary and secondary cases of Raz's narrow legal reasoning as narrow$_a$ and narrow$_b$, respectively. In considering how the legal epithet applies to narrow legal reasoning, it is simpler to dispose of the case of narrow$_b$. The *reasoning* here is syllogistic. The content of the law provides our major premise—an unwritten agreement to sell land is not a contract; the factual situation supplies our minor premise—this is an unwritten agreement to sell land; from which we derive our conclusion—this is not a contract. As to the *legal* quality of the reasoning, we can refer to the fact that our major premise comes from a body of legal principles, but this is not sufficient in itself to make the reasoning legal. Simply because we had a major premise coming from the principles of dentistry, we would not refer to dental reasoning. And although mechanical reasoning does convey something metaphorically, we would not use the phrase to capture the fact that we had diagnosed the fault in a car engine by using as our major premise one of the principles governing the workings of the internal combustion engine.

Nevertheless, it may be that the phrase "sound mechanical reasoning", or "sound dental reasoning", does convey something by expressing the fact that our reasoning is based on sound mechanical principles, or sound principles of dentistry. However, in this case the mechanical or dental epithet still strictly applies to the content of the premise rather than the reasoning. And the phrase "sound mechanical reasoning" is really a compression of the phrase "reasoning based on sound mechanical premises", or to put it another way, the "mechanical" is a transferred epithet, transferred from the content of the premise to the reasoning that involves that premise. The same conclusion applies to the phrases "legal reasoning", or "sound legal reasoning", in the context of narrow$_b$ reasoning: "legal" is a transferred epithet, which applies to the content of the major premise employed in the reasoning process, indicating that it is legal, or, constitutes a sound legal premise.

The case of narrow$_a$ reasoning is not so straightforward. It does not simply involve the recognition that the factual situation arising in a particular case falls within the described factual situation found in the content of a legal principle, yet essentially the same point applies. In reasoning to the conclusion that the content of the law is such and such, we recognise that the law with such and such content satisfies the test (in terms of descriptive social fact) that allows us to recognise it as a law. This time the major premise is composed of the test for recognising a law, the minor premise is that the putative law with such and such a content satisfies that test, and the conclusion is that such and such is indeed the content of a law. Now we could apply the legal epithet to the major premise in one or both of two ways. We could speak of it as comprising a legal test, either in the sense of being a test for law, or in the sense of being a test that is itself legally recognised as the correct test. In either or both of these senses, however, the epithet strictly applies to the content of the major premise, not to the reasoning process. And in talking here of legal reasoning, we are again applying a transferred epithet.

Turning now to Raz's broader case of legal reasoning, if we consider the features displayed in the previous section,[28] then neither (a) nor (b) is capable of making the reasoning *legal*, since they identify general characteristics that this form of legal reasoning may share with other forms of reasoning that are not legal. Feature (c) covers the possibility of narrow$_a$ reasoning being involved, and so for the considerations just provided, this is insufficient to make the reasoning legal. Although feature (d) broadens the reasoning out to allow moral and other evaluative premises, even in the looser use of the transferred epithet this would only permit us to describe the reasoning as moral, etc, and so is no basis for providing a legal quality to the reasoning. We must therefore conclude that it is feature (e) that the legal epithet of Raz's broader reasoning depends upon. It is legal reasoning because it is undertaken "according to law".

This feature of reasoning *according to law* is filled out by Raz in two respects. First, it is reasoning that is undertaken by those to whom the law has given the task of resolving disputes that require legal resolution: "undertaken according to law, for the law requires courts to reach decisions through such [ordinary evaluative] reasoning."[29] But secondly, it is also necessary that those to whom the law has given the task perform this task by employing ordinary evaluative reasoning in a manner that the law permits: "reasoning according to law, reasoning that imports moral and other premises in accordance with the role they have by law, or at any rate consistently with the law."[30]

In the first respect of what it means to reason according to law, we are simply saying that those so engaged in reasoning are authorised by the law to do so. This in itself does not make the *reasoning* legal, even in the transferred sense considered above, any more than by authorising only the chief mechanic to work on the managing director's car we would ensure that his reasoning was mechanical in even the loosest sense.

Yet it will be the case that the *outcome* of the reasoning engaged in by those authorised by the law to do so will count as legal. It will count as legal in the dual sense of being recognised both by the law, and as law. Still this does not make the *reasoning* legal. Indeed, if we do focus exclusively on this first respect, and the courts are given plenipotentiary authority to determine cases that come

---

[28] Text at nn. 14–19 above.

[29] Raz, above n. 1, at 5. It is worth pointing out that for Raz the legal requirement to use the reasoning does not mark off a distinctive case of evaluative reasoning that can be labelled legal. Although the law may restrict the scope of such reasoning (see point following in main text), the law is providing an opportunity (however so restricted) to engage in "ordinary" evaluative reasoning. Elsewhere Raz expresses his belief about why it is appropriate to engage in ordinary evaluative reasoning on such occasions. There exists a general background reason: there is a natural need to employ such reasoning when determining issues that affect the well-being of others (above n. 20, at 311–12). There may be a specific reason found in the explicit use of an evaluative term in the legal materials (*ibid.* at 227; cp above n. 3, at 75). There is also a simple pragmatic reason: there is nothing else other than ordinary evaluative reasoning that could do the job (above n. 20, at 314–17).

[30] Above n. 1, at 6. That both requirements are necessary is made clear by Raz in considering the possibility of a perverse judgment, made by an authorised judge in an unauthorised manner, which would not be a case of reasoning according to law.

before them, we might sensibly talk of the reasoning of judges, the autonomy of the judges, and even, in a transferred sense,[31] the autonomy of judicial reasoning. But we cannot talk here of a distinctive sense of legal reasoning, or talk sensibly of the autonomy of legal reasoning.

Taking in the second respect of what Raz considers it means to reason according to law, the legal qualification of the reasoning process clearly moves us away from a position of complete judicial autonomy, or (more loosely) the autonomy of judicial reasoning. However, to require that a judge "imports moral and other premises in accordance with the role they have by law, or at any rate consistently with the law" only reduces the latitude of judicial discretion in prioritising moral (or other) premises or criteria, which will be employed in the reasoning process. It circumscribes the judge's authority to engage in a reasoning process whose outcome will count as legal in the sense indicated. The amount of latitude allowed by the law to this reasoning process may vary, but still in no case will this make the *reasoning* legal.

Taken to the extreme case, importing moral and other premises in accordance with the role they have by law will completely close down judicial autonomy because that role will be so tightly drawn as to itself determine the decision that the court will reach. However, this amounts to a more sophisticated form of narrow$_b$ reasoning, in that instead of the content of a single legal provision, we now have the contents of one or more moral or other premises ordered in accordance with the role that the law permits them to perform; this provides a definite amalgamated content, sufficient to govern the outcome of the case that the court is to decide. Apart from this extreme case,[32] judges will retain a greater or lesser degree of autonomy in their evaluative reasoning, selecting from and ordering together moral and other evaluative premises, within the confines permitted by the law. Some recognition that the latitude of judicial discretion may vary is found in Raz's alternative formulation of the legal check: "or at any rate consistently with the law".[33] This suggests that in some cases there will be a wider scope for judicial discretion in selecting from and ordering together the moral and other evaluative premises.

In all these cases we can sensibly address the issue of the extent of judicial autonomy allowed by the law; we can speak of the judge's reasoning, of the judge's reasoning being authorised by law, of the legal outcome of the judge's reasoning. There is, however, no basis for talking of a distinctive sense of legal reasoning or for talking of the autonomy of legal reasoning.

---

[31] Strictly speaking it is the judges who are autonomous in selecting the premises, or criteria, to employ in their ordinary evaluative reasoning.

[32] Differing views can be found as to whether the extreme case ever exists, and if so how common it is. It is interesting to note that Raz provides an example of reasoning from determinate moral premises as stipulated by the law, above n. 20, at 230, though I shall argue below that he does not allow for the full significance of the possibility.

[33] See text at n. 30 above.

Our survey of Raz's forms of legal reasoning must conclude that in each of them the legal epithet is strictly speaking inappropriate. In narrow legal reasoning, it is a transferred epithet which is transferred from the content of the major premise employed in the reasoning process (the legal test in narrow$_a$ reasoning, and the legal principle in narrow$_b$ reasoning). In broader legal reasoning, the legal epithet depends on feature (e), that the reasoning is according to law. This feature turns out to be a complex one which yields a number of ways in which the legal epithet can be traced, but in none of them does it relate to the reasoning itself; it relates rather to the authorisation of those engaged in the reasoning, to the outcome of the reasoning, and to the restriction (of a greater or lesser extent) placed upon the manner in which the reasoning may proceed.

SOME IMPLICATIONS

I want now to begin to consider the implications of the close attention we have paid to the legal character of the reasoning found in the different forms of legal reasoning recognised by Raz. I shall commence by looking at the implications for his view of the autonomy of law. This will serve to develop the significance of relating the sources thesis to the legal reasoning thesis, and will lead naturally to a reconsideration of the conundrum I articulated earlier. In turn this will open up questions concerning the way Raz seeks to place within the broader umbrella term *legal reasoning* a variety of instances of reasoning related to law, whilst on the other hand restricting his use of the term in some cases. I shall argue that a revision of Raz's position does lead us towards a meaningful general use of the term *legal reasoning*, but one that is sensitive to a greater variety of forms than Raz has acknowledged.

So far as the issue of autonomy goes, Raz's characterisation of narrow legal reasoning as autonomous can be recast in the light of a stricter reference point for the legal epithet. We should now speak not of the autonomy of legal reasoning, but rather of reasoning from premises whose content is restricted to the application of (non-evaluative social fact) tests of legal sources—in the principal case (narrow$_a$) the major premise is constituted by such a test, and in the secondary case (narrow$_b$) the major premise is the outcome of solely applying such a test. This goes so far as to make law autonomous in the sense of being identifiable by a process of reasoning which does not depend on moral or other evaluative argument, and is free accordingly from a further moral check—which requirement lies at the heart of Raz's sources thesis. But this clarification of legal autonomy as expressed through the sources thesis severely limits a doctrine of the autonomy of law in two ways.

First, legal autonomy of this sort depends upon our being able to rely entirely on a major premise constituted either by a non-evaluative social fact test of legal sources (narrow$_a$ reasoning) or by what is solely the outcome of applying such a test (narrow$_b$ reasoning). Secondly, the legal autonomy we have identified with the reliance on such a premise has no relevance beyond the acceptance of that premise. That is to say, it tells us nothing about what factors (evaluative or otherwise) operate prior to the acceptance of the major premise constituted by a non-evaluative social fact test of legal sources: it does not state why we have this test rather than that one. Nor does this kind of autonomy say anything about what factors (evaluative or otherwise) operate to determine the content of those legal sources prior to their being identifiable by such a test: although identifying them by the test necessarily identifies the content they have, it does not indicate how it is that they have come to have such a content.

From the first point in the previous paragraph it follows that any legal operation that does not rely entirely on such a major premise falls outside the scope of this kind of legal autonomy. This means that when we turn to what is, for Raz, the more important broader legal reasoning, it is not simply a matter, as he portrays it, of being unable to accept the autonomy of legal reasoning. We can no longer support the autonomy of law as established by Raz in the case of narrow legal reasoning. The condition (of depending entirely on a major premise constituted directly or indirectly by a non-evaluative social fact test of legal sources) is no longer satisfied.

Taken together with the qualifications noted in the second point made above, this does much to diminish the scope of a claim that law is autonomous. Moreover, our enquiry into the role of the legal epithet in the case of broader legal reasoning confirms the idea that the issue here is not one of the autonomy of legal reasoning at all. A more rigorous application of the legal epithet reveals that the issue is this, how autonomous are *the judges* in exercising their ordinary evaluative reasoning in determining particular legal outcomes?

This question relates to the conundrum raised earlier concerning the problem of recognising a court's judgment as a legal norm when the content of the norm has been fixed by moral or other evaluative argument. The analysis in the previous section of the appropriate roles for the legal epithet in the case of broader legal reasoning separated the following elements:

   (i) the *legally authorised position*[34] of the judge to reach a decision;

  (ii) the *ordinary evaluative reasoning* employed by the judge in reaching a decision;

  (iii) any *legal constraints* upon that reasoning (and hence on the authorised position to reason);

  (iv) the *legal outcome* of such reasoning.

---

[34] I use "authorised position" here to cover the twin aspects of *power* to give a legally binding judgment and *duty* to exercise that power. The detailed content of both aspects of the judicial position must contain some reference to exercising that power or performing that duty as the law requires—a judge passing judgment in favour of a party in return for a bribe would be in breach of that duty and would not be exercising that power—though if unchallenged the judgment may remain valid as fulfilling a legal *condition* of being delivered by a judge in accordance with the legal formalities. On the distinction between exercising a power and fulfilling a condition, see ch. III of Andrew Halpin, *Rights and Law—Analysis and Theory* (Oxford, Hart Publishing, 1997).

Unless (iii) is so restrictive as to take us to a sophisticated form of narrow$_b$ reasoning,[35] then the specific judgment of the court, (iv), becomes a legal norm because it is the outcome of the *reasoning* of a person authorised by the law to reach a decision in this case. As the judge reasons towards the content of the legal norm that comes into existence as the outcome of his reasoning, we can say that the *existence and content* of this legal norm is being determined by moral or other evaluative argument ((ii) as constrained by (iii)), and so the test in the sources thesis (on which Raz's notion of legal autonomy depends) is being denied.

However, once we get to the point where the judge has determined the existence and content of this norm, then others may identify the existence and content of the norm purely by referring to (i–authority) and (iv–outcome), ie, without engaging in any moral or other evaluative argument. Only at this point is Raz's sources thesis upheld, and so able to provide the status of a legal norm to the judgment in accordance with it. Significantly, Raz's pre-emption thesis only bites at this point too. For if we consider the position of a citizen who is considering how to behave in accordance with the law that a judge *will* establish to dispose of his dispute, it is impossible for this citizen to decide how to act without considering extra-legal factors that might shape the decision of the judge.[36]

Raz effectively conceals the significance of the conundrum by using the *legal* epithet for the whole process of reasoning covered by (i)–(iv), and by emphasising that it is a process entirely undertaken "according to law". This fails to isolate the two distinct processes that may be involved: first in the judge's determining the legal answer to the issue facing the court in a particular case, requiring (ii–evaluation) and (iii–constraint); and subsequently in identifying the legal answer given by the court to the issue in a particular case by focusing only on (iv–outcome).

Through avoiding the full implications of the different elements involved, Raz may appear to provide a solution to the conundrum. However, this appearance is achieved either by relying entirely on (iv–outcome) in identifying the existence and content of the legal norm,[37] or by switching the focus to where a judge complies with a prior norm to engage in the process of reasoning. This is the norm (whose existence and content can be identified in accordance with the sources thesis) found at (i–authority), requiring the courts to determine the case before them, and so to act "according to law".[38] The ordinary evaluative reasoning of the judges in determining the content of the legal norm used to dispose

---

[35] See text preceding n. 32 above.

[36] This is recognised by Raz elsewhere, above n. 20, at 232.

[37] This is included as a case of narrow$_a$ reasoning, Raz, above n. 1, at 5, and is explained in detail, *ibid*. at 14–16, as being the basis for discovering the content of the court's decision that is "established as precedent".

[38] *Ibid*. at 5; and similarly, at 18. Cp Raz's notion of a "directed legal power" discussed in the following note.

of the case before them, together with its implications, somehow slips away between the subsequent recognition of the outcome and its prior authorisation.[39]

Raz's strategy raises a number of related questions. Why link elements (i–authority), (ii–evaluation), (iii–constraint) and (iv–outcome) together within the broader form of legal reasoning? Why not focus on the separate legal norms found at (i–authority) providing authority to engage in reasoning to reach a decision, and at (iv–outcome) indicating established law guiding future cases? If one is concerned to uphold the sources thesis, why bother to maintain any *legal* link between (i–authority) and (iv–outcome), rather than severing our legal interest at (i–authority) and waiting in a state of suspended animation for (iv–outcome) before recommencing our concerns as legal theorists?[40] On the other hand, if one does find good cause to maintain the legal link between (i–authority) and (iv–outcome) by identifying a process of legal reasoning, why be content to stop there rather than to explore further the different forms of legal reasoning that occur at (ii–evaluation) and (iii–constraint)?

To answer these questions is in general to recognise that the process involved at (ii–evaluation) and (iii–constraint) in making the link between (i–authority) and (iv–outcome) does possess features which give it a legal character, whichever form it takes. We can go further and suggest that it is impossible to isolate the legal concerns attached to (i–authority) and (iv–outcome) from the process involved at (ii–evaluation) and (iii–constraint). However, providing satisfactory answers does require us to confront the different forms of the legal reasoning process that may occur at (ii–evaluation) and (iii–constraint). Such an approach precludes the possibility of sheltering under an umbrella term of broader legal reasoning, unconcerned with the detail of the processes that might be involved at (ii–evaluation) and (iii–constraint) and the implications they might have for the legal environment around us.

Let us start with the simplest possible process that might link (i–authority) and (iv–outcome), a case of narrow$_b$ legal reasoning. Although Raz banished this to the hypothetical in his response to Postema, I have argued above that there are grounds for reinstating it as an actual occurrence in English law, and

---

[39] In an earlier treatment of a similar "puzzle" Raz provided a solution which on the one hand boldly eradicated the legal significance of elements (ii–evaluation) and (iii–constraint) by pronouncing that prior to reaching stage (iv–outcome), there simply was no law, whilst on the other hand maintained a link between stages (i–authority) and (iv–outcome) in terms of the judge reasoning to the conclusion in (iv–outcome) in accordance with a directed legal power provided in (i–authority). Significantly, this solution is undergirded by treating the Sources Thesis as axiomatic. It is interesting to note that although the "puzzle" is attributed to the concerns of other theorists, Raz is willing to provide a solution to it, indicating the general importance of the puzzle. Above n. 20, at 223, 228–32. I discuss Raz's use of a "directed legal power" further in n. 50 below.

[40] The link is maintained by Raz both by recognising the broader form of legal reasoning, and by the argument built around directed powers, referred to in the previous footnote. The alternative, of treating only the narrow form of legal reasoning as strictly falling within the concern of the law, was perhaps at one time entertained by Raz in making a distinction between the legal and moral roles of a judge, see n. 20 above.

noted also that Raz acknowledges it as a possibility elsewhere in his writings.[41] In a case of narrow$_b$ legal reasoning we saw that the legal epithet strictly applied to the content of the major premise, to which was added a factual minor premise, in order to reach the legal conclusion:

Syllogism 1

major premise:	(legal principle) an unwritten agreement to sell land is not a contract
minor premise:	this is an unwritten agreement to sell land
conclusion:	this agreement is not a contract

This form of legal reasoning could be engaged in by a judge authorised to determine a case so as to reach a conclusion (and thereby provide a link between (i–authority) and (iv–outcome)). It could equally be engaged in by a citizen, or that citizen's legal adviser, so as to indicate how the law would be applied by the judge in a case where the law was so clear that litigation would be futile (the handshake in the pub). It may also arise in a case where litigation does occur due to a dispute over the facts, on the common assumption by both parties as to what the legal outcome will be depending on the determination of the factual dispute (I have what appears to be a written agreement signed by you to sell me your land, which you claim I have forged).

Although I have suggested that Raz does recognise such a case of narrow$_b$ legal reasoning where a factual premise is added to the legal principle contained in the major premise, Raz clearly balks at allowing that one could similarly reach a valid legal conclusion where the minor premise involved not a factual premise but a moral one. The example he provides is:

Syllogism 2

major premise:	(legal principle) a contract tending to corruption in public life is illegal
minor premise:	this is a contract tending to corruption in public life
conclusion:	this is an illegal contract.

In this case Raz insists we must await the decision of the court before reaching the legal conclusion as to the status of the contract.[42]

One might assume that what lies behind Raz's insistence here is the indeterminacy of the moral test in the minor premise, given which we must await its authoritative determination by the court. This is not the case, however, for Raz has constructed this particular hypothetical on the assumption that the moral test is determinate on this occasion.[43] Raz's misgivings go deeper. He argues that we must wait for the court's decision, because the minor premise calls for

---

[41] See nn. 25 and 26 above, and text accompanying.

[42] Above n. 20, at 232. This is the occasion for Raz's pronouncement of no law prior to the court's decision, remarked on in n. 39 above. It occurs in juxtaposition to Raz recognising but not pursuing a different possibility where a *factual* premise is involved (see n. 25 above).

[43] *Ibid.* at 230.

moral reasoning and hence we cannot reach the conclusion without relying on moral argument. In this way we uphold the sources thesis, waiting for the social fact of the court's decision rather than relying on moral argument, in order to conclude what the law is.[44]

However, in the case where the moral test in the minor premise is determinate, Raz's objection can be overcome. If, as in Raz's hypothetical where there is no indeterminacy in applying the moral test, it is generally accepted in society that contracts to provide election funds in return for favours after being elected do tend to corruption in public life, we can speak of the fact of how such contracts are regarded. Although moral reasoning might be required in order to apply a moral test, the outcome of that reasoning can be reported as a factual statement. If, on a particular occasion, the outcome of the moral test is determinate, we can then factually report this determinacy by stating what the outcome of the test is (without needing to wait for any authoritative determination). On such occasions it is, accordingly, possible to substitute a factual premise as the minor premise. That "this is a contract tending to corruption in public life" is accepted as a factually true statement of how contracts to provide election funds in return for favours are morally regarded in our society.

In the case where the moral test in the minor premise is determinate, we can in this way find a factual premise and recognise an instance of narrow$_b$ legal reasoning in the same way as where the factual character of the minor premise is overt. To be completely rigorous we should acknowledge that we are reading into the legal principle found in the major premise as implicit a reference to the moral standard as accepted in our society, but it is necessary to find some reference point and it is difficult to think of a more appropriate one in a case where society does have a determinate moral standard.[45] The syllogism then reads:

Syllogism 3

major premise: (legal principle) a contract [regarded in our society as] tending to corruption in public life is illegal

minor premise: this is a contract [regarded in our society as] tending to corruption in public life

conclusion: this is an illegal contract.

This syllogism does not, however, deal with the case where the moral test is indeterminate. Must we accept that at least here Raz's objection holds? We must acknowledge that in the case of moral indeterminacy we cannot reach a definite conclusion as to what the law is, but this does not prevent us from having a stab

---

[44] *Ibid.* at 232.

[45] Referring to the common standards of society is a frequent judicial practice. The danger is that judges can purport to be doing it in a case where there are no common standards, and hence the moral test found in the law is not determinate. I discuss an example of this in relation to dishonesty in the Theft Acts in "The Test for Dishonesty" [1996] *Criminal Law Review* 283. However that is not to say that no clear common standards exist—consider a case of a severe beating of a toddler resulting in broken bones in applying the common law test of "moderate and reasonable" physical chastisement.

at it. However, in engaging in this broader form of legal reasoning, which does require us to undertake ordinary evaluative reasoning,[46] we are not simply engaging in the ordinary evaluative reasoning that we might indulge in if we woke up one morning to discover that we had been given the job of deciding the outcome of every case as we thought it should be.[47] We are either adopting a confident posture of counsel in thinking our own moral argument would be sufficient to persuade the court to accept that this contract is one that tends to corruption in public life, or the insightful posture of a commentator who is confident of predicting that the court will determine that this contract is one that tends to corruption in public life. Otherwise, if we are honest, we will admit that it is utterly impossible to conclude what the law is in this case of moral indeterminacy.

Lawyers might sometimes reach this extreme point of honesty. I suspect that more often they adopt one of the two preceding postures, with greater or less confidence. But these two postures approximate closely to a case of narrow$_b$ legal reasoning: they are both trying to fill in the minor premise with the fact of what the court will accept (rather than the fact of what is accepted by all in a case of moral determinacy). The further amended syllogism then reads:

Syllogism 4

major premise:	(legal principle) a contract [regarded in our society as] tending to corruption in public life is illegal
minor premise:	{the court will find that} this is a contract [regarded in our society as] tending to corruption in public life
conclusion:	this is an illegal contract.

---

[46] Raz stresses that this sort of reasoning can be undertaken by judge or citizen, above n. 20, at 311.

[47] We should remind ourselves that the moral test is indeterminate and hence there exists a number of possible answers that ordinary evaluative reasoning could provide (cp Raz, above n. 3, at 199, in acknowledging that two people sharing the same moral view and information may exercise their moral judgements with different outcomes). This opens up consideration of an ambiguity in the legal reasoning thesis. Raz speaks of what the court "should decide" if a case were before it. The "should" is ambiguous as to the probable or normative. In the case where the law contains an indeterminate moral test, my *legal* reasoning as to what the court should decide must involve reading the "should" as a matter of probability—I am otherwise indulging myself in moral reasoning as to what I would decide if I were the judge, which given that I am not may have nothing to do with the law. In the case where the law contains a determinate moral test both readings will lead to the same result—the probable outcome will ride on the back of the determinate moral outcome. The legal reasoning thesis accordingly makes sense as a thesis of *legal* reasoning if we generally take the "should" in the probability sense, bearing in mind that calculations of such probability may require us to engage in such ordinary evaluative reasoning that we could expect of the court.

Two further points need to be made. If we accept the possibility of a determinate moral test, then we must acknowledge the possibility of a probability of 1, ie a certain outcome in applying ordinary evaluative reasoning. A more far reaching consequence of examining the role of "should" in the Legal Reasoning Thesis is to open up a possibility of tensions between what the judge considers he should (normatively) decide, what I consider the judge should (probability) decide, and what I consider the judge should (normatively) decide—which makes the Thesis in its present form inadequate. These tensions will be explored in detail in the following section.

The family resemblance is perhaps sufficient to persuade us to allow such a case of broader legal reasoning to share the common appellation of legal reasoning with narrow$_b$ legal reasoning of an overt fact type and narrow$_b$ legal reasoning of a determinate moral test type, and to account for Raz's bringing elements (i–authority), (ii–evaluation), (iii–constraint) and (iv–outcome) together under the umbrella term legal reasoning. But the connections between these three forms of reasoning and the common appellation can be traced in a different way, in that whether we have a case of narrow$_b$ overt fact legal reasoning, of narrow$_b$ determinate moral test legal reasoning, or of broader indeterminate moral test legal reasoning, can itself be a matter for argument amongst lawyers.[48] There exists a more general arena of reasoning relating to the law in which these very distinctions are worked out, and into which other factors may enter.

There are two further reasons why if we are dealing with a case of broader legal reasoning we cannot isolate the ordinary evaluative reasoning that occurs at (ii–evaluation) so as to exclude it from the concerns of the law. One is evident in Raz's analysis from the presence of legal constraints in element (iii–constraint) alongside element (ii–evaluation), and also more generally from the background body of law into which the position of the judge in element (i–authority) fits. The requirement upon the judge to determine whether this contract tends to corruption in public life is to be read not only in the context of the particular legal provision that provides this requirement but also in the context of the wider body of existing law.[49]

The second may similarly be discerned in elements (iii–constraint) and (i–authority) though arises not from the background body of legal doctrine but on the latitude allowed to the judge to depart from that doctrine in engaging in ordinary evaluative reasoning. I have argued against Raz that this cannot be captured in a single legal proposition that judges are free in every case to consider whether there is anything in the situation that would justify modifying the law. There may, however, be legal principles that have some bearing here, such as those which alter the degree of latitude considered permissible depending on the court involved or the subject matter of the case.

It now seems that much complexity may lie behind the parenthetical clause, {the court will find that}, in the minor premise of Syllogism 4. The discussion so far would suggest that having recognised the looseness of the legal epithet, we may return to a general employment of the term *legal reasoning* to cover a variety of forms, each of which is related to the law, so long as we do not lose sight of the complexity that lies beneath. We have not as yet satisfactorily explored that complexity. The burden of clarifying the implications of this complexity for a theoretical model of law will be taken up in the next section. There are already

---

[48] Raz shows how a test for inflation might be regarded as factual or evaluative, and speaks of determinate and indeterminate outcomes of evaluative tests without providing any clear guidance on how we can recognise one rather than the other, above n. 20, at 228–31.

[49] Cp Raz, *ibid.* at 233, 223, 237.

implications for our understanding of the nature of the reasoning involved prior to a decision by a court. Although the discussion so far upholds some sense of broader legal reasoning, it does so through denying the possibility of isolating elements (ii–evaluation) and (iii–constraint) and banishing them to a no-law zone until a judgment of a court is reached.[50] This also has implications for Raz's sources thesis.

WIDER ISSUES

In this final section I want to expand the observations that have been made both on legal reasoning and the autonomy of law and briefly consider some of the consequences for an adequate theoretical model of law. Before tying in some concluding remarks on the exchange between Raz and Postema, I will enumerate a number of points building on the previous discussion. I hope that in their present concise form they will serve to elucidate the distinctions between the different forms of legal reasoning, whose recognition I have suggested lies at the heart of a more general understanding of legal reasoning and thus of our grasp of the nature of law.

(1) *There is a diversity of reasoning processes that may be engaged in relating to law.*

At the very least we must distinguish among the following:

---

[50] It is worth making briefly some further comment on two of the arguments Raz employs in order to suggest the existence of the no law zone (see n. 39 above). One is the argument on directed powers, already referred to. The argument depends on establishing an analogy between a directed legislative power and a directed judicial power (*ibid.* at 228) but this analogy fails. Raz is right to point out that there is no law in the former case until the legislative power has been used to bring it about (so that nobody could purport to be acting lawfully or complain that another is acting unlawfully in accordance with such law until it is enacted: see, in particular, Raz's discussion of EC directives that do not have direct effect, *ibid.* at 235). However, in the case of a directed judicial power, law does exist prior to the exercise of the power, which can be employed to guide behaviour and be used to complain about the unlawful behaviour of another, even as a preliminary to the very exercise of that directed power in the case in which the complaint is made. Raz acknowledges the distinction (*ibid.*, at top of 235) but fails to allow for its significance, relying on the uncertainty that sometimes accompanies the exercise of a directed judicial power (*ibid.* at 235–6)—but this is uncertainty as to what the law is, or whether the existing law will survive a challenge to overturn it, not certainty as to there being no law. (See further, n. 64 below.)

The second argument is related to the first, suggesting that there is no law for the citizen until the point judgment is reached. This leads on to an acute problem that Raz faces in his exchange with Postema (above n. 1, at 18–20). How can any norm be regarded as binding on a citizen if it is capable of being challenged in the courts, and upon challenge there exists no norm until judgment is given? Raz's response to the problem is to rely on the limited motivation and practical opportunity to engage in litigation. This ducks the issue because it fails to address all those cases where citizens do not consider litigation where they share a common perception of what the law is without needing a judge to determine it. It also fails to address what happens in those cases where litigation does occur and arguments are mounted as to the *existing* law, and remedies sought on the basis of its existence at the time of the wrongs alleged.

(a) formal deductive reasoning, grounded in a test of legal sources, in order to reach a conclusion that a norm with such and such content is a legal norm;

(b) formal deductive reasoning upon the basis of a recognised legal norm with such and such content to derive a conclusion that a particular case should be legally disposed of by a court through a decision that such and such applies;

(c) ordinary evaluative reasoning by a judge, who is authorised by the law to decide a particular case, used to reach the conclusion that in that case such and such applies;

(d) (as a case of (a)) formal deductive reasoning, from a test of legal sources recognising precedent as a source of law, to a conclusion that a norm with such and such content is a legal norm because a case has been decided by a court on the basis that such and such applies;

(e) (ancillary to (d)) textual analysis of the judgment of a court, which may include speculation regarding the ordinary evaluative reasoning employed by the judge, to reach the conclusion that the case has been decided by a court on the basis that such and such applies;

(f) ordinary evaluative reasoning to reach the conclusion that a judge, authorised by the law to dispose of a particular case, should decide it on the basis that such and such applies;

(g) speculation that a judge, authorised by the law to dispose of a particular case, will employ ordinary evaluative reasoning to reach the conclusion that the case should be decided on the basis that such and such applies.

Further variants of the above may be identified along the following lines:

$(c_1)/(d_1)/(e_1)/(f_1)/(g_1)$ . . . where relevant legal materials not otherwise determinative of the case are referred to alongside moral or other evaluative factors;[51]

$(c_2)/(d_2)/(e_2)/(f_2)/(g_2)$ . . . where there are no relevant legal materials and recourse is had only to moral or other evaluative factors;[52]

---

[51] This variant covers a number of types of situation. One is where the legal material contains an abstract proposition which must be subjected to moral or other evaluative factors before determining whether it should be instantiated in a particular concrete case, I have discussed this in relation to rights in chs V and VI of Halpin, above n. 34. Another is where linguistic imprecision in the legal material permits the court to invoke moral or other evaluative factors in considering whether a legal principle should apply to a particular case, e.g. the statutory provision considered earlier requiring contracts for the sale of land to be in writing explicitly provides that this will be satisfied "where contracts are exchanged". The question whether this phrase covered the final stages of an agreement concluded by written letters fell to be decided (in the negative) by the Court of Appeal in *Commission for the New Towns* v. *Cooper (G.B.) Ltd* [1995] Ch 259. Overt evaluative reasoning on this point is to be found at 287. Reasoning by analogy may also be found here (overlapping, if not a separate type of situation). On this see Raz, above n. 3, at 201–6, and the extensive discussion by Scott Brewer in "Exemplary Reasoning: Semantics, Pragmatics, and the Rational Force of Legal Argument by Analogy" (1996) 109 *Harvard Law Review* 923. Both conclude that reasoning by analogy from legal materials is not itself determinative of the issue.

[52] An explicit admission that the case before them fell into this category was made by the House of Lords in *Airedale NHS Trust* v. *Bland* [1993] AC 789, at 879–80 *per* Lord Browne-Wilkinson.

$(c_3)/(d_3)/(e_3)/(f_3)/(g_3)$ . . . where relevant legal materials otherwise determinative of the case are discarded on the grounds of moral or other evaluative factors—in circumstances where the court is legally permitted to do so;[53]
$(c_4)/(d_4)/(e_4)/(f_4)/(g_4)$ . . . where relevant legal materials otherwise determinative of the case are discarded on the grounds of moral or other evaluative factors—in circumstances where the court is not legally permitted to do so.[54]

(2) *The role of legal sources in determining the existence and content of legal norms is dependent on a number of factors.*

In particular we should note:

(a) that the nature of the existing legal materials may make them inadequate to determine the legal outcome of a particular case;
(b) that the extent to which existing legal materials are used to determine the legal outcome of a particular case may be affected by the attitude taken to existing materials by those authorised to reach that decision;
(c) that the fact that the legal outcome of a particular case is determined by those who are authorised by a legal source to determine that outcome does not make the content of that outcome determined by a legal source.

(3) *The role of moral and other evaluative factors in determining the existence and content of legal norms may vary in a number of ways.*

In particular we should note:

(a) that moral and other evaluative factors may enter the process of ordinary evaluative reasoning by a judge which leads to the content of an authoritative legal norm in cases (1)(c), including variants (c_1)–(c_4);
(b) that, although the process of reasoning in case 1(f) is strictly distinct from the process of reasoning in case 1(e) or 1(g)—1(f) is unrestricted ordinary evaluative reasoning, the other two cases ((e) and (g)) involve speculation as to how someone else has engaged in, or will engage in, ordinary evaluative reasoning,[55] the speculative nature of this reasoning will leave open the

---

[53] The paradigm setting in English law is the *Practice Statement (Judicial Precedent)* [1966] 1 WLR 1234, which permits the House of Lords to depart from their own previous decisions when they consider that "it is right to do so", making overt the ordinary evaluative reasoning involved.

[54] For an effective denunciation of the House of Lords for subverting statutory material, see Glanville Williams, "The Lords and Impossible Attempts, or *Quis Custodiet Ipsos Custodes?*" (1986) 45 *Cambridge Law Journal* 33. I have argued that the English Court of Appeal acted in breach of the principles of precedent in altering the basis for assessing damages for defamation, in "Law, Libel and the English Court of Appeal" (1996) 4 *Tort Law Review* 139.

[55] Cp Raz, above n. 1, at 14–16. Raz labels what I refer to in 1(e) "reconstructive argument", but does not fully discuss the 1(g) scenario. This may be attributed to Raz subsequently focusing on a case of the court changing previously clear law (variant (c_3)) rather than clarifying unclear law (variant (c_1) or (c_2)), marginalising even this prospect, and stressing that the law is anyway binding either side of the change (*ibid.* at 18–20). Similarly, in above n. 20, at 323–4, Raz narrows down the discussion to an either–or between judicial evaluative (moral) reasoning in deviating from legal doctrine, and the application of legal doctrine.

possibility of bringing in ordinary evaluative reasoning as found in 1(f),[56] and so allow moral and other evaluative factors to enter the process of reasoning in cases (1)(e) and (1)(g), including variants (e_1)–(e_4) and (g_1)–(g_4);

(c) that moral and other evaluative factors may enter the preliminary process of ordinary evaluative reasoning engaged in by a court in deciding whether to engage in a process of formal deductive reasoning of type (1)(b) or of ordinary evaluative reasoning of type (1)(c_3) or (1)(c_4) in discarding relevant legal materials;[57]

(d) that moral and other evaluative factors may be used to determine or speculate on the existence of a legal norm in the preceding cases (3)(a)–(c) only in the weak sense of determining or speculating on *the existence of a legal norm with a particular content* as opposed to a legal norm existing with a different content, but not in the strong sense of determining or speculating that a norm with such content has *an existence as a legal norm*; that would be a conclusion which could only be reached by recognising the legal source of the norm, i.e., through engaging in formal deductive reasoning from a test of legal sources;[58]

(e) that although the existence and content of a legal norm can be discovered without recourse to moral or other evaluative factors, through engaging in a process of formal deductive reasoning in case (1)(a), 1(b), or (1)(d), the

---

[56] In the context of "reconstructive reasoning" Raz concedes that "we often rely on our ideas of what is reasonable in reconstructing other people's thought", but limits the legitimacy of this to occasions when we have reason to believe that the person whose reasoning we are reconstructing shares our view of what is reasonable (above n. 1, at 15–16). The scope for bringing in our own evaluative reasoning is actually greater than Raz allows for a number of reasons: (i) the full range of speculative reasoning extends beyond Raz's case of reconstructive reasoning, taking in (1)(g) as well as (1)(e) with variants (g_1)–(g_4) and (e_1)–(e_4)—including dealing with the situations illustrated in n. 51 above; (ii) even if we are attempting to reconstruct the evaluative reasoning of a single judgment, the material we are working on may not be consistent or coherent, permitting us to choose those parts we find reasonable; (iii) this opportunity is greatly increased when we have multiple judgments to reconstruct; (iv) a similar point applies when we have a variety of precedents to select from. The practical demonstration of this occurs in just about every appellate court case, where counsel learned in the law are able to argue on opposing sides constructions or reconstructions of the law employing evaluative reasoning favourable to their clients.

[57] As in *Jones* v. *Secretary of State for Social Services* [1972] AC 944, where the House of Lords considered it inappropriate to exercise their power to depart from a previous decision.

[58] This is the converse of point 2(c). It also provides a significant contrast with point 1(b) in which the existence *and* content are given by formal deductive reasoning from a norm recognised by a test of legal sources. For further discussion of how a norm may be said to exist without a clear content, see n. 50 above and n. 64 below. The requirement in 3(d) of a recognition of a legal source means that in the case of speculative legal reasoning the opening for ordinary evaluative reasoning is restricted to that which speculates about what a court might actually decide. Hence such reasoning is not elevated over legal sources, and, as I shall discuss below, such finality as they may provide. In relation to the judicial reasoning in 3(a) or 3(c) this requirement cannot offer a bootstrap lift to provide a legal source to the judiciary of that material which will be recognised as having a legal source by their determining it. However, the reasoning so engaged in is not completely unrestricted ordinary evaluative reasoning, not least because it is undertaken in discharging the requirement to provide a formally recognised source of law, and also due to the general intermeshing of doctrinal argument and evaluative reasoning (see further n. 63 below).

content of that norm may still be traced to a process of ordinary evaluative reasoning which involved moral or other evaluative factors.[59]

(4) *The role of legal sources, or of moral and other evaluative factors, in determining what is regarded as lawful conduct,*[60] *may vary.*

In particular we should note:

(a) that if we consider our circumstances to be governed by legal materials which are inadequate or likely to be so regarded by the courts, as noted in (2)(a) and (2)(b),[61] we may have recourse to case (1)(g) (speculative reasoning) which may slip into case (1)(f) (unrestricted ordinary evaluative reasoning) (see (3)(b)), and so allow ourselves to be swayed by moral and other evaluative factors in considering whether our conduct is lawful;

(b) that, in any case, after the event in these sort of circumstances, a court may authoritatively determine the issue of whether our conduct is lawful through a consideration of moral and other evaluative factors, in a number of ways as noted in (3)(a).

One general inference to draw from these points is that any plausible attempt to construct a theoretical model of law must be capable of capturing the dynamic, even unstable, nature of law. Present in these points are a diversity and contingency which combine in a volatile character that cannot be contained in a formulaic structure, whether the formulae seek to relate law to non-evaluative social tests of legal sources or to external moral or other evaluative tests.[62]

---

[59] Cp Raz, above n. 1, at 5: "moral . . . in the sense that they embody . . . moral considerations"; and above n. 3, at 40.

[60] The question being considered is how one should behave according to the law.

[61] A wider possibility than Raz considers, see nn. 43 and 44 above. Nor is a reasonable reluctance to become involved in litigation necessarily an impediment (Raz, above n. 1, at 20), since a position may sometimes be taken up as lawful where the burden of litigating to establish otherwise is on the other side.

[62] The remark applies equally to an attempt to combine the evaluative with the non-evaluative in a version of soft positivism, so far as that too seeks to rely on a formulaic approach. Some recognition of the possible limitations of soft positivism from a perspective in favour is provided by Matthew Kramer, "Coming to Grips With the Law: In Defense of Positive Legal Positivism" (1999) 5 *Legal Theory* 171 at 193–200 in recognising that there may be cases where "soft positivism is unfeasible" where general perception of a correct moral answer, or at least institutional unanimity on the answer to be given, does not occur. Criticism of the limitations of soft positivism from a hostile perspective is provided by Eleni Mitrophanous, "Soft Positivism" (1997) 17 *Oxford Journal of Legal Studies* 621, particularly concerned with the inability of soft positivism to draw a line between the morality that can be incorporated into law and the morality that remains outside. Both authors see limitations on the basis of a failure by soft positivism to provide a workable formula by which law can be identified.

The position taken by Mitrophanous is that adopted by Raz, above n. 3, at 47 n8. It is interesting to note that in taking up Raz's challenge WJ Waluchow, *Inclusive Legal Positivism* (Oxford, Clarendon Press, 1994) 226–9, suggests a distinction between morality incorporated into law and morality that remains outside operating within a realm of judicial discretion, on the basis of whether the moral test within the law is determinate or not. However, in addressing the problem of resolving whether the test on a particular occasion is determinate Waluchow resorts to relying on how it is seen by the judge who applies the test. This simply leaves open at a point of prior formulation the

Turning more specifically to the issues arising in the exchange between Raz and Postema, the above points would suggest in some cases modifications to the positions endorsed by these authors, in other cases rejection. The sources thesis requires modification in the light of points (1)–(3), but taking particular account of point (3)(d), it does not require outright rejection. The key modification relates to the *content* of legal norms which can no longer be regarded as being determined "entirely without appeal to moral or evaluative argument" in all instances. A modified sources thesis[63] can be proposed:

> *Modified sources thesis*: membership in law's limited domain [of practical reasons or norms] is determined by criteria which are defined exclusively in terms of non-evaluative matters of social fact (about their sources), such that the membership of norms can in all cases be determined entirely without appeal to moral or evaluative argument, though the content of member norms may be determined only in some cases by the same criteria and in other cases will be determined by moral or evaluative argument engaged in by those authorised by those criteria to determine that content.[64]

indeterminacy Waluchow seeks to satisfy Raz in closing: it will now be indeterminate which cases are regarded as determinate by the judge. Waluchow thus reinforces Raz's request for a formulaic test of law without succeeding in providing one. His approach also conceals the danger mentioned in n. 45 above. Recognition of some occasions of determinate moral tests in the law does not mean that we can clearly identify every occasion—which tells against a formulaic approach to law of whatever persuasion.

[63] It is worth reminding ourselves of the twofold rationale provided by Raz for his original Sources Thesis, above n. 3, at 48–52: first it is supposed to reflect a distinction between different conditions the law can be in (settled/unsettled) as mirrored in the different abilities judges must possess in order to fulfil their roles (doctrinal/moral); secondly, it is supposed to capture a fundamental characteristic of law, that it marks off authoritative rulings which set a limit to the possibility of continuing to challenge the justification of those rulings. It is the "explanatory power" that dominates the first rationale, but this can be rebutted in three ways, by our observations of the artificiality that it entails in dividing one form of legal reasoning from another, in the creation of the no law zone, as well as in the purported distinction between judicial roles (rather than recognising that the one slips in practice into the other—as Raz does himself elsewhere, above n. 20 at 319). This last point can cause further confusion by portraying a realm of judicial activity that is objectively doctrinal, which may well be used to cover activities that are anything but. For an illuminating discussion on this phenomenon in relation to the use of the doctrine of the Rule of Law by the Israeli Supreme Court, see Alon Harel, "The Rule of Law and Judicial Review: Reflections on the Israeli Constitutional Revolution" in David Dyzenhaus (ed.), *Recrafting the Rule of Law: The Limits of Legal Order* (Oxford, Hart Publishing, 1999). For a further illustration of the use of "objective principles of law", see n. 76 below. As to Raz's second rationale, I seek below (text at n. 70) to develop this further by distilling out of the sources thesis the quality of finality, whilst suggesting that in its original form it goes beyond the purely descriptive (n 74 below).

[64] The distinction between judicial and legislative law making, in relation to filling out the content of legal norms, consists in this. Even though for every matter that may be disputed the courts are required to pass judgment, it is not the case that every such matter must be covered by an act of the legislature. Hence, in every such matter there is a potential legal norm in the judgment of the court, the content of which, though not predetermined by existing legal sources, will be determined by the ordinary evaluative reasoning of the courts. Such a potential legal norm does not necessarily exist in legislative activity. Accordingly, it is possible in relation to a certain matter, in the case of a judicially created norm to state that a norm will be recognised as existing, but not know for sure the content of the norm until judgment is given. On the other hand, we cannot say that a legislatively created norm will come into existence in relation to a certain matter until legislation is passed—which will determine simultaneously both the norm's existence and its content.

The recognition that legal sources will not of themselves necessarily determine the content of every legal norm, but that in some cases the content will be determined by moral or evaluative argument engaged in by those authorised to determine that content, means that we can acknowledge the possibility of reasoning speculatively, (1)(g),[65] prior to the authorised ordinary evaluative reasoning which determines the issue, (1)(c). If we also acknowledge the possibility of other cases being clearly determined by recognised legal norms, (1)(b),[66] then we have three key forms of what might loosely be called legal reasoning to consider and the legal reasoning thesis requires modifying accordingly:

Modified legal reasoning thesis: reasoning to conclusions which entail that, according to law, if a matter were before a court the court should decide thus and so, may take one of three forms: (i) formal deductive reasoning from a recognised legal norm which clearly determines the case; (ii) ordinary evaluative reasoning undertaken by a judge authorised to decide that case; (iii) speculative reasoning as to how a judge will undertake ordinary evaluative reasoning to decide the case.

In turn this leads us to question the pre-emption thesis, which states that reasons in law's limited domain preclude acting for certain other reasons falling outside that domain.[67] For the pre-emption present in this thesis is dependent upon the possibility of reasons already recognised as members of law's limited domain applying exhaustively to determine how we should act in a matter that is capable of coming before a court for judgment, and our modified legal reasoning thesis indicates that this need not always be the case, as reflected by point (4). This means that pre-emption will apply only some of the time, and therefore that the pre-emption thesis needs to be modified accordingly:

Modified pre-emption thesis: reasons in law's limited domain operate in practical reasoning as pre-emptive reasons (that is, reasons which preclude acting for certain other reasons falling outside the domain) in cases where it is accepted that reasons already recognised as members of law's limited domain would determine how a court would decide the matter before it; but in other cases, where it is not accepted that reasons already recognised as members of law's limited domain would determine how a court would decide the matter

---

[65] Such speculative reasoning may range over a number of factors. It may be largely doctrinal, on the assumption that the law in the area of concern is currently developing a coherent doctrine. It may be more evaluative, on the assumption that evaluative factors embedded in existing law can point the way, or on the assumption that the values established in previous law are likely to be departed from. It may even rely on knowledge of the character and inclinations of the individual judge involved, so as to predict the likely outcome. I considered some empirical evidence of this last possibility in ch. 2. The possibility is noted by Raz, above n. 20, at 232.

[66] See text following n. 22 above.

[67] Raz, above n. 1, at 7, again, following Postema's formulation, which is attributed to Raz himself: Postema, above n. 2, at 114 n21.

before it, recourse to moral and other evaluative factors will be required as reasons for acting in a lawful manner.[68]

In all of this no further mention has been made of the autonomy of law. Nor is it obviously helpful to talk in such terms. The crude proclamation of autonomy considered at the commencement of this article was rejected peremptorily as facile. But the points enumerated in this section, and the subsequent modifications proposed to the sources, legal reasoning, and pre-emption theses, suggest that even a more sophisticated notion of legal autonomy is more likely to obscure than clarify issues.

In place of autonomy, we should perhaps speak of the finality[69] of law: the capacity of law to provide a final determination in matters that require determination to avoid uncertainty or dispute in our social relations. It is this quality of finality that precludes further recourse to moral or other evaluative argument—it prevents further recourse to any argument. But it says nothing as to what moral or other evaluative argument may enter into or lie behind that final determination. The precise location of this finality is not to be found in legal sources alone, or in legal reasoning, for it is dependent ultimately not on the comprehensive nature of legal sources, or on the exhaustive nature of legal reasoning, but on the possibility of identifying an authorised court which can have the final say on the matter. Although in some cases we can confidently rely on legal sources and legal reasoning to settle how the authorised court would determine the matter, in other cases we cannot.[70]

Acknowledging this latter possibility (as expressed in the modified theses) is of fundamental significance in constructing any theoretical model of law. In particular, it emphasises that the role of law in providing social coordination is

---

[68] In reality, practical reason may be used in this context not simply to address the issue of how to act lawfully (as I have assumed here), but also the issue of how to act expediently. In particular, if there is some doubt about how the court may determine a case, we may be thinking as much along the lines of whether we can risk getting our speculation about the outcome wrong, as anything else. Taking it a stage further, even if we are confident about what the eventual outcome will be, we may still be concerned with the expediency of being involved in protracted litigation. Raz shows some sensitivity to these wider considerations in the passage cited in n. 61 above.

[69] Raz regards the pursuit of finality as part of the sources thesis, above n. 1, at 13–14; cp Raz, *The Concept of a Legal System* 2nd edn. (Oxford, Clarendon Press, 1980) 215–16. Postema incorrectly takes Raz's position on finality as being linked to excluding a "range of moral and evaluative considerations" (above n. 2, at 93), whereas it is about *ending the debate* on such considerations.

[70] If both parties are prepared to rely on a common understanding of the law the ultimate finality of the law may be taken for granted. Where one party is prepared to challenge the understanding of the other party, then the ultimate basis for the finality of law will be revealed in the judgment of the court which is given the final say on the matter. An extreme illustration of this point is to be found in a Swedish case, discussed by Dennis Töllborg in "Law as Value" (1998) 84 *Archiv für Rechts- und Sozialphilosophie* 489, in which a Swedish first instance judge refused to uphold a constitutional right for the public to be given access to evidence that had been used in a trial, despite two rulings by the Court of Appeal that she should do so. The evidence requested constituted child pornography. Since the appeal court could only order the first instance judge to make the order, she thus had the final say over whether the order was made—a finality confirmed ultimately by the Government's decision not to remove her from office but to change the law.

dependent upon being able to identify a judge to deliver final judgment on a matter, not necessarily by being able to identify beforehand what the final judgment will be, or in being able to identify neutral principles (or principles acceptable to all parties) that will determine the judgment. Postema errs in taking that as his starting point.[71] Even if the search for such principles is plausible,[72] this would, as Raz indicates, not necessarily be a task for law.[73]

The ideal of law as a method of social coordination possesses a technical feature of there being a clear legal answer to every conflict that may arise in social relations, followed closely by a practical feature that such clear legal answers should be complied with by citizens and applied by those who have the authority to administer the law. But how do we go about the task of constructing a theoretical model of law that is less than ideal? One way is to ensure that our model secures as much of the ideal that our imperfect laws have so far achieved. Arguably the key role of Hart's rule of recognition and of Raz's sources thesis is to ensure just that: we can identify the law that we do have and thus ensure that in practical terms it can be given the respect it merits as law.[74] Another way is to use our model to show the potential of our imperfect law to grow closer to the ideal. Arguably Postema's conjunction of law's role of social coordination

---

[71] For fuller discussion of Postema's assumption about law's "defining task", see Raz, above n. 1 at 2–4. The appeal of Postema's view is indicated in the prominence given to it in Henrik Palmer Olsen and Stuart Toddington, *Law in Its Own Right* (Oxford, Hart Publishing, 1999) 10–12. For present purposes, it suffices to make three simple points. First, a fundamental flaw in Postema's characterisation of the defining task appears in his initial conjunction: "designed to unify public political judgment and co-ordinate social interaction" (Postema, above n. 2, at 80). It simply is not the case that coordinating social interaction depends on unifying public political judgment. It depends on being able to state with finality whose political judgment counts. Second, the tradition of thinking about law "from Cicero to the present day" (*ibid.*), which Postema cites as authority for his defining task, is simply not matched by the practical experience of law from beyond Cicero to the present day. The golden age of Roman law did depend on being able to state with finality whose political judgment counted, but had nothing to do with unifying public political judgment. Law flourished while the political judgment of plebeians, women generally, and slaves, was not taken into account. Indeed (and this takes us into the third point), Postema himself acknowledges that modern society has "problems of social co-operation caused, in part, by the absence of a common public language of deliberation and justification" and concedes that it "may not be possible to construct a framework for common deliberation and public justification in societies deeply divided about matters of fundamental value and principle" (*ibid.* at 111–12). However, Postema does not suggest that modern society suffers from a failure to coordinate social interaction, or an absence of law. Third, if we have a problem of discovering a basis for unifying public political judgment, this is a political (or moral) problem, not primarily a legal one. If the problem is solved, the answer will be reflected in our law. Equally, if the problem is not solved we will still have law that reflects that state of affairs. To suggest that there is an issue as to whether law and political morality should be approached by a strategy of isolation or integration (*ibid.* at 111) as a means of dealing with the problem of finding a basis for unifying public political judgment misses the point.

[72] Note the scepticism expressed by Postema himself, cited in the previous note.

[73] Raz, above n. 1, at 12–13.

[74] There is an aspirational as opposed to descriptive character to both of these features of the respective theories, see HLA Hart, *The Concept of Law* 1st edn. (Oxford, Clarendon Press, 1961) 92, with a view to remedying uncertainty; Raz, above n. 3, at 52, in order to provide "publicly ascertainable standards"; and cp WJ Waluchow, above n. 62, at 119–23, 184, 188–90, on the evaluative rather than descriptive ascription of function.

with a consensual public political judgment has this as its aim: the potential for clear legal answers that will be effectively practised depends on being able to identify the principles which would provide those answers, and so the pursuit of those principles needs to be integrated within our model of law.

In their very different ways both of these models assume progression towards the ideal. The first model assumes that we can identify the progress that we have made so far. The second model assumes that we are making progress. Neither may be the case. We may have to acknowledge that there is no master test by which we can always identify what law we have, but instead only a test to identify who will provide an answer to the question.[75] We may have to acknowledge that there are no accepted master principles by which we can identify what law to have, but only those persons we can identify who will have the say on what law we have.

A theoretical model of law, as we experience it, must seek to depict accurately the certainty we seek from the law by also coming to terms with the dynamic and unstable nature of the phenomenon, and the role of those individuals who are permitted to develop, change, and destabilise the law. Even if this means acknowledging that a judge is only sometimes a herald, that sometimes a judge is even more than a rogue herald, and that sometimes a judge gets to take the place of a king.[76]

---

[75] Hart, in his imaginative but far from historically accurate account of the transition from a pre-legal to legal world, above n. 74, at 89–91, draws attention exclusively to rules. Raz, above n. 3, at 51–2, does speak of "authoritative rulings" but these are made synonymous with "rules" or "ascertainable standards". The preoccupation with rules ignores the role of the ruler.

[76] The recognition of dual roles for the courts in passing judgment is to be found in ch. 10 of Raz, above n. 3. Judges themselves are often more reluctant to acknowledge them. The impending incorporation of the European Convention on Human Rights into UK law led to an outpouring of judicial theorising, tending to dampen fears that incorporation would somehow increase judicial discretion in shaping UK law. One example is the Ganz Lecture in Public Law delivered at Southampton University in November 1997 by Sir John Laws, "The Limitations of Human Rights" (subsequently published in [1998] *Public Law* 254). Sir John develops an argument that regards rights as legal constructs in order to free them from an underlying concept of morality, so as to reach the conclusion that judges may be trusted to interpret the rights of the Convention, because in so doing they are only performing their traditional function of dealing with objective principles of law thus reaching a position that Postema, above n. 2, could only portray as mythical. For (sceptical) discussion of earlier examples of judicial theorising, see John Griffith, "Judges and the Constitution" in Richard Rawlings (ed.), *Law, Society, and Economy* (Oxford, Clarendon Press, 1997) 289; and for general reflection on the transition from *Rechtsstaat* to *Justizstaat*, see Neil MacCormick and Robert Summers (eds.), *Interpreting Precedents* (Aldershot, Dartmouth, 1997) 549–50.

4

A Study on the Judicial Role

INTRODUCTION

THIS CHAPTER FOCUSES on the role played by the judge in legal reasoning. Legal reasoning has, at least in the common law world,[1] always been quintessentially the activity of the judge. Other lawyers, as practitioners and commentators, may engage in legal reasoning but only in a role that is subordinate to or supplementary to the judicial determination of the law in court. Any attempt to probe the nature of legal reasoning must pay attention to the role of the judge, and even investigate the possibility of different roles being performed by the judiciary, in determining and developing the law. The central practical significance of the common-law judge is mirrored in the celebrity status granted to the judge within Anglo-American legal theory, whether by attracting undue attention to the mundane routines of the judge's life (what the judge ate for breakfast[2]) or by approaching apotheosis of the judge's attributes.[3]

---

[1] The Roman jurist with imperial authority to give a determination of the law never found a common law counterpart, see WW Buckland, *A Text-book of Roman Law*, Peter Stein (ed.), rev 3rd edn. (Cambridge, Cambridge University Press, 1975) 20–5; RC Van Caenegem, *Judges, Legislators and Professors: Chapters in European Legal History* (Cambridge, Cambridge University Press, 1987) 53–65, 96–101.

[2] Charles Yablon, "Justifying the Judge's Hunch: An Essay on Discretion" (1990) 41 *Hastings Law Journal* 231 at 236 n16, suggests that this phrase may have developed from Roscoe Pound's description in 1905 of a cadi administering justice "tempered by the state of his digestion". Joseph Rauh, "Lawyers and the Legislation of the Early New Deal" (1983) 96 *Harvard Law Review* 947 at 950 reports that Thomas Reed Powell in his 1935 constitutional law class at Harvard observed that the determination of cases usually turned on "the nature of the breakfast the judges have in the morning".

[3] There is something remarkable about Dworkin's use of Hercules. He is used as a paradigm of what a judge might be, and hence for Dworkin what a judge should aspire to. However, since Dworkin candidly admits that the attributes of Hercules are possessed by no human judge (*Taking Rights Seriously* (London, Duckworth, 1977) 105; *Law's Empire* (London, Collins, 1986) 239), the more obvious investigation to pursue is what it is that sets mortal judges below Hercules, and how their lesser attributes might contribute to them performing a rather different judicial role to that which is open to one possessed of Hercules' attributes. Dworkin's response to such a criticism is wholly inadequate, in brazenly asserting that Hercules provides an accurate model of the hidden structure of the judgments of mortal judges, despite acknowledging their different attributes— *Law's Empire* 265. (On which, see further, David Luban, "Reason and Passion in Legal Ethics" (1999) 51 *Stanford Law Review* 873 at 895–6.) Moreover, since the whole of the past body of judge-made law has been the work of lesser mortals not blessed with the key attributes of Hercules, it is astonishing to suggest that their collective handiwork will fit into a grand political theory such as a judge as skilled as Hercules might develop (or to suggest that it will display the "integrity" that might be expected to be found in the uniform code of which Hercules was the sole author). For further discussion of the contrast between Hercules and actual judges, see JW Harris, "Unger's

In the previous chapter there was more than a suggestion that the role we attribute to the judge serves to indicate how we characterise the law itself. A central concern of the present study is to demonstrate the tendency lawyers have, even when they disagree about the appropriate description of the judicial role, to find parameters for that role which can be accounted for in some sort of legal manner. Following the doubt expressed in the previous chapter over the possibility of finding a distinctive form of legal reasoning, I shall argue here that the role of the judge cannot be cast exclusively in legal terms.

An area of law which readily lends itself to an investigation of legal reasoning and the judicial role is the English law relating to judicial review. This is a particularly fertile area to study because it has seen unparalleled growth through judicial development;[4] it has given rise to fierce theoretical debate; and the controversy surrounding this area of law has attracted the open engagement of the views of the judiciary. In part fuelled by the impending enactment of legislation bringing the European Convention of Human Rights into domestic UK law,[5] there has in recent years been a wider discussion of the judicial role which has prompted the self-examination of members of the judiciary, notably Sir John Laws and Sir Stephen Sedley.[6]

THE THEORETICAL CONTROVERSY CONCERNING JUDICIAL REVIEW

The controversy concerning the theoretical basis for judicial review is a matter of importance that extends beyond the particular concerns of public lawyers. Embracing as it does the fundamental relationship between the legislature and the judiciary and their respective constitutional roles, it brings into sharp focus issues which have a bearing on our wider understanding of the nature of law and its practice. The way the controversy has developed provides a particularly striking opportunity to consider the benefits of relating together academic and practitioner perspectives, and to consider the value of theoretical insights for our understanding of the practice of law. The course this particular controversy has taken also raises general questions about the nature of academic debate, and the the way that academic and practitioner alike are inclined to represent the law. Accordingly, a wide variety of readers should be grateful to the Centre for Public Law at the University of Cambridge, its Assistant Director Christopher Forsyth, and Hart Publishing, for bringing together in one volume the key contributions to the debate

---

Critique of Formalism in Legal Reasoning: Hero, Hercules, and Humdrum" (1989) 52 *Modern Law Review* 42; Adrian Vermeule and Ernest Young, "Hercules, Herbert, and Amar: The Trouble with *Intratextualism*" (2000) 113 *Harvard Law Review* 730.

[4] In their Preface, Michael Supperstone and James Goudie (eds.), *Judicial Review* 2nd edn. (London, Butterworths, 1997) comment that during the 1990s the developments of English administrative law have been proceeding unabated with the most noticeable progress "on a daily basis" being in the area of judicial review.

[5] See further, n. 74 below.

[6] See, in addition to the references in this chapter, ch. 2 n. 52; ch. 3 n. 76.

on the "Foundations of Judicial Review", both those which preceded and those which were delivered at a conference of that title held at the Centre in May 1999.[7]

That many eminent lawyers have engaged in so much heated debate with such fierce disagreement remaining, raises the naive but awkward question whether these lawyers know what they are talking about. The nature of the disagreement between the two approaches to the basis for judicial review is one that bewildered some of the participants at the conference,[8] yet the erudition of those maintaining the opposing positions in the debate can leave no doubt that they know their subject matter.[9] Still the unresolved dispute does raise the possibility that there is more to what they are talking about than they know or recognise as lawyers. It is this possibility that I shall eventually pursue here. First it is necessary to gain a sense of the point the debate has reached.

THE TWO MODELS OF JUDICIAL REVIEW

During the course of debate a certain amount of refinement has occurred to each explanation of the basis for judicial review, but it is helpful to start with the extreme versions of the two models. This provides a clear picture of the ground between the two approaches before undertaking the more difficult task of clarifying the real nature of the dispute that now remains. In their extreme forms[10] the two models take their respective positions as follows.

---

[7] Christopher Forsyth (ed.), *Judicial Review and the Constitution* (Oxford, Hart Publishing, 2000). Unattributed page references given subsequently will be to this volume, and I shall subsequently use "this volume" or "Forsyth (ed.)" to refer to the book, in which most of the material under discussion is to be found. I shall also provide a reference to the alternative source of those chapters which have been published elsewhere prior to the conference, or, in some cases following the conference but prior to the publication of this volume, on each occasion that the chapter is first cited.

[8] TRS Allan, "Comment: The Rule of Law as the Foundation of Judicial Review" in Forsyth (ed.) (2000); Michael Taggart, "Comment: *Ultra Vires* as Distraction" in Forsyth (ed.) (2000). Christopher Forsyth's good humoured self-deprecation in using as an image for the debate the Lilliputian controversy over which end to crack open a boiled egg also testifies to this point, "Heat and Light: A Plea for Reconciliation" ch. 18 in Forsyth (ed.) at 396–7.

[9] The principal supporters of the *ultra vires* model (taking the baton from Sir William Wade) are Christopher Forsyth and Mark Elliott; and of the common law model, Dawn Oliver, Paul Craig and Sir John Laws.

[10] It is not altogether clear that either model in its extreme form has gained unalloyed support. The extreme form of the *ultra vires* model is associated with Sir William Wade: Mark Elliott, "The *Ultra Vires* Doctrine in a Constitutional Setting: Still the Central Principle of Administrative Law" (also published in (1999) 58 *Cambridge Law Journal* 129) ch. 5 of Forsyth (ed.) at 84. The extreme form of the common law model is thought to have surfaced in what Lord Irvine has described as some "extra-judicial romanticism" (quoted in this volume at 45 and 394) of Lord Woolf and Sir John Laws (referred to at 126–7). Reasons why it is difficult to find a pure expression of either model in its extreme form include the varied range of contexts in which judicial review is sought, the confusing range of uses to which the term *ultra vires* has been put (on which see the useful discussion in David Feldman, "Convention Rights and Substantive *Ultra Vires*" ch. 11 in Forsyth (ed.)), and the speculative nature of some of the discussion (what the courts might do, if Parliament were to . . .). Nevertheless, even if the two models in their extreme forms represent hypothetical theoretical positions, they have their value in marking out the nature of the gap which has been narrowed in subsequent theoretical positions actually adopted by participants.

The *ultra vires* model sees the basis for judicial review as being the courts fulfilling their ancillary role to ensure that a power granted by the sovereign Parliament should not be exercised beyond the limits set by Parliament when it granted the power. The principles of judicial review are accordingly just those principles which mark out the limits found in the explicit or implicit intention of Parliament in granting the power.

The common law model (again in its extreme form) sees the principles of judicial review as a self-standing common law creation, a judicial construct to ensure the proper exercise of power, which could even be used to strike down a grant of power explicitly and unequivocally intended by Parliament that was in breach of these principles.

It is readily apparent that the ground between these two models in their extreme forms does not simply cover the principles of judicial review but also the constitutional fundamental of the sovereignty of Parliament. In their modified forms, however, the sovereignty of Parliament is not an obvious issue, and nor is the creativity of the judiciary.

The modified *ultra vires* model still maintains the role of the courts as subordinate to the sovereign Parliament but now acknowledges a creative judicial role in working out the detailed principles of judicial review. These roles of Parliament and the courts are kept in harmony by positing an implied legislative intent that all statutory powers should be exercised in accordance with the principles of judicial review which Parliament has authorised the courts to apply.

The modified common law model openly acknowledges the sovereignty of Parliament by admitting that the principles of judicial review could not be effective against an explicit clear statutory statement of Parliamentary intent that they should not prevail on a particular occasion, but still maintains an independent common law source for the principles, which are regarded as having come into being irrespective of Parliamentary intention.

What is apparent now is the common ground between the two models. Although impartial contributors to the debate find it less easy to see what the remaining differences are,[11] in the eyes of the leading proponents of the two models the distinction is still very real. In exploring the nature of this remaining distinction I shall seek to concentrate on the core features that make the two models what they are, rather than to examine some of the secondary arguments that seek to put one model in a more attractive light than the other—such as historical lineage,[12] or ability to accommodate related doctrines (notably, the

---

[11] See n. 8 above.

[12] Stimulating discussion on this is to be found in Paul Craig, "*Ultra Vires* and the Foundations of Judicial Review" (previously published in (1998) 57 *Cambridge Law Journal* 63) ch. 3 of Forsyth (ed.); and Sir Stephen Sedley, "Public Power and Private Power" (from *Freedom, Law and Justice*, 1999 Hamlyn Lectures (London, Sweet & Maxwell, 1999) ch. 13 of Forsyth (ed.). However, doubt is cast on the existence of an unbroken historical lineage for judicial review by Stephen Bailey, "Comment: Judicial Review in a Modern Context" in Forsyth (ed.); and Martin Loughlin, "Comment: Whither the Constitution?" in Forsyth (ed.).

treatment of ouster clauses, and the availability of collateral challenge[13]). It is not that these arguments are without weight or relevance. They bring a number of important insights into the broader picture in which this debate is set. However, it is my contention that we will be in a better position to unravel the unresolved issues at the heart of judicial review, and consequently to deal with any outstanding doctrinal implications in the law, by keeping our focus on the distinctive characters of the two models.

THE "UNDISTRIBUTED" OR "EXCLUDED" MIDDLE

One central issue affecting the core features of the two models surfaces in one form or another at various stages in the debate, and is alluded to by both Paul Craig and Christopher Forsyth in their concluding contributions as still very much a part of what divides the two approaches. Craig in his assessment of the remaining difference between the two models has this to say:[14]

"It should be remembered that the central kernel of the argument [for the *ultra vires* model] is that where Parliament does not prohibit it must be taken to authorise expressly or impliedly. It is for this reason that legislative intent must be found in order to legitimate the imposition of any constraints on the way in which power is exercised. . . . The common law model holds that the principles of judicial review are developed by the courts. . . . If the omnipotent Parliament does not like these controls then it is open to it to make this explicitly clear. . . . There is therefore nothing in the common law model which involves a strong challenge to sovereignty."

The perspective on the difference from the other side of the debate is provided by Forsyth in these words:[15]

"The difference between [the two models] is simply over the articulation of what is plainly an artificial construct: the intention of Parliament. Should Parliament be presumed to have authorised the application by the judges of the principles of good administration or should that authorisation come from the common law? . . . The concepts of ultra vires and intra vires are mutually exclusive: a decision-maker either acts within or outside his or her powers, there is no middle ground. . . . If, say, a decision-maker in denying a hearing in certain circumstances, acts within the powers granted by Parliament the common law cannot impose a duty of fairness upon that decision-maker without challenging parliament's power to allow him or her to make valid decisions without a hearing. Otherwise you have the position where every requirement for validity laid down expressly or implied by Parliament is satisfied yet the common law

---

[13] The position of ouster clauses figures prominently throughout the debate. I make a brief concluding reference to them in n. 73 below.

[14] "Competing Models of Judicial Review" (also published in [1999] *Public Law* 428) ch. 17 of Forsyth (ed.) at 378, 382–3; similarly at 384, and 388 n. 37, "It is perfectly plausible to suggest, both empirically and conceptually, that the legislature might have no specific intent one way or the other as to the incidence or intensity of review in a particular context."

[15] 396, 402.

is imposing an additional requirement for validity. That is a challenge to parliamentary supremacy."

The issue arising in these extracts is whether the intention of Parliament in relation to the grant of a power it has made to another body comprehensively covers the conditions under which that power is to be exercised, or whether it leaves a gap for the courts to impose conditions on their own authority. This is the issue of the so called undistributed or excluded middle as it impinges on our understanding of Parliamentary intention relating to the conditions attached to a power it has granted.

Both turns of phrase lend serious philosophical weight to the debate, but in themselves add nothing to the argument. In fact, as we shall see, the first phrase is misconstrued,[16] and the principle covered by the second phrase is misused. Nevertheless, it is worthwhile pausing over the technicalities. Although dispelling the confusion over the use of philosophical terminology does not resolve the issues at the heart of the distinction between the two models, it does help to clarify what the real issues are.

The logical law of the excluded middle asserts that something must either be or not be the case $(p \vee \sim p)$. There is no room for a situation in the middle of these two alternatives where something both is and is not the case (or, neither is nor is not the case).[17] Forsyth calls upon the notion (though not the terminology[18]) of an excluded middle in making his argument in relation to Parliament's intention in granting the power:[19]

"The analytical difficulty is this: what an all powerful Parliament does not prohibit, it must authorise either expressly or impliedly. Likewise if Parliament grants a power to a minister, that minister either acts within those powers or outside those powers. There is no grey area between authorisation and prohibition or between empowerment and the denial of power."

---

[16] Clear explanations of both "undistributed middle" and "excluded middle" are to be found in Simon Blackburn, *The Oxford Dictionary of Philosophy* (Oxford, Oxford University Press, 1994) and Ted Honderich (ed.), *The Oxford Companion to Philosophy* (Oxford, Oxford University Press, 1995).

[17] There is disagreement among logicians as to whether the law of the excluded middle is a universal law. Both Blackburn and Honderich, above n. 16, in their entries on "excluded middle" and the related principle of "bivalence" refer to suggested counter-examples. Whether these counter-examples hold depends both on how one understands the principle and the purported counter-example. For discussion see WV Quine, *Philosophy of Logic* (Englewood Cliffs, NJ, Prentice-Hall, 1970; 2nd edn. Cambridge, MA, Harvard University Press, 1986) at 83–7.

[18] Forsyth uses the form of the excluded middle $(p \vee \sim p)$, "There is no grey area between authorisation and prohibition or between empowerment and the denial of power" ("Of Fig Leaves and Fairy Tales: The *Ultra Vires* Doctrine, the Sovereignty of Parliament and Judicial Review" (also in (1996) 55 *Cambridge Law Journal* 122) ch. 2 of Forsyth (ed.) at 40), and similarly, "no middle ground" (text quoted at n. 9 above). Although Forsyth employs the terminology of "mutual exclusivity" to characterise his argument (401–2), he furnishes by analogy a clear case of the excluded middle, pregnant or not pregnant (402). Strictly speaking, mutual exclusivity is a wider principle dealing with the relationship between two different things $(p \rightarrow \sim q)$, for example a person cannot be a "brother" and a "sister", whereas the law of the excluded middle indicates a person must be either a "brother" or "not a brother".

[19] 39–40.

Sir John Laws on the other hand lays claim to an application of the principle of the undistributed middle in arguing that there can indeed be a case in between the cases of "Parliament authorises" and "Parliament prohibits":[20]

> "Forsyth's argument is vitiated by an implicit mistake: the mistake of assuming that because Parliament can authorise or prohibit anything, all authorities and prohibitions must come from Parliament. It is a *non sequitur*. It neglects what the logicians call the 'undistributed middle'—an obscure, but useful, academic expression, meaning that although X and Y may be opposites, like praise or blame, they do not cover the whole field; there might be Z, which involves neither."

The terminology is misplaced for the principle of the undistributed middle technically refers not to the middle that was excluded by $p \vee {\sim}p$, but to the middle term in a syllogism, making the point that if that term is undistributed (i.e. not taken to cover all of its instances) then the syllogism is flawed.[21] Nevertheless, the gist of Laws' argument is clear. He is denying that we have a case of an excluded middle. Sometimes it is the case that Parliament neither authorises nor prohibits.

Now it is important to be clear that in denying that we have a case of the excluded middle we are not necessarily denying the law of the excluded middle. We may simply be pointing out that the case of suggested alternatives does not fall under $p \vee {\sim}p$ because the one alternative is not the negation of the other: we do not have a case of p and ${\sim}p$, and hence the law of the excluded middle is not relevant on this occasion. This is certainly the position with the analogy that Laws draws with praise or blame. Blame is not formed by the negation of praise—from the fact that I do not praise you it does not mean that I blame you. So on this occasion we do not have a case of $p \vee {\sim}p$ to fall under the general law.

By contrast, the analogy used by Forsyth, pregnant or not pregnant,[22] is a perfect illustration of the law of the excluded middle—we reach the one alternative by the negation of the other, and $p \vee {\sim}p$ holds. The crucial question is what is the nature of the alternatives when we are considering the intention of Parliament in relation to the conditions attached to the power it has granted.

Let us drop the technical terminology for the moment. It is perfectly intelligible to say of a person that he:

(1) wants something to happen, or
(2) wants something not to happen, or
(3) has no wishes one way or the other

[20] "The Problem of Jurisdiction" (excerpted from Michael Supperstone and James Goudie, above n. 4) ch. 4 of Forsyth (ed.) at 78.
[21] For example, an argument to prove that all sharks are lawyers—

> All lawyers can bite;
> all sharks can bite;
> therefore, all sharks are lawyers.

—is flawed because the middle term, "can bite", is undistributed (i.e. does not cover all of its instances).
[22] See above, n. 18.

—for example, in relation to seeing a particular film at the cinema this evening. It would similarly seem wholly appropriate to say of Parliament that it may:

(1) intend something to happen, or
(2) intend something not to happen, or
(3) have no intention one way or the other.

These demonstrations do not breach the law of the excluded middle, for in both of the above examples (1) and (2) are separate propositions, each of which with its negation can satisfy the law of the excluded middle. In the first example we can say in relation to (1) that it must be the case that the person wants to go to the cinema to see *The Flintstones,* or does not want to go to the cinema to see *The Flintstones; and* in relation to (2) it must be the case that the person wants not to go to the cinema to see *The Flintstones*, or does not want not to go to the cinema to see *The Flintstones.* The reason why this seems tedious and pedantic in the extreme is that in everyday speech we do not normally bother to make a distinction between the negation of (1) and the affirmation of (2), or between the negation of (2) and the affirmation of (1). The same phrase, respectively, "I do not want to go to the cinema to see *The Flintstones*", or, "I do want to go to the cinema to see *The Flintstones*", is happily used for both, so avoiding the awkward locutions that I have just reproduced. However, the distinctions do exist and on occasion we force ourselves to recognise them—"Are you saying that you positively want to see *The Flintstones* [affirmation of (1)] or that you do not mind seeing *The Flintstones* [negation of (2)]?" Though, as this example illustrates, when doing so we take care to make our language less cumbersome.

The precise logical structure of our desires in relation to seeing *The Flintstones* may seem laboured but it is necessay in order to understand not merely the relationship between propositions (1) and (2) but also their relationship to proposition (3). Recognition of the distinct negations of (1) and (2) is a prerequisite to the recognition of (3), which is formed by the conjunction of the negations of (1) and (2): "I neither positively want to see *The Flintstones*, nor positively want not to see *The Flintstones*. I am indifferent to *The Flintstones*."[23]

We can similarly provide a fuller presentation[24] of the range of possibilities in the second example, as follows:

(1a) P intends something to happen, or
(1b) P does not intend something to happen.

---

[23] Since most readers by now are probably indifferent to *The Flintstones* in the sense of feeling callous disregard towards them, I should point out that I am using indifference here in the neutral sense of not caring one way or the other about watching them. For those readers who do tire of *The Flintstones*, the same exercise can be done in relation to eating chocolate mousse.

[24] The case of both (1a) and (2a) holding is impossible due to one content of the intentions being the negation of the other and hence making the intentions inconsistent. To join (1a) and (2b), or (2a) and (1b), is technically possible but otiose.

(2a) P intends that something does not happen, or

(2b) P does not intend that something does not happen.

and where both (1b) and (2b) hold

(3) P has no intention one way or the other.

Forsyth's confusion is promoted by the looseness of everyday language which fails to discriminate between (1a) and (2b), and between (2a) and (1b), which makes it easy to misrepresent (1a) and (2a) as being p and $\sim p$ in the law of the excluded middle. The slip is further eased by the actual words used by Forsyth to represent (1a) and (2a), "authorisation and prohibition",[25] due to the solecism that "prohibition" is the negation of "authorisation". The true relationship between authorisation and prohibition is more complex, following precisely the above analysis of intending something to happen and intending something not to happen (given that an authorisation involves a particular instance of the intention that something does happen—from the viewpoint of the body capable of expressing a mandatory will upon the matter; and similarly, with prohibition and the intention that something does not happen).[26] The point that prohibition is not simply the negation of authorisation can be reached in a less tortuous manner by reflecting on the possibility of a body having the capacity to prohibit something but not having the capacity to authorise it, as in the case of the Senate's veto over the appointment of a Supreme Court judge. Simply because it does not prohibit the appointment of a Justice it does not follow that the Senate can authorise the appointment.[27]

When Parliament grants a power, it is possible, for example, that:

(1a) P intends the power to be exercised reasonably, or

(1b) P does not intend the power to be exercised reasonably.

(2a) P intends that the power should be exercised unreasonably, or

(2b) P does not intend that the power should be exercised unreasonably.

---

[25] See text quoted at n. 19 above.

[26] The same analysis can be reached by relating the authorisation and prohibition to the positions of the subject in a scheme of deontic logic. In Hohfeldian terms a person authorised will enjoy a liberty and a person prohibited will be under a duty, but the liberty to do something is not the negation of a duty to do something—on which see further, Glanville Williams, "The Concept of Legal Liberty" (1956) 56 *Columbia Law Review* 1129 (also in Robert Summers (ed.), *Essays in Legal Philosophy* (Oxford, Basil Blackwell, 1968)); Andrew Halpin, *Rights and Law—Analysis and Theory* (Oxford, Hart Publishing, 1997) ch. II. The same point gives rise to the recognition of a liberty to do something and a distinct liberty not to do something, or what Joel Feinberg has referred to as half-liberties—*Rights, Justice and the Bounds of Liberty* (Princeton, NJ, Princeton University Press, 1980) at 157.

[27] Confusion is further confounded in the passage quoted at n. 19 above by Forsyth treating as like cases: (i) authorisation and prohibition; (ii) acting within a power and outside a power; (iii) empowering and denying power. The case of (ii), unlike (i), does involve a true negation, and like the analogous pregnant and not pregnant (n. 18 above) does follow the law of the excluded middle. The case of (iii), however, is ambiguous in the use of "denying power" between being regarded as a synonym for prohibition, in which case it follows the analysis of (i), and being regarded as synonymous with the weaker "not granting power", in which case we have a true negation and the analysis of (ii) can be followed.

and where both (1b) and (2b) hold

> (3) P has no intention whether the power should be exercised reasonably or not.

It is important to stress that proposition (3), which I have illustrated above with a case of indifference to the outcome, is not necessarily the product of reflective consideration of the issues. It may be the case that after being confronted with the issues a couldn't-care-less attitude emerges, and this would fall under (3). But a case could equally fall under (3) through the issues not being broached, or because due to some extraneous factors it was not possible to reach an intention one way or the other on the matter. Proposition (3) emerges as a logical possibility whenever both (1a) and (2a) fail to arise, whatever the reasons for these failures. I shall for convenience continue to refer to cases falling under (3) as cases of indifference but shall refer to a case of "conscious indifference" when it is indifference in the strict sense. It is worth stressing this in the context of our present study because one of the arguments advanced in favour of the *ultra vires* model has been to suggest that if Parliament is not regarded as having intended that the power should be exercised reasonably, the implausible conclusion necessarily follows that Parliament intended the power should be exercised unreasonably, or at least Parliament was consciously indifferent to the power being exercised unreasonably.[28] Neither conclusion follows as a matter of logic,[29] and without further consideration of how the imputed intention, or conscious indifference, to act unreasonably actually arose we cannot assume it.

This then takes us to a recognition of what is logically possible and leaves us to consider other factors in order to decide what actually is the case, or what should be the case. Confused use of philosophical terminology should not be allowed to obscure the real issues, and I shall now attempt to address some of the issues that do affect our understanding of judicial review.

"AN ALL POWERFUL PARLIAMENT"

Establishing that the law of the excluded middle does not make it logically impossible for Parliament to have no intention one way or the other, in relation to placing a condition on the exercise of a power it has granted, does not end the debate. There may be further reasons why Parliament should be regarded as having closed down all possibilities for the making of conditions other than those it has itself authorised.

---

[28] Elliott at 94, 356; Forsyth at 401.

[29] The errors are: in the stronger case confusing (1b) with (2a); and in the weaker case assuming a case of (3) has to be accompanied by conscious indifference instead of considering how it arose in the specific factual circumstances, a point I will take further in the following sections.

It is clear that for Forsyth, and the other supporters[30] of the *ultra vires* model, the mainstay of their argument is the threat to parliamentary sovereignty that they regard is entailed by abandoning their model in favour of the common law model. Forsyth in his concluding contribution regards it as the principal strength of the *ultra vires* model that it "provides a firm constitutional foundation for judicial review" by treating the principles of judicial review as not a threat to parliamentary sovereignty but as impliedly authorised by Parliament.[31] Mark Elliott stands on the same ground[32] and from this position has articulated the ultimate challenge to the other side:[33]

> ". . . so long as the common law accords a legislative supremacy to Parliament, it must be possible to reconcile the courts' public law jurisprudence with this constitutional principle. It is the interpretive methodology of ultra vires—and *only* this methodology—which is capable of securing this reconciliation."

This challenge assumes certain things about the nature of parliamentary sovereignty. Following the clarification of the logical possibility that Parliament could be in a position of indifference as to the imposition of a condition on a power it had granted, the argument on the side of the *ultra vires* model has to place all its weight on an understanding of parliamentary sovereignty capable of excluding the logical possibility conveyed by proposition (3). In examining this further we will need both to consider the understanding of parliamentary sovereignty involved, and also to look in more detail at the practical factors which might bring about a case falling under proposition (3).

Taking the latter topic first, I have already emphasised that there may be a number of reasons why a case falls under proposition (3). In relation to parliamentary intention concerning a matter capable of being governed by law, it may be the case that Parliament has considered the matter and decided upon a neutral stance towards it (conscious indifference).[34] It may be the case that

---

[30] Mark Elliott is a particularly strong ally on this point: "The *Ultra Vires* Doctrine in a Constitutional Setting: Still the Central Principle of Administrative Law" (also published in (1999) 58 *Cambridge Law Journal* 129) ch. 5 of Forsyth (ed.); "The Demise of Parliamentary Sovereignty? The Implications for Justifying Judicial Review" (1999) 115 *Law Quarterly Review* 119; "Fundamental Rights as Interpretative Constructs: The Constitutional Logic of the Human Rights Act 1998" ch. 12 of Forsyth (ed.); "Legislative Intention Versus Judicial Creativity? Administrative Law as a Co-operative Endeavour" ch. 16 of Forsyth (ed.).

[31] 408, 404.

[32] 368–9.

[33] 109.

[34] The objection that Parliament by adopting a position of indifference is in fact adopting an intention in favour of the status quo, and so can never be truly indifferent, assumes that there exists a legal status quo. This is certainly not always the case. It is not the case where the existing law is unclear and Parliament adopts a position of indifference as to its future course by declining the opportunity to enact a law to clarify it one way or the other (some would see the failure to codify the criminal law as a matter of parliamentary indifference). Nor is it the case where a change in the law is brought about with uncertain consequences and Parliament adopts a position of indifference as to which of those future consequences will prevail by declining the opportunity to deal with the matter in the legislation (whether in leaving it to the courts, or in leaving it to a statutory instrument to fill in the details).

Parliament has not had the opportunity even to consider the matter—there has never been an occasion when Parliament has debated anything even remotely connected to the matter—or the particular matter was not thought about at the time a related subject was being debated. It may be the case that although there was general awareness of this particular matter, it was not brought to Parliament's attention or even implicitly taken into account when related legislation was passed. It may be the case that although the matter was raised in Parliament the timetable of parliamentary business precluded a parliamentary intention being formed on that particular matter before the related legislation was enacted; or even that it was expedient not to resolve a parliamentary intention in relation to that particular matter before the vote was taken.[35]

Parliamentary sovereignty is a subject which can provide theorists with a number of stimulating issues to pursue.[36] It may be as much an artificial construction as parliamentary intention,[37] but even so may perform the function of covering, albeit figuratively, doctrines of practical importance. For our present interests we may fortunately reduce the subject matter of parliamentary sovereignty to a small number of practical concerns.

It is one thing to invoke the doctrine of parliamentary sovereignty in proclaiming that Parliament cannot bind its successors, or in asserting that what Parliament enacts is supreme. In the anthropomorphic language so readily used of Parliament, this amounts to saying that Parliament can change its mind, or that nobody can tell Parliament what to do. It is, however, something else entirely to claim that an aspect of parliamentary sovereignty requires us to conclude that nobody can do anything without Parliament authorising it. This at the very least turns Parliament into an interfering busybody. In fact, it requires of Parliament super-human capacities even in its anthropomorphic guise. It would mean that Parliament had the capacity to consider each past circumstance and each future eventuality, and to formulate an appropriate authorisation to deal with it. It would require the capacity to eradicate all of the cases that we have just catalogued as leading to a recognition of proposition (3). This needs more than an "all powerful Parliament". We would need a legislative

---

[35] The skill of the draftsman is occasionally called upon to word legislation that is ambiguous as to the determination of such a matter, so that every side within the apparent parliamentary consensus can be appeased. Louis Jaffe, *Judicial Control of Administrative Action* (Boston, MA, Little, Brown & Co, 1965) at 37–8 suggests that the inability to reach a detailed consensus within the legislature on controversial matters may be a good reason for delegating power to an administrative body.

[36] For some recent examples, see Jeffrey Goldsworthy, *The Sovereignty of Parliament: History and Philosophy* (Oxford, Clarendon Press, 1999); Neil MacCormick, *Questioning Sovereignty: Law, State, and Nation in the European Commonwealth* (Oxford, OUP, 1999); NW Barber, "Sovereignty Re-examined: The Courts, Parliament, and Statutes" (2000) 20 *Oxford Journal of Legal Studies* 131; Paul Craig, "Public Law, Political Theory and Legal Theory" [2000] *Public Law* 211 at 211–30; Martin Loughlin, *Sword and Scales: An Examination of the Relationship between Law and Politics* (Oxford, Hart Publishing, 2000) at 136–40, 151–7.

[37] It was once regarded as "almost entirely the work of Oxford men": RFV Heuston, *Essays in Constitutional Law* 2nd edn. (London, Stevens & Sons, 1964) at 1.

body displaying omniscience and capable of acting beyond temporal constraints. It is not sufficient to rely on the sort of default intention enthusiastically adopted by Austin, that what a sovereign Parliament has not overturned it has implicitly authorised, for at the best this is another instance of the error of equating the absence of a prohibition with a positive authorisation, and at the worst it is a blatant fiction to remedy the defects in Austin's theory.[38] In reality no body can be said to have authorised something on which it has not had the opportunity to form a view.[39]

Recognising that Parliament has neither the time nor the capacity to exercise its sovereignty in such an officious manner does not lead us to deny other aspects of its sovereignty. The common law model adopts a practical view of parliamentary sovereignty which recognises that nobody can tell Parliament what to do, and that Parliament can always have the final say, but considers that until Parliament sees fit to proclaim otherwise the courts will get on with their business of formulating and applying the principles of judicial review.[40] "If the omnipotent Parliament does not like it, it can say so." (To slightly paraphrase Craig's retort.[41])

Admittedly, this view of parliamentary sovereignty acknowledges that the courts continue to go about their business on the sufferance of Parliament: that the sovereign Parliament if it wished could take away all the business of the courts, and hand it over to popular tribunals; and could undo all the past work of the courts by enacting a comprehensive code to replace all existing law. Still this view does not recognise that the conduct of each element of the court's business is authorised by Parliament. It is rather like, in a more primitive context, trying to account for the continuing validity of the laws of Rex I after his death upon the succession of Rex II. Given that Rex II could have repealed all the laws of Rex I but has not done so, their continuing validity is on the sufferance of Rex II. However, it would be absurd to suggest that Rex II authorised the laws that Rex I made.[42]

It is part of the common ground between the modified *ultra vires* and common law models that the details of the principles of judicial review are created by the courts, so neither side is suggesting that in some way parliamentary sovereignty requires Parliament to authorise the material content of the principles

---

[38] John Austin, *The Province of Jurisprudence Determined*, Wilfrid Rumble (ed.) (Cambridge, Cambridge University Press, 1995) at 35. The case of fiction is suggested by Austin's remark that rules made by judges are "established by the sovereign legislature"; the case of error by his talking of an authority imparted "by way of acquiescence".

[39] The case of authorising *someone* is another matter, but not at issue here. The argument is not that Parliament has authorised the courts, but that Parliament has authorised the principles of judicial review. (A case of offering *carte blanche* to someone may be regarded as authorising the person, or, in some circumstances authorising any of a limited range of possibilities which the person will subsequently select—in which case the authorising body has formed the view that any option contained in that range is acceptable.)

[40] I leave for later discussion of the nature of this business.

[41] Text quoted at n. 14 above.

[42] See HLA Hart, *The Concept of Law* (Oxford, Clarendon Press, 1961) 60–64.

of judicial review. Yet there remains a point of issue between the two models over the matter of who has authorised the principles of judicial review. Are they created under the authority of Parliament, or by the courts' own authority?

What exactly are the practical implications of the view of parliamentary sovereignty required by the *ultra vires* model? Since it is not being suggested that Parliament authorises the material content of the principles of judicial review, how exactly does its purported authorisation of the principles bite in a practical way? An important qualification that has been suggested from the *ultra vires* side is that the issue of authorisation only arises in the context of the courts dealing with the conditions that are to be attached to a *statutory* power.[43] This recognises that the courts on their own authority get on with the business of developing and applying the principles of judicial review for non-statutory bodies, but insists that any conditions attached to a power granted by Parliament must be authorised by Parliament itself at pain of threatening parliamentary sovereignty.

However, the recognition of proposition (3) and the variety of ways in which a case may fall under it,[44] means that there is no direct challenge to the will of Parliament until Parliament has had and exercised the opportunity to express an intention upon each of the conditions that might or might not be regarded as an appropriate limitation of the power. On a smaller scale the super-human qualities required by the doctrine of parliamentary sovereignty in its unrealistic hyper-officious form would be needed here to maintain the position that all the conditions attached to a power granted by Parliament must be authorised by Parliament itself. Yet it is implicit in the acknowledgment by the *ultra vires* side that the material content of the principles of judicial review are the creation of the courts that this is not presumed.

One way out of the apparent lack of an effective notion of parliamentary sovereignty on the *ultra vires* side is to resort to a romantic view of parliamentary sovereignty. It is strictly speaking unnecessary to be conscious of parliamentary sovereignty when the courts are working out the practical determination of the principles of judicial review, but to restrict our perspective in this way misses out on the beauty of the broader picture. The courts are not simply doing their own thing but working in harmony with principles that Parliament also embraces and fully endorses. Something like this seems to be the impetus for Elliott's heartfelt request:[45]

> "In order to acknowledge that the credit lies with the courts for the translation of these norms into enforceable legal principles, it is not necessary to deny that Parliament has long been taken to respect those values. There is no shame in admitting that judicial development of administrative law is consistent with the legislative intention of Parliament. . . . it is, rather, the characteristic of a mature democracy in which respect for the most fundamental values permeates each branch of the constitution."

[43] See Elliott's discussion of this point at 90–1.
[44] See text at nn. 34 and 35 above.
[45] 368–9.

If it were known that a sovereign Parliament endorsed certain values, then there could be something in an argument that suggested the courts were offering an affront to parliamentary sovereignty (displaying impudence rather than overt contempt) by adopting any other values in applying principles of judicial review.[46] However, this takes the *ultra vires* model onto much weaker ground, relying on romantic appeal rather than logical argument, and, as I shall argue in the following section, it is the sort of romantic appeal that again links the *ultra vires* model with fairy tales.

A RETURN TO THE REALM OF FAIRY TALES

Reference is made to two sorts of values by the supporters of the modified *ultra vires* model, which it is confidently assumed can be regarded as governed by parliamentary intention: the standards of reasonableness, and the values of the rule of law. Essentially the same point can be made about both in revealing the flimsiness of their romantic appeal. They both have an intangible quality when it comes to the point of capturing them in concrete situations. I shall concentrate on reasonableness here, reserving comments on the rule of law[47] for the following section.

The question whether a power has been exercised reasonably is usually raised by a victim of the exercise of that power, who wishes to challenge it. In court the standard defence in such an action for judicial review is not that the body exercising the power enjoyed the authority to exercise it unreasonably, but rather that the power had been exercised reasonably. This alone should be sufficient to alert us to the fact that the standards of reasonableness are not settled. Moreover, even if we narrow it down to reasonableness in the context of what purposes the power was granted to achieve, the points of contention simply multiply. What exactly are the purposes? How far is it envisaged that those purposes should be achieved at the expense of competing considerations?[48]

---

[46] The impudence would lie in creating law that was known to be against the wishes of Parliament and which it would be presumed Parliament would wish to strike down, rather than contempt which would occur in creating law known to conflict with the law that Parliament had made. I make no comment here as to whether the courts are ever impudent or in contempt in these ways, but the nice aspect of the romantic vision portrayed by Elliott is that the presumed harmony with Parliament's intention in whatever values the courts have adopted makes any finding of even impudence impossible.

[47] Elliott does suggest that reasonableness is one of the requirements of the rule of law (96) but this view is not necessarily a part of the argument whenever it is asserted on the *ultra vires* side that the requirement of reasonableness must be regarded as being governed by parliamentary intention.

[48] The problems of reasonableness are discernible in the formulation of the *Wednesbury* test, which moves to a test of *un*reasonableness and then limits residual cases of unreasonableness to those which are so obvious that everyone would recognise them ([1948] 1 KB 223 at 230, 234 *per* Lord Greene MR: "so unreasonable that no reasonable authority could ever have come to it"). Yet even so, the test's dependence on what can be regarded as relevant or irrelevant factors means that there may still be conflicting views on the matter by the two parties to the dispute. Lord Greene dealt with the views of the applicant by suggesting to counsel that he was really asking the court to

If uniform standards of reasonableness existed, it really would not matter a whit whether we took those standards as internal to the grant of power or externally imposed on the grant. The question whether Parliament intended the power to be exercised reasonably or the courts had imposed the condition would be redundant for all practical purposes (and probably for all theoretical purposes too) *if* there existed a uniform set of standards of reasonableness known to all. For when Parliament granted the power it would know exactly under what conditions, subject to that uniform set of standards, the grant would take place. And when the courts reviewed the exercise of the power they would simply apply that uniform set of standards to the case before them (and presumably litigation in this area would dry up to leave only disputes over the facts).

It is in this hypothetical realm that it would be possible to fill the logical gap reached at the end of the section before last, by the factual assertion that Parliament knew full well what standards of reasonableness could be applied as conditions to the power it had granted, so as to reason that if Parliament had not included them it must have been at least consciously indifferent to the power being exercised unreasonably. Any reasoning to the conclusion that Parliament was consciously indifferent to, or intended, the power being exercised unreasonably requires us to inhabit a hypothetical realm where there exists a body of standards of reasonableness known to Parliament which it has reached a state of conscious indifference towards or has rejected.

Let us be clear where the telling of fairy tales is taking place. Only a cynic would suggest that every human endeavour to behave reasonably is a transparent illusion. Nor would it be so fanciful to hold a general presumption that people are capable of behaving reasonably, and in a trivial sense retain the expectation that all will behave reasonably. However, what is being imputed to Parliament is not a lofty view of mankind but an authorisation of a set of standards of reasonableness used for the principles of judicial review, by which hard decisions are made as to which exercise of power was reasonable and which was not. It does not require a cynic to point out that no human effort has so far achieved an intelligible set of standards of reasonableness to determine what amounts to reasonable behaviour in any given situation. It is nothing more than

substitute its own view of *reasonableness* (at 230), but Lord Greene's application of the test is premised on "Nobody, at this time of day, could say that the well-being and the physical and moral health of children is not a matter which a local authority. . . can properly have in mind" (*ibid*). For doubts as to whether the issue of reasonableness in *Wednesbury* would be resolved in the same way in a later sitting of the House of Lords, see JAG Griffith, "The Brave New World of Sir John Laws" (2000) 63 *Modern Law Review* 159 at 161–2. And for judicial reconsideration of how concerned local authorities should be about the moral welfare of their residents, see Sir John Laws' dicta in *R v. Somerset CC, ex p Fewings* [1995] 1 All ER 513 at 530: "if Parliament intends to confer power on a subordinate body to regulate the morals of other people, it will choose words which make it plain beyond peradventure". Further unsettling of the *Wednesbury* test through acknowledging the question of how relevant purposes are to be weighed in relation to competing considerations is evidenced in the suggestion of the "super-*Wednesbury* test" when competing considerations involve the protection of human rights (discussed in this volume by David Feldman at 252).

a fairy story to suggest that Parliament has worked out and adopted a set of standards of reasonableness, and a bigger story to suggest that Parliament shares the same set of standards with the courts. Breaking the spell of these illusions leads to a number of conclusions.

First, the absence of a settled set of standards of reasonableness means that there exists the possibility of dispute over what precise standards should be applied, how they should be prioritised and how they should affect the outcome, in a particular concrete situation. The dispute may be between the views of the parties to the litigation. It might arise between the view of the court and the view of Parliament[49] *if* Parliament had had the opportunity to reach a considered view on the matter.[50] Secondly, it is worth repeating that without a settled body of standards (unless Parliament works through all practical eventualities and forms its own view upon them), the absence of an intention that a power should be exercised reasonably should not lead us to infer that Parliament was consciously indifferent to the power being exercised unreasonably. Thirdly, we may properly characterise reasonableness as encompassing standards to be worked out before they can be applied, as involving a deliberative endeavour not a communicative requirement.[51]

This characterisation of reasonableness has implications not only in considering how realistically Parliament's intentions are being portrayed, but also for realistically assessing the courts' actions. I shall consider this point more fully in the concluding section, but having examined the fairy stories the treatment of this subject would be incomplete without considering what has happened to the fig leaf.

REPLACING FIG LEAVES

The criticism that the reliance on an implied Parliamentary intention was nothing more than a fig leaf used to cover up the courts' own creative role, in

[49] I leave aside here further enquiry on differences between the views of reasonableness of one judge and another. For fierce exchanges on this, see Richard Revesz, "Environmental Regulation, Ideology, and the D.C. Circuit" (1997) 83 *Virginia Law Review* 1717; Harry Edwards, "Collegiality and Decision Making on the D.C. Circuit" (1998) 84 *Virginia Law Review* 1335; Richard Revesz, "Ideology, Collegiality, and the D.C. Circuit: A Reply to Chief Judge Harry T. Edwards" (1999) 85 *Virginia Law Review* 805. Revesz claims that his empirical study indicates that judges are likely to vote ideologically particularly on cases involving procedural challenge to EPA policies adopted through notice-and-comment rulemaking, and when other judges on the panel share their party affiliation. That such challenges effectively question the reasonableness of the EPA's behaviour is indicated by Edwards at 1362.

[50] After the event we might well have a situation where Parliament (or, more realistically, the Government) does form the view that the power should have been available to be exercised unreasonably *applying the court's view of reasonableness*.

[51] In some specific contexts it may be clear to both parties what is regarded as reasonable, due to a common familiarity with the standards of behaviour that hold in that context, and hence the exhortation to be reasonable is not an invitation to engage in protracted deliberation but a communicative requirement. Such contexts are far removed from the contentious issues arising in an action for judicial review.

producing principles of judicial review to set the conditions to the powers that Parliament had granted, is less stinging in the light of the modifications that the two theoretical models of judicial review have undergone. Both now acknowledge a creative role for the judiciary. As we have seen, the point of issue remaining between the two models is about who authorises the principles of judicial review that the courts apply with their creative ingenuity to the situations arising before them. Both sides also have described the principles, that each from its own perspective gives different credit for authorising, as amounting to the values of the rule of law.[52] As I indicated in the previous section, it would I think be possible to take the values of the rule of law through the same argument that was employed there on the standards of reasonableness. The result would be to show that the claim by the *ultra vires* side that Parliament must be taken to have authorised the values of the rule of law as used by the courts in judicial review is as much a fairy story as the claim in relation to the standards of reasonableness.[53] However, I think that there is a more worthwhile exercise to be undertaken in considering how the rule of law has been used in this debate. This arises out of the observation that the use of the rule of law differs between the two models. If its use as a prop in a fairy story falls to the *ultra vires* side, I shall suggest its use as a fig leaf is now more evident on the common law side. I shall actually suggest that the common law side is outdoing the *ultra vires* side by collecting a wardrobe of fig leaves.

On the *ultra vires* side the use of the rule of law (as with reasonableness) is as an instrument to connect Parliament to the principles of judicial review applied by the courts. The fact that this instrument happens to be a set of values is secondary to the fact that it is regarded as being held in common by both, so that Parliament can be taken to have implicitly authorised what the courts engage in creatively applying. I shall rely on the suggestion made above that the argument developed in the previous section can meet this particular contention. On the common law side, by contrast, the rule of law is used precisely because it amounts to a set of values. This set of values provides an authority for the business of the courts. The different uses of the rule of law relate directly to the outstanding point at issue between the two models. The *ultra vires* side sees the sovereignty of Parliament as providing the authority for the principles of judicial review so has no need to rely on values in the rule of law to provide authority. The common law side in denying that the authority comes from Parliament,

---

[52] Craig's preference for justice as a more appropriate term is noted below.

[53] That the values (or even the doctrine) of the rule of law are not settled appears from two contributions to this volume: David Dyzenhaus, "Form and Substance in the Rule of Law: A Democratic Justification for Judicial Review" ch. 7 in Forsyth (ed.); and TRS Allan, "Comment: The Rule of Law as the Foundation of Judicial Review" in Forsyth (ed.). For further discussion, see the contributions to David Dyzenhaus (ed.), *Recrafting the Rule of Law: The Limits of Legal Order* (Oxford: Hart Publishing, 1999). A particularly pertinent contribution to that volume by Alon Harel criticises the use of the rule of law to portray a realm of judicial activity that is objectively doctrinal in an illuminating discussion of the use of the rule of law by the Israeli Supreme Court: "The Rule of Law and Judicial Review: Reflections on the Israeli Constitutional Revolution".

and wishing to divert our gaze from the possibility that the principles are nothing but bare judicial constructs, has recourse to the values seen as inherent in the
rule of law to provide authority for the principles that the courts employ. The
old fig leaf of parliamentary intention has been replaced by a new fig leaf of
the rule of law.

This distinction between the two uses of the rule of law is apparent in the
following passages. For the *ultra vires* side Elliott states:[54]

"It is the simple—and wholly plausible—assumption that Parliament intends to legislate consistently with the rule of law *which bridges the apparent gulf* between legislative silence and the developed body of administrative law . . ."

On the common law side, however, Craig states:[55]

"Supporters of the common law model have made it clear that they believe that the
content of judicial review should be decided in accordance with the rule of law, or normative considerations of justice, *which warrant the imposition* of constraints on the
exercise of discretion."

This purported derivation of authority from the rule of law presumes, as
much as did the purported derivation of authority from parliamentary intention
on the *ultra vires* side, a settled body of values through which the authority can
be transmitted. Once we acknowledge the contentious nature of the rule of

[54] 96 (emphasis added). The "bridge" holds for Elliott even where changes occur in the principles
of judicial review, because these are still linked to the evolution of "the constitutional principle of
the rule of law" and the "changing constitutional norms" it provides (101), and Parliament has been
regarded as legislating consistently with the constitutional principle of the rule of law (96). The idea
that Parliament and the courts march in tune on either side of this bridge to the unheard music which
reflects the pace and direction of our changing constitutional norms, is an idea whose credibility
Elliott does not pause to explore. This is possibly due to the fact that Elliott has already relied on a
relationship existing between legislative intention and the principles of judicial review as a matter
of logic (95), and hence is not seeking to question the relationship but is merely looking for an apt
way of describing it. The failure of the logical basis for the relationship makes it appropriate to think
again. However, Elliott's credulity on the relationship between Parliament and the courts is not limited to the context of judicial review. He asserts that a similar relationship exists when the courts
interpret other statutory terms: "No one would question the existence of a relationship between the
intention of Parliament and the courts' jurisprudence on the meaning of terms . . ." (97, 101–2). To
assume that Parliament accepts that the detailed meaning of legislative provisions will fall to the
courts to decide, and that the courts may form different views on the meaning of terms as the courts'
perceptions of social conditions change, does not lead to the assumption that Parliament has authorised within its legislative disposition the meaning reached by the courts. Far from no one questioning this matter, any reader of this volume has reason to consider the possibility of Parliament and
the courts having a discordant relationship over the meaning of statutory provisions, when a judge
can declare that he is acting in accordance with parliamentary intention only to be rebutted immediately thereafter by legislation to overturn his decision: the *Joint Council for the Welfare of
Immigrants* case and its statutory aftermath, cited by Forsyth at 400.

[55] 376 (emphasis added). Similarly: "normatively justified on the grounds of justice, the rule of
law, etc." (383); "normatively warranted in terms of justice, the rule of law, etc." (392). The substantive justification for the principles of judicial review is regarded by Craig as following the analysis of judge-made principles in other areas of law, which Craig considers to derive their formal
validity from the fact that courts have pronounced them, but their substantive authority from their
intrinsic normative quality: "the normative principles which comprise their content", "pre-existing
concepts . . . which have a normative force of their own" (379–80).

law,[56] no such settled body of values can be found. At one point, Craig himself acknowledges "the different meanings attached to the concept of the rule of law" as grounds for his personal preference for "justice" as a more appropriate term. However, it is clear from his following words that this is not due to the belief that justice provides a settled body of values. Craig wishes only to avoid certain connotations of the rule of law,[57] stating himself to be "perfectly happy to employ the terminology of the rule of law, provided that it is understood that the substantive concept of the rule of law necessarily entails *some* vision of justice and rights."[58] Whose vision of the rule of law (or justice, or rights) is to prevail?

In the absence of a settled body of values, invoking the rule of law as authority for the substantive scope of the principles of judicial review can be revealed as a sham by the simple technique of setting against a particular application of the principles of judicial review a hypothetical, pleaded, or dissenting application with the contrary result. The only thing that can determine whether the actual application on a particular occasion or its contrary has normative force is the authority of the court which decides it.[59] The common law model's portrayal of the normative force of the rule of law is as much a fig leaf as the *ultra vires* model's portrayal of derived normative force from parliamentary intention.

The rule of law is not the only device used on the common law side to cover up judges acting on their own authority to determine the scope of the law. Sir John Laws in his second contribution to this volume[60] makes use of two devices. His first suggestion is that the authority of the common law in general and its development of judicial review in particular is based on social consent or public confidence.[61] However, the unreliable nature of this covering for judicial authority is indicated by Laws himself within the same paragraph, when he remarks that "public opinion is a many-headed hydra, and what issues from its innumerable mouths is so unformed, various, quixotic and self-contradictory . . .".[62]

Before abandoning this device Laws reaches for another, the notion of principle. Principle is a word with loud and reassuring connotations, which has been selected on other occasions by other authors to take advantage of those connotations, but Laws provides us with a careful investigation of the nature of legal

---

[56] See above n. 53.

[57] For Craig's detailed views on the rule of law, see "Formal and Substantive Conceptions of the Rule of Law: An Analytical Framework" [1997] *Public Law* 466.

[58] 376 (emphasis added).

[59] Craig does seem to waver a little when attempting to defend some remarks by Sir John Laws which might have suggested that the courts rely on their own authority when deciding the scope of judicial review (386). On this occasion, he suggests that "in making that determination the courts should use justice, the rule of law, etc as guiding criteria."

[60] "Judicial Review and the Meaning of Law" ch. 8 in Forsyth (ed.).

[61] 174.

[62] *Ibid.*

principle with a view to convincing us that it provides a "process [which] confines the judge's own views in a strict and objective context".[63] However, Laws'
four building blocks of principle—arguments from logic, from consequences,
from precedent, and from ideals—only serve to underscore the essentially contentious nature of principle, or perhaps more accurately that principle serves a
role subservient to whichever body of doctrine, ideological or otherwise, is
selected. For none of these building blocks can provide a definite foundation,
nor an architectural plan for the building to be constructed.[64] Principle may be
used as a form in which to express the finished product of the judges but it is
another device of concealment to suggest that principle provides the substantive
authority for their work.

A rather more elaborate device is to be found in the discussion on the common law side of a particular set of principles, the "principles of good administration".[65] I need not dwell on the point that what is considered to be good
administration is also contentious, and that these also amount to a fig leaf if
used to provide authority for the principles of judicial review developed by the
courts. The same point can be made in relation to what may be regarded as a
synonymous expression, "the duties of considerate decision making".[66]
However, in these two cases it is important to distinguish between two ways in
which these principles or duties can be discussed. It is possible to regard them as
providing the authority for judicial decisions,[67] but it is also possible to engage
in fruitful discussion under these headings of what factors might be available to
be taken into account, and what objectives it might be thought worthwhile to
pursue, in formulating principles and in applying them to cases of judicial
review.[68] As valuable as the latter discussion might be it should be regarded as

[63] 189. Edwards, above n. 49, provides an example of having recourse to the reassuring connotations of principle. For warning against the blandishments of principle, see Stanley Fish, *The Trouble
with Principle* (Cambridge, MA, Harvard University Press, 1999): "the vocabulary of neutral principle can be used to disguise substance so that it appears to be the inevitable and nonengineered
product of an impersonal logic" (at 4).

[64] The suggestions that logic provides us with a "discipline", and that precedent shapes the use
of the building blocks into "a common enterprise" (183), cannot help. The discipline of logic may
alert us to what decisions are available, or to what are the consequences of beliefs that we hold, but
does not determine which decisions to take or which beliefs to accept. And although precedents once
determined may land us all in a particular common enterprise, that is not to say that they have been
determined from an enterprise that we have chosen to pursue in common.

[65] Dawn Oliver, "Is the *Ultra Vires* Rule the Basis of Judicial Review?" (previously published in
[1987] *Public Law* 543) ch. 1 of Forsyth (ed.) at 3–4.

[66] Dawn Oliver, "Review of (Non-Statutory) Discretions" ch. 14 in Forsyth (ed.) at 307–8.

[67] This role is apparent in Oliver, above n. 65, treating the principles of good administration as
an alternative to *ultra vires* for the basis of judicial review, particularly at 25–6. Similarly, in "The
Underlying Values of Public and Private Law" in Michael Taggart (ed.), *The Province of
Administrative Law* (Oxford, Hart Publishing, 1997) she treats "the key values as keystones" (at
218).

[68] This role is at the same time apparent in Oliver's work. In her contribution to Taggart (ed.),
above n. 67 at 224, she perceptively acknowledges that the key values "have to contend with other
considerations in the law and legal policy" and that upholding them in relation to the claims of one
individual "may involve weighing up the competing claims to these values of other individuals."
And also that, "It also involves consideration of the wider implications of giving precedence to such

quite distinct from the provision of a settled set of values that can be regarded as underlying the principles of judicial review and authorising their application by the courts. The reason for this is that no matter how many relevant factors or worthwhile objectives are identified, it remains contentious as to how these factors and objectives are to be related and prioritised in particular situations, and hence they themselves cannot form the basis for the courts getting on with the business of doing just that.

CONCLUDING REMARKS

A common thread has run through the dissatisfaction I have expressed with the "fairy stories" told on the *ultra vires* side and the "fig leaves" employed on the common law side. This is their dependence on a non-existent, settled set of values, which could realistically be linked to the principles of judicial review used by the courts whether as a bridge between parliamentary intention and the principles of judicial review, or in order to provide authorisation for the principles of judicial review.

Something else that can be seen as common to the two models, despite their fierce dispute, is an effort to fix the principles of judicial review within the law. On the *ultra vires* side there is an attempt to subordinate the principles of judicial review to the sovereignty of Parliament, but this is done in a way which does not merely uphold fundamental constitutional doctrine. By tracing the authority for the principles of judicial review used in determining the scope of a particular power to an implied intention regarded as part of the statutory creation of that power, there is retained an appearance of legality to the conditions that the courts impose upon the power.[69] In a very different way, the common law side makes a claim for the legality of these conditions, invoking the rule of law, or some other source of intrinsic legal value. What neither side is prepared to countenance is the prospect that the law enacted by Parliament, or found in the

---

values." Similarly, in above n. 66 at 307, she admits that "countervailing considerations" may prevail against duties of considerate decision-making. Oliver's concern in these essays, and in her book, *Common Values and the Public-Private Divide* (London, Butterworths, 1999), to identify considerations or values that are common to both sides of the traditional divide between public law and private law, although it may illuminate the development of the doctrines on either side of the traditional divide, does not of itself provide a justification or basis for the doctrines that emerge. In particular, the identification of common underlying *abstract* values (see Taggart (ed.) at 218, 224–5) does not perform this latter function, otherwise Justinian's identification (*Institutes* i.1.3) of the most abstract values of the law—to live honestly, to harm no-one, and to give each his due—would suffice. The problem is that they would suffice to form the basis of a number of conflicting systems of law.

[69] Sir William Wade sees this as providing an important motive for judges to adopt the *ultra vires* model if only as a matter of expediency: "Comment: Constitutional Realities and Judicial Prudence" in Forsyth (ed.). Jeffrey Jowell, "Of *Vires* and Vacuums: The Constitutional Context of Judicial Review" (also published in [1999] *Public Law* 448) ch. 15 of Forsyth (ed.), suggests that just such a motive may have been behind judicial dicta supporting the *ultra vires* model (337).

principles of the common law, does not provide an answer to what conditions should attach to the exercise of a power that Parliament has created. Why not?

If this possibility were acknowledged, how could the debate between the two sides continue? It would be nullified. If it were admitted that the law did not provide an answer, there could be no pre-existing substantive legal authority for the answer, and hence there would be no subject for a debate focusing on where that authority was to be found.

The defects discovered in the efforts of both sides to provide an answer do support raising the issue as to whether this question existed to be answered in the first place. Lawyers may be reluctant to raise this issue, for it implies uncomfortable things for lawyers. One is that if the conditions attached to the exercise of a power granted by Parliament are not in a particular case[70] to be found in the law, it follows that it is not necessarily the job of lawyers to determine them. The second is that if it happens that lawyers are given the job to set these conditions, they should recognise that in doing so they are operating as more than lawyers learned in the law. From this second point follows a third which raises questions about what skills or qualities we should look for in the lawyers who are handed this task.[71]

One way of looking at this task emerged in our earlier discussion of reasonableness but can be regarded as characteristic of each of the various abstract depictions referred to as governing this task. It was suggested there that

---

[70] In some cases conditions might be clear from the statutory provision or from general conditions that have already been established as part of administrative law. However, such cases are not fuel for the debate we have been considering, which deals with the question of what gives authority to the principles of administrative law before they have been established, and which operates outside the scope of explicit statutory conditions.

[71] Louis Eisenstein, "Some Iconoclastic Reflections on Tax Administration" (1945) 58 *Harvard Law Review* 477 at 523–6, 534–43, argued that judges lacked the abilities to deal with the essentially non-legal issues of working out the details of tax provisions which should be entrusted to an administrative body possessing the appropriate technical skills. John Bell, in ch. X of *Policy Arguments in Judicial Decisions* (Oxford, Clarendon Press, 1983), suggested that recognition of a "creatively political aspect" of the judicial function had a number of implications, particularly for the manner of selection of judges. More recently, Andrew Fraser, "Beyond the Charter Debate: Republicanism, Rights and Civic Virtue in the Civil Constitution of Canadian Society" (1993) 1 *Review of Constitutional Studies* 27, has suggested as a radical solution to concerns that an unaccountable judiciary has been given too much power in interpreting the Canadian Charter that judges should be elected by the legal profession and academia subject to popular ratification. Fraser sees it as an advantage of this proposal that academic critics would be confronted by their civic responsibility. Political aspects of the appointment of Supreme Court Justices are considered in two books, Terri Jennings Peretti, *In Defense of a Political Court* (Princeton, NJ, Princeton University Press, 1999) and David Alistair Yalof, *Pursuit of Justices: Presidential Politics and the Selection of Supreme Court Nominees* (Chicago, IL, Chicago University Press, 1999), reviewed in John Yoo, "Choosing Justices: a Political Appointments Process and the Wages of Judicial Supremacy" (2000) 98 *Michigan Law Review* 1436. Yoo considers, "By constitutionalizing more areas of life and by pursuing the notion of judicial supremacy, the Court itself has shunted normal political activity from the world of policy into the world of Court appointments." (at 1461). In order to counter this, he suggests that the appointments process should be used to select new Justices who are prepared to "deny the Court's own supremacy." (at 1467). The general point is also raised in Fredman, below n. 74, and in Kate Malleson, *The New Judiciary: The Effects of Expansion and Activism* (Aldershot, Ashgate, 1999).

reasonableness as a general objective enjoined a deliberative enterprise rather than a communicative requirement. It was Aristotle who suggested that "to lay down a law about things that are subjects for deliberation is an impossibility. Therefore men do not deny that it must be for a human being to determine such matters."[72] However, Aristotle was not a lawyer.

If these suggestions do have some bearing on the nature of judicial review,[73] the theory of that subject should be concerned not with the authority for the conditions attached to the power that Parliament has granted, but with the issue of whose deliberations beyond the law should determine the scope of the power; in particular, when the scope should be set by the body granted the power, and when by the judges in the courts. This would give prominence to a more careful consideration of the role of the judiciary within the theory of judicial review.[74]

---

[72] Aristotle, *Politics*, III.xi.8. I use the translation from the Loeb edition by H Rackham (Cambridge, MA, Harvard University Press, 1932) except that I prefer "determine" to "judge" in the second sentence. Either translation is appropriate for the Greek *krinounta*, but the former avoids the connotation that we are dealing with a judicial judgment, rather than a human determination. The emphasis on general human determination rather than an exercise of judicial skill is evident from Aristotle's use of *anthrōpon* here in contrast to the use of *archōn* (translated by Rackham as "official", a term used of the chief magistrates at Athens) in the following passage.

[73] If they do, they also have a bearing on the doctrinal implications of the subject. I am not in a position to survey here all outstanding doctrinal issues, but would suggest that following the way that the doctrinal implications for ouster clauses have been used by both sides in the debate, that the adoption of a particular view of substantive authority for the principles of judicial review does not help to dispose of the matter; and further, that by taking the issue of ouster clauses out of this debate we are more likely to face the real concerns that ouster clauses raise over to what extent, and how, a legislative body should be able to delegate power to a subordinate body to be exercised without review by the courts.

[74] Treatment of the judicial role has long been a prominent part of discussion of judicial review in the United States, see e.g., Learned Hand, "Chief Justice Stone's Conception of the Judicial Function" (1946) 46 *Columbia Law Review* 696. That constitutional discourse in the UK may operate to blur our understanding of the judicial role is commented on by Neil Walker, "Setting English Judges to Rights" (1999) 19 *Oxford Journal of Legal Studies* 133 at 145. That consideration of the judicial role may gain greater prominence by the enactment of the Human Rights Act 1998 is indicated by suggestions already being made that the practical impact of the Act in a number of areas will depend upon the role performed by the judges, see Helen Fenwick, "The Right to Protest, the Human Rights Act and the Margin of Appreciation" (1999) 62 *Modern Law Review* 491; Gavin Phillipson, "The Human Rights Act, 'Horizontal Effect' and the Common Law: a Bang or a Whimper?" (1999) 62 *Modern Law Review* 824; Stephanie Palmer, "Human Rights: Implications for Labour Law" (2000) 59 *Cambridge Law Journal* 168. And see generally, Sandra Fredman, "Judging Democracy: The Role of the Judiciary Under the Human Rights Act 1998" (2000) 53 *Current Legal Problems* 99.

5

Excluded Middles, Right Answers and Vagueness

INTRODUCTION

T HE LAW OF the excluded middle (or the principle of bivalence[1]), which surfaced in the previous chapter, has a pedigree going back to Aristotle and has
long been established as an elementary law of logic. Despite some doubts as to
its universal standing,[2] its stark simplicity and apparently self-evident sound-
ness must have seen it explicitly invoked or tacitly assumed in countless arguments in all manner of contexts. In this chapter I want to consider further
appeals to the law of the excluded middle taken from arguments found in two
contexts of significant importance for an understanding of legal reasoning. The
first of these contexts is the debate over whether the law provides right answers
in hard cases which has attracted considerable attention following the efforts of
Ronald Dworkin to provide an affirmative answer to this question.

I shall take this discussion of the law together with the study of judicial review
in the previous chapter as a means of inviting more general deliberation over the
law of the excluded middle. I shall undertake this in the belief that a modification to the law (or, more strictly speaking, a modification to the application of
the law), which can be discerned in these two contexts, has wider significance.
The modification arises in both cases due to the recognition that a purported
application of the law of the excluded middle requires more careful analysis: an
attempted singular application of the law is erroneous in concealing a situation
where two applications of the law are possible. The spurious singular application produces a false conclusion, contrary to the result obtained when a more
rigorous analysis involving a dual application of the law is carried out. The
practical setting for the error I describe is such that the respective subject matters for the two applications of the law are so closely related that it is easy to
make the mistake of viewing them as a single subject matter requiring a single
application of the law. I suggest that in order to avoid error in this sort of
case it would be appropriate to recognise a particular application of the law of
the excluded middle, which might conveniently be referred to as the law of
the excluded middles, so emphasising the dual application of the law to the two

---

[1] For the purposes of this chapter I shall regard the two expressions as synonymous, though technically the latter is an application of the former to the truth or falsity of propositions.
[2] See ch. 4 n. 17.

distinct "middles" involved. Furthermore, I suggest that the analysis captured in the law of the excluded middles might assist in our understanding of some of the counter-examples that doubters have brought forward to question the universality of the law of the excluded middle. In particular, in the concluding section of this chapter I attempt to show how this analysis could be used to deal with the alleged counter-example of vagueness, which provides the other context of particular relevance for legal reasoning.

RIGHT ANSWERS TO HARD CASES

Ronald Dworkin has persistently[3] and imaginatively defied the conventional jurisprudential wisdom which holds that in certain cases of a particularly complex or novel character the law does not provide a definite answer. In denying that judges in hard cases have a discretion to determine what the law is, Dworkin has argued instead for the judicial use of public standards or principles in a way that is capable of providing the right legal answer. The process of reaching a right answer in hard cases obviously differs from the process of reaching the legal answer in easy cases. Dworkin is not suggesting that hard cases are an illusion. He is at his most imaginative in seeking to portray the process of judicial reasoning in hard cases which is more subtle than the straightforward application of a clear legal rule yet is still capable of delivering the right legal answer. He draws metaphorically on literary criticism (answering questions about characters where the relevant information is not explicitly provided by the author on the basis of narrative consistency), and literary creation (different authors writing a chain novel so as to achieve narrative coherence). He draws upon a mythical judge of his own creation (Hercules who has the superhuman intellectual stamina to fit together past and future legal decisions within the unified scheme of a political theory).

Dworkin's burden to describe this process of reaching the right answer in hard cases is shouldered on the premise that a right answer *must* exist. None of his imaginative devices operates as an effective argument to demonstrate this, though they may act as striking images to help people to see what reaching a right answer in hard cases might be like, on the assumption that it exists. Its

---

[3] In "Pragmatism, Right Answers, and True Banality" in Michael Brint and William Weaver (eds.), *Pragmatism in Law and Society* (Boulder, CO, Westview Press, 1991) at 382 n. 1, Dworkin maintains his "one-right-answer claim" citing as key essays in which he has advanced it: *Taking Rights Seriously* (Cambridge, MA, Harvard University Press, 1977) chs 4 and 13; *A Matter of Principle* (Cambridge, MA, Harvard University Press, 1985), cited hereinafter as MofP, chs 5 and 7; *Law's Empire* (Cambridge, MA, Harvard University Press, 1986) ch. 7. An incipient form of Dworkin's thesis is to be found in "Judicial Discretion" (1963) 60 *Journal of Philosophy* 624. More recently, Louis Wolcher has suggested in "Ronald Dworkin's Right Answer Thesis through the Lens of Wittgenstein" (1997) 29 *Rutgers Law Journal* 43 at 43 n 2 that the thesis can also be found related to constitutional values in Dworkin's *Freedom's Law: The Moral Reading of the American Constitution* (Cambridge, MA, Harvard University Press, 1996) at 15.

existence is taken by Dworkin to be "an ordinary, commonsensical, extremely weak proposition of law" which he has repeatedly indicated he would not have taken the trouble to point out if it had not been denied by so many legal theorists.[4] Given Dworkin's own confident posture on there being no need for detailed argument to support his thesis, it is not surprising that the voluminous discussion on the right answer thesis has over the years proved entertaining and distracting but failed to reach resolution.[5]

There is, however, some serious argument to be found for reaching the conclusion that there must be right answers in hard cases, in contrast with mere assertion and illustration of what is purported to be a common sense view of the law. It arises in an essay first published in 1977 and involves Dworkin's attempt to employ the law of the excluded middle to demonstrate the untenability of the opposing position held by supporters of the no-right-answer thesis.[6] This argument more often than not has simply been ignored in the literature growing out of Dworkin's right answer thesis.[7] My case for revisiting it is based on the view

---

[4] Above n. 3, "Pragmatism, Right Answers" at 359. Significantly, Gerald MacCallum, "Dworkin on Judicial Discretion" (1963) 60 *Journal of Philosophy* 638 (a response to Dworkin's paper, above n. 3) points out Dworkin's reliance on the premise that people have an entitlement to the correct decision in all cases.

[5] Dworkin himself has shown some signs of impatience with the debate, see "Pragmatism, Right Answers" above n. 3, at 360. Nevertheless, the debate continues, see, for recent examples, Richard Markovits, "Legitimate Legal Argument and Internally-Right Answers to Legal-Rights Questions" (1999) 74 *Chicago-Kent Law Review* 415, JM Balkin and Sanford Levinson, "Getting Serious About 'Taking Legal Reasoning Seriously'" *ibid.* 543, Richard Markovits, "'You Cannot Be Serious!': A Reply to Professors Balkin and Levinson" *ibid.* 559, Michael Quinn, "Argument and Authority in Common Law Advocacy and Adjudication: An Irreducible Pluralism of Values" *ibid.* 655, among a number of contributions to a Symposium on Taking Legal Argument Seriously.

[6] "No Right Answer?" in PMS Hacker and J Raz (eds.), *Law, Morality and Society* (Oxford, Clarendon Press, 1977) ch. 3, revised in (1978) 53 *New York University Law Review* 1, reproduced as "Is There Really No Right Answer in Hard Cases?" in MofP ch. 5. The argument using the law of the excluded middle is in MofP 120–34. It follows from my suggestion that these pages contains Dworkin's real argument for the right answer thesis, that I view his discussion of the third argument for the second version of the no-right-answer thesis (the argument from controversy) at pp 137*ff.* as not providing an *argument* for the existence of right answers. This section seeks to illustrate how facts of narrative consistency might (metaphorically) appear in the law on the assumption suggested in the previous section that law resembles a literary exercise designed to produce right answers (141), and then invokes Dworkin's earlier "description of our legal enterprise" (142) premised on there being right answers. Nevertheless, an interesting criticism of what can be regarded as Dworkin's implicit argument in his discussion of controversy in the law is to be found in Jacob Janzen, "Some Formal Aspects of Ronald Dworkin's Right Answer Thesis" (1981) 11 *Manitoba Law Journal* 191.

[7] Some discussion of it is to be found in Kevin Saunders, "What Logic Can and Cannot Tell Us About Law" (1998) 73 *Notre Dame Law Review* 667; Michael Moore, "Metaphysics, Epistemology and Legal Theory" (1987) 60 *Southern California Law Review* 453; Joseph Raz, "Legal Reasons, Sources, and Gaps" (1979) *Archiv für Rechts- und Sozialphilosophie, Beiheft* 11, 197, reproduced as ch. 4 of *The Authority of Law* (Oxford, Clarendon Press, 1979), considered below nn 13, 20.

Timothy Endicott, *Vagueness in Law* (Oxford, OUP, 2000) at 64–72, provides a discussion of that part of Dworkin's argument which deals with vagueness. In his book Endicott argues for a reformulation of vagueness to avoid the conventional "neither true nor false" representation, and the problems associated with the law of the excluded middle. He concludes that vagueness in law is unavoidable and suggests that resolution of vagueness is a duty of judges, in a manner that resembles Raz's judgment "according to law", considered in ch. 3 above.

that a proper analysis of the points it raises actually supports the possibility of a no-right-answer thesis, and moreover that it does so in a way that embraces the common sense positions that Dworkin has misappropriated to lend credibility to his own view of the law.

The use made by Dworkin of the law of the excluded middle is at first sight extremely thorough. He divides the opposing arguments into two versions of a no-right-answer thesis. Both versions, according to Dworkin, "deny that the bivalence thesis holds for important dispositive concepts."[8] For example, both would deny that in every case a particular contract must be either "a valid contract" or "not a valid contract". The difference between the two versions, as Dworkin sees it, lies in the way that the two versions reject the law of the excluded middle, $p \vee \sim p$.

The first version of the no-right-answer thesis considers that there is a third possibility, perhaps "an inchoate contract", so that to see the only possibilities as "a valid contract" or "not a valid contract" is to make the sort of mistake made by a person who sees "young" or "old" as exhausting the logical space available in describing the age of a man and failing to recognise the possibility of "middle-aged". The second version does not rely on a third possibility but considers that there are some cases that it is not possible to locate as either "valid" or "not valid", which cannot clearly be said to be the one or the other. For example, the requirements for a valid contract include its not being sacrilegious, and it is unclear whether a particular agreement should be regarded as sacrilegious or not. These cases, Dworkin suggests, would be like a case of someone who is on the border between youth and middle age.

More formally, Dworkin treats the first version as denying the excluded middle by considering there to be cases of p, $\sim p$, and (non-$p = r$); and the second version as denying the excluded middle by considering there to be cases of p, $\sim p$, and (neither p nor $\sim p$).[9]

An initial response to this more formal rendering of Dworkin's representation of the first version would be to suggest that if a case of (non-$p = r$) does not amount to $\sim p$, then as between p and (non-$p = r$), or more simply between p and r, the law of the excluded middle is not under threat at all. It is irrelevant, as much as it is between praise and blame, or in the analogy Dworkin provides between young and old. Blame is not the negation of praise; old is not the negation of young; r is not the negation of p. Such a response is encouraged by the way that Dworkin depicts the first version. A significant problem is that he relies on analogies to illustrate the way that the first version breaches the law of the

---

[8] MofP 120*ff*.

[9] MofP 121–2. In his detailed discussion that follows Dworkin divides his opponents further by taking three arguments that might be used to support the second version (from vagueness, from positivism, from controversy) and further still by taking four forms of positivism that might be maintained. So in all there are potentially at least seven variants of the no-right-answer thesis to consider. However, Dworkin himself occasionally recognises that these versions are not discrete and that the argument may sometimes slip from one to the other.

excluded middle although the law does not even come into consideration within the situation covered by the analogy. This is so with the analogy of young, old and middle-aged. It also applies to Dworkin's analogy with a hypothetical legal system where we have p representing a valid contract (where the parties are aged over twenty-one), and r representing an inchoate contract (where a party is between sixteen and twenty-one).[10]

The law of the excluded middle does not apply to the question of whether a valid or inchoate contract is present, since an inchoate contract is not the negation of a valid contract. For example, we may have a case of an agreement with a fifteen year old, which is not a valid contract but is not an inchoate contract either. The mere fact that if we have a case of r then we can be sure that we do not have a case of p is immaterial: r is not equal to ~p. The idea of a case of ~p sometimes but not always also being a case of r is uncontroversial. We can have a case of not-praise where there is blame, and also a case of not-praise where there is not-blame. More formally, we can have $(\sim p \wedge r) \vee (\sim p \wedge \sim r)$. This actually upholds the law of the excluded middle, for $r \vee \sim r$, in the set of cases where there is ~p.

However, Dworkin seems to insist in his representation of the first version of the no-right-answer thesis that it goes a step further in treating r as a case of "non-p" distinct from ~p, rather than being a special case of ~p which would amount to $(\sim p \wedge r)$.[11] If this is the case Dworkin wishes to make, then again his analogy is misleading. For in the hypothetical legal system if contracts are divided according to the ages of the parties into three discrete categories— "valid", "inchoate", and "invalid" (where the parties are respectively both over twenty-one, one between sixteen and twenty-one, one under sixteen), then it follows that both "inchoate" and "invalid" contracts so defined amount to subsets within the set of cases of ~p, taking "valid" to be p. We have effectively $(\sim p \wedge r)$ for "inchoate" and $(\sim p \wedge q)$ for "invalid", and neither is distinct from ~p.

Moreover, within this analogy the law of the excluded middle is upheld in three ways: generally, as between $p \vee \sim p$; and in the particular cases for $r \vee \sim r$ within $(\sim p \wedge r) \vee (\sim p \wedge \sim r)$ as above, and similarly for $q \vee \sim q$ within $(\sim p \wedge q) \vee (\sim p \wedge \sim q)$.

Leaving analogies to one side, Dworkin's unillustrated formal representation of the first version of the no-right-answer thesis in fact collapses into his formal representation of the second version. Whatever non-p is meant by Dworkin to

---

[10] MofP 123. It is remarkable that at the conclusion of the paragraph introducing this analogy, Dworkin states that in the case of this hypothetical legal system it would be "wrong to appeal to the bivalence thesis" because we do not have a case of p and ~p, but nevertheless commences the next paragraph by saying that the first version argues that "our own legal system is really like that". The difference between Dworkin's treatment of the hypothetical legal system and his treatment of "our own legal system" is commented on further below.

[11] The evidence for this is twofold: (1) in providing his formal representation at MofP 122 Dworkin moves from (non-p) not being identical with (~p), which would still allow for treating "non-p" as a special case of ~p, to the tighter suggestion that "(non-p) ... is not the negation of (p)"; (2) Dworkin's talk of the "third possibility" (MofP 121).

convey it is clear that it is not a case of *p*. So we actually have as *r* something that is not only not ~*p* but also is not *p*; i.e. is (neither *p* nor ~*p*). Yet for Dworkin this represents the supposedly distinct form of the second version of the no-right-answer thesis.

If we consider now more carefully the practical example that Dworkin provides for the first version, we can see how it has to be viewed in order to avoid it conforming to the law of the excluded middle. Remember an "inchoate" contract is distinct from both a "valid" contract (where both parties are over twenty-one years of age), and from an "invalid" contract (where one party is under sixteen).[12] In the case of an inchoate contract (where one party is between sixteen and twenty-one) the judge has a discretion as to whether to enforce it or not. It is implicit in Dworkin's representation that the decision of the judge may turn the contract into a "valid" contract.[13] If this were not possible an inchoate contract would have to be regarded from the outset as one form of the negation of a "valid" contract, and the law of the excluded middle would be upheld in just the ways we noted in relation to the hypothetical legal system, where there were legally stated to be three discrete categories of contract. The same point can be made in relation to having to view the decision of the judge as being capable of turning the inchoate contract into an "invalid" contract in order to prevent it being regarded as a form of the negation of an "invalid" contract from the outset.[14] Hence at the point prior to the judicial determination of its status the inchoate contract is represented as (neither *p* nor ~*p*) only on the understanding that at the subsequent point of judicial determination its status will be fixed as *p* ∨ ~*p*. Dworkin's representation of the first version of the no-right-answer thesis as denying the law of the excluded middle is, accordingly, at its strongest a temporary postponement of the recognition of the law.

What is happening when we try to view Dworkin's example of the first version in this way, so as to uphold his claim that the law of the excluded middle is

---

[12] The terms "inchoate" etc are used twice by Dworkin—once in the analogous hypothetical legal system, and then again for an example of how the first version would represent "our own legal system" (MofP 123). The relationship between the latter and the former is given in terms of it being "really like that". If this means it is "exactly like that", then Dworkin's representation of the first version suffers from the defects of the analogy just given. Assuming a weaker relationship with the analogy, I examine now how the example would have to be regarded in order to maintain a breach of the law of the excluded middle within it.

[13] This point is overlooked by Moore, above n. 7 at 479 and n. 102, in his attempt to reconstruct Dworkin's right answer thesis from his representations of the no-right-answer thesis, which leads him to suggest three possible dispositions (*s*, *t*, *v*) relating to the three types of contract, rather than the two (valid, invalid).

[14] Note that if "invalid" has been legally defined as a technical term of law, so that it cannot be regarded as equivalent to not-valid (the negation of valid), it can, of course, still be a particular case of not-valid (i.e. (~*p* ∧ *q*)), as indicated in the analysis of the hypothetical legal system above. However, according to Dworkin's representation, at the point of resolution the inchoate contract is determined by the judge as being enforceable or not, which must be regarded as making it "valid" or "invalid" for the reasons just given in the main text. If this were not the case, at the point of resolution we would have to retain as distinct categories "enforceable valid" and "enforceable inchoate", "unenforceable invalid" and "unenforceable inchoate", so retaining the three underlying discrete categories of contracts which, as we have seen, uphold the law of the excluded middle.

being breached? What puts this case outside our analysis of that law being upheld in the hypothetical legal system? The crucial difference is that in the earlier analysis we took the hypothetical legal system at its word in defining the three discrete categories of contracts as "valid", "inchoate" and "invalid"; whereas, in considering the example of the first version of the no-right-answer thesis we only allowed ourselves to recognise two ultimate categories, "valid" and "invalid" and regarded "inchoate" as a mid-way stage between these two.

This seems to support Dworkin's claim that the first version of the no-right-answer thesis breaches the law of the excluded middle, because at this mid-way stage an inchoate contract is neither valid nor invalid. Even so, two important qualifications have to be acknowledged. First, as we have noted, the breach is only a temporary one. Secondly, the breach is recognised at the expense of forfeiting the distinction between the first and second versions of the no-right-answer thesis. We have had to give up the recognition of "inchoate" contracts as a discrete third category so as to avoid replicating the analysis of the hypothetical legal system which upholds the law of the excluded middle. Hence the first version collapses into the second version, as our remarks on the purely formal representations of the two versions indicated above: the so-called third possibility turns out to be nothing more than a convenient label for (neither p nor $\sim p$).

We have now reached the stage in our attempts to vindicate Dworkin's claim that the two versions of the no-right-answer thesis breach the law of the excluded middle, where we have had to join his two versions in order to maintain his position. The position does nevertheless seem maintainable for those cases which fall under (neither p nor $\sim p$) subject to the reservation made that this has to be regarded as only a temporary breach of the law. I now want to suggest that even this limited apparent vindication of Dworkin does not withstand further examination.

The need to clarify the picture further arises from the key point that prevents Dworkin's example of the first version[15] being treated *exactly* like his analogy of the hypothetical legal system, in which the law of the excluded middle was upheld. This is the recognition that what is treated as an inchoate contract prior to judicial determination of its status must be capable of acquiring the status of a valid or invalid contract consequent upon that judicial determination.

This means that two things hold for what is conveniently labelled as an "inchoate contract" within Dworkin's example, formally represented as (neither p nor $\sim p$). First, it is inherent in its initial recognition as (neither p nor $\sim p$) that its status can be transformed. Secondly, taking together its initial status and the potential status that even at the initial momentary point we are forced to recognise, there are three forms that this contract may take: (i) unresolved (neither p nor $\sim p$); (ii) resolved p; (iii) resolved $\sim p$.

---

[15] Or, as we should now acknowledge, of the no-right-answer thesis *simpliciter*, given that we have recognised the collapse of the distinction between the two versions.

These three states of the contract, far from breaching the law of the excluded middle, fit into an analysis which upholds the law. This follows from the recognition that these three states are the product of a process of transformation occurring or not occurring over two alternative positions. For it is possible to cover all three of the states we have recognised by considering whether each of the potentially resolved states ((ii) or (iii)) has been resolved as such or not. The analysis proceeds in the same way as that provided in the previous chapter for Parliamentary intention:

(1a) contract is resolved as valid, or
(1b) contract is not resolved as valid
(2a) contract is resolved as invalid, or
(2b) contract is not resolved as invalid

and where both (1b) and (2b) hold

(3) contract is not resolved as valid or invalid

This clearly shows the law of the excluded middle being upheld both with proposition (1a) and its negation (1b), and again with proposition (2a) and its negation (2b). The three forms of the contract given above are also recognisable within this analysis:

(i)   unresolved (neither p nor $\sim p$)—case (3);
(ii) resolved p—case (1a);
(iii) resolved $\sim p$—case (2a).

Since Dworkin's distinction between his representations of the first and second versions of the no-right-answer thesis has collapsed,[16] this should be regarded in general as a satisfactory analysis to rebut Dworkin's assertion that the no-right-answer thesis breaches the law of the excluded middle.[17]

The analysis does more than this. It serves to show how the no-right-answer thesis can be regarded as plausible in a way that is compatible with an "ordinary, commonsensical" approach to the practice of law. For the possibility of there being no settled right answer as to the status of a contract, covered by (3) in this analysis, is compatible with recognition of "the fact that lawyers treat the claim that a contract is not valid as the negation of the claim that it is valid"[18] since lawyers will only *claim* on behalf of their clients that (1a) or (2a) should be

---

[16] Dworkin's insistence on a clear distinction between the two forms of the no-right-answer thesis is worked to his own advantage in separating the claims to plausibility of each (notably, MofP 132–3). Having represented the two versions as denying the law of the excluded middle in distinct and incompatible ways, Dworkin forces his opponents to either resolutely maintain the existence of legal categories (the third possibilities such as the "inchoate" contract) which cannot be found in the practice of the law, or to persist with the ineffable quality of neither-nor in the face of the law's relentless determination of either–or.

[17] The analysis can be applied to the example Dworkin provides for what he regards as the second version, commencing with: (1a) contract is resolved as sacrilegious, or . . . etc.

[18] MofP 126.

held to be the law, and so in this practical context the one claim amounts to the negation of the other. Moreover, the fuller analysis offered here does nothing to deny that there is no middle ground between "a valid contract", and its negation "an invalid contract".[19] Those are precisely the only options that are available to be recognised. The further question that a full analysis needs to accommodate is not whether there is some other option beyond these two but whether recognition in either of the two cases has yet been given by the law.[20]

Dworkin himself actually gets very close to recognising the existence of this further question in considering an argument that both of the following statements could be false: "The law provides that Tom's contract is valid" and "The law provides that Tom's contract is not valid".[21] However, he dismisses the possibility by asserting that it amounts to personifying the law. This evasive strategy does not work. For however one regards legal materials as arising, and whatever one takes to constitute them, it is possible to recognise that those materials are insufficient to provide an affirmative confirmation of either of the propositions just given, without needing to personify the law. In fact Dworkin himself concedes the possibility subsequently[22] in relation to his imaginary literary exercise that it may be appropriate from the limited material we have to work on to conclude that there are no reasons either way to reach the conclusion that David Copperfield had type-A blood or not, though if a conclusion could be reached in conformity with the law of the excluded middle it could only be "type-A" or "not type-A".[23] Dworkin's belief[24] that in the case of a modern

---

[19] See MofP 123, 127.

[20] Saunders, above n. 7, at 668–9 points out that Dworkin has committed a logical error in substituting p for (p is a proposition of law) in his discussion of the argument from positivism. This can be related to the matter raised here in insisting on the need to address the issue of whether legal recognition has been given to p. However, Saunders does not press the point, preferring to suggest that the debate should not depend on an unquestioning adherence to the law of the excluded middle.

Moore, above n. 7 at 488ff, overlooks the flaw that Saunders draws attention to and instead exploits it to turn Dworkin's argument back on him so as to favour a position of metaphysical realism. Moore's earlier advocacy of this position (at 484–5) does acknowledge the need for some sort of issue of ultimate recognition to be addressed, but by restricting the issue of recognition to *justification* of the use of bivalent semantics, Moore suppresses the question of whether recognition has been given, and readily concludes that only metaphysical realism can provide the underlying reality required.

Raz, above n. 7, considers a number of strategies for avoiding Dworkin's conclusion in his discussion of the argument from positivism. Although Raz does not directly raise Saunders' objection, his own preferred strategy of recognising a kind of prima facie legal proposition requires further determination by the court before it is possible to say whether, e.g., a contract is valid or invalid (at 75). Raz's treatment of these cases is consistent with the analysis proposed here but his approach is more restrictive in denying the possibility of gaps in the law due to the law being silent—for this he relies on closure rules (at 75–7). This reliance may, however, be misplaced: consider applying the rule, "whatever is not legally prohibited is legally permitted" in a case involving conflict between two incompatible uses of land.

[21] MofP 126.

[22] MofP 142.

[23] MofP 134.

[24] MofP 143.

legal system there is always sufficient material (taking in the wide scope he allows for that term) to provide a right answer must stand or fall on its own credibility. It cannot be shored up by relying on a common sense view of the practices of lawyers[25] or by invoking the law of the excluded middle.

SOME GENERAL REFLECTIONS

The two case studies offered so far suggest a general framework for the law of the excluded middles, covering a situation where two closely related propositions have the semblance of themselves being alternatives of negation such that the possibility of neither holding seems at first sight to produce a third possibility which denies the law of the excluded middle. A full analysis reveals that there is a distinct negation for each proposition, providing two pairs of negations, each satisfying the law of the excluded middle. The apparent "third possibility" is then seen to be one outcome of this fourfold analysis, combining the distinct negations of each proposition. In the case studies above we have referred to the two propositions with their distinct negations as respectively (1a) & (1b) and (2a) & (2b), and then shown how the apparent third possibility, (3), is constituted by the conjunction of (1b) and (2b).

Apart from the law of the excluded middle being upheld in relation to each proposition taken as a whole, it is also the case that it applies to the key element central to the illusion that the law has been broken, when that element is taken in isolation. We can apply the law of the excluded middle to (reasonable exercise of power) ∨ ~(reasonable exercise of power), for example in the first case study, or to (valid contract) ∨ ~(valid contract) in the second case study. The full propositions involve an additional element such that the single application of the law to the key element is no longer appropriate. In the first case study this further element was provided by "Parliament intending" (or not); in the second case study by "the law resolving" (or not). We could in fact find yet another application of the law of the excluded middle in relation to this further element taken in isolation: Parliament has either formed an intention or it has not; the law has either resolved the matter or it has not.

A critical point arising in the second case study was that there had to be the possibility of resolving an "inchoate contract" as a valid contract, otherwise we could state from the outset that we had a simple application of the law of the excluded middle in relation to (valid contract) ∨ ~(valid contract). Whatever an

---

[25] The two particular practices of lawyers relied on by Dworkin are those commented on in the preceding paragraph, suggesting that they are compatible with the no-right-answer thesis. That a wider consideration of the practices of lawyers lends support to the no-right-answer thesis is suggested by Kent Greenawalt, "Discretion and Judicial Decision: The Elusive Quest for the Fetters that Bind Judges" (1975) 75 *Columbia Law Review* 359; and that a complete reliance on the practice of lawyers to support the right answer thesis should lead Dworkin to abandon theory altogether is proposed by Wolcher, above n. 3.

inchoate contract amounted to, if there was no possibility of it being resolved as a valid contract, we could say that both an "inchoate contract" and also an "invalid contract" satisfied ~(valid contract), and hence (valid contract) ∨ ~(valid contract) would exhaust all the logical space. This particular point has wider significance. For we can say in general that if we are putting forward a case of (neither *p* nor ~*p*) we must be considering there is a possibility of resolving our case so depicted into *p*. If it were not so then we would again be able to say at the outset that we had a case of ~*p* due to the fact that the case could never be resolved into *p*. (And, similarly, we must be leaving open the possibility of resolving the case into ~*p*.)

The general implications of putting forward an unresolved case, popularly represented as (neither *p* nor ~*p*), can be explored with the aid of the framework provided to accommodate the law of the excluded middles. What is represented by (3) is clearly the unresolved case, produced by the absense of both the alternative resolved states, (1a) or (2a). The nature of the relationship between the two elements whose combinations go to making up the propositions found in (1a) and (2a) can be stated in general terms, taking account of the existence of the unresolved case. The second element indicates some form of resolution (or not) of the first element (or its negation). Taking *p* as the first element (e.g. *valid contract*) and P as the second element which may operate upon it so as to resolve its status (e.g. *the law resolving*), we may then formally represent the framework for the law of the excluded middles as follows.

$$P p \lor \sim P p \qquad [(1a) \text{ or } (1b)]$$
$$P \sim p \lor \sim P \sim p \qquad [(2a) \text{ or } (2b)]$$
$$P p \lor P \sim p \lor (\sim P p \lor \sim P \sim p) \qquad [(1a) \text{ or } (2a) \text{ or } (3)]$$

This framework, as has been remarked, also upholds $p \lor \sim p$ and $P \lor \sim P$. It does not, however, support the illusion of (neither *p* nor ~*p*).

One further general observation needs to be made arising out of the different applications of this framework which are illustrated in the two case studies that we have undertaken. The potential for the unresolved case (3) to reach resolution, in the form of one of the possible alternatives (1a) or (2a), may remain active or it may be exhausted. That is to say the opportunity to reach resolution may still be open: as we saw with the inchoate contract, whose final status was yet to be fixed by the determination of the court; or, the occasion for resolution may have passed; as we saw with the case of Parliament having failed to resolve how it wished a power it had granted to be exercised (or the case of my being indifferent about going to see *The Flintstones*). The illusion of (neither *p* nor ~*p*) finds fertile ground with a case where the potential resolution remains open because it conveys, albeit inaccurately, that neither of the alternatives has yet been resolved and since the process of resolution (i.e. P) has not as yet taken place this is easily left out of the picture. However, in a case where the potential has been exhausted the natural tendency is not to put forward the bare form of (neither *p* nor ~*p*), because the passing by of the opportunity for resolution is evident and looms large in the portrayal of the case. We allow into the picture Parliament's failure to express its intention, my indifference to watching *The Flintstones*, or the law's failure to provide for a particular case.[26] The framework provided above underlines that whether we anticipate a resolution of the unresolved case or recognise no further opportunity to reach resolution, the absence of resolution is a material element of a full analysis.

I now want to briefly consider whether this framework has any further applications, particularly in relation to cases used as counter-examples by those doubting the universality of the law of the excluded middle. As a preliminary point, it can be shown to apply to the case offered by Aristotle himself as being beyond the scope of the law of the excluded middle—the case of what may happen in the future.[27] The framework requires that instead of simply analysing our present perspective on whether there will be a sea battle tomorrow, our analysis takes in the fuller picture of whether or not it has been resolved that a sea battle takes place on such and such a date. We can then apply the law of the excluded middles in a straightforward manner, taking P to refer to *it is resolved* and *p* to refer to *a sea battle occurred on such and such a date*. That it is legitimate to offer an analysis of what I have called the fuller picture in this way rests upon the argument that to offer only an analysis of our present perspective on the future is to offer an analysis that is inherently restricted, since to take a present perspective on the future only makes sense on the assumption that the future is capable of being resolved. The analysis of Aristotle's sea battle example then proceeds in familiar fashion:

(1a) It is resolved that a sea battle occurred on such and such a date.

(1b) It is not resolved that a sea battle occurred on such and such a date.

(2a) It is resolved that a sea battle did not occur on such and such a date.

(2b) It is not resolved that a sea battle occurred on such and such a date.

and where both (1b) and (2b) hold

(3) It is not resolved whether a sea battle occurred or not on such and such a date.

Aristotle's concluding remarks in his discussion of future events[28] gives some indication of the need to take account of the fuller picture without offering a detailed analysis of it. He states in respect of the alternatives that, e.g., a sea battle will occur or a sea battle will not occur, that:

> "Though it may be that one is more probable, it cannot be true yet or false. . . . For the case of those things which as yet are potential, not actually existent, is different from that of things actual."

---

[26] As is seen in the case discussed by Dworkin, text at n. 21 above.

[27] *On Interpretation*, IX. Translation is taken from the Loeb edition, in *The Organon* I, Harold Cooke (trans), (Cambridge, MA, Harvard University Press, 1938).

[28] *Ibid.*

Aristotle's emphasis on it being a case of not true of false *yet* indicates we are considering it possible to resolve our case into either p or ~p. His insistence that statements relating to things that are potential must be regarded as different to those relating to things that actually exist supports the approach adopted within the framework for the law of the excluded middles, which leaves no room for a case to be described in terms of (neither p nor ~p). For this expression misuses terms for representing alternative states of what actually is the case, either p or ~p, in attempting to convey what is not yet the case. An accurate depiction would have to be in terms of (neither p *yet* nor ~p *yet*). It is precisely this additional element of yetness that the framework offered here seeks to capture.[29]

The next obvious subject to consider as a possible application for the framework is three-valued logic, since the problems of Aristotle's discussion of the sea battle provided the setting for its development by Jan Łukasiewicz.[30] The analysis of the sea battle within the framework provided above can be contrasted with its analysis in terms of Łukasiewicz's three-valued logic, under which (1a) would correspond to the sea battle occurring with a value of 1, (2a) would correspond to the sea battle not occurring with a value of 0, and (1b) and (2b) would respectively correspond to the possibility of the sea battle occurring, or not, and each have a value of ½.

The construction of the framework for the law of the excluded middles has in common with Łukasiewicz's development of three-valued logic a recognition that alternative perspectives taken on an unrealised potential event occurring or not are not contradictory. These are the propositions represented here by (1b) and (2b), whose conjunction forms (3). Łukasiewicz similarly considers the two perspectives taken at instant t regarding whether or not John will be at home tomorrow noon, and denies that they are contradictories.[31] However, a number of advantages can be suggested for the framework analysis, most notably the capacity of retaining within bivalent logic the analysis of material that three-valued logic purports to exclude from its scope.

More specifically, advantages can be found in avoiding the technical difficulties that a switch to three-valued logic entails. One such problem of dealing with

---

[29] That Aristotle's analysis is more sensitive to change in tense (more specifically, recognises the distinction between past-present and future) than the favoured timeless approach to modern logic has been noted by AN Prior, "Three-Valued Logic and Future Contingents" (1953) 3 *Philosophical Quarterly* 317, and Ronald Butler, "Aristotle's Sea Fight and Three-Valued Logic" (1955) 64 *Philosophical Review* 264. It goes beyond my present objectives to enquire too deeply into the matter here, but this does raise questions as to what sort of general assumption (or as Butler puts it at 271, 273–4, metaphysical presupposition) modern logic makes about the existential quantifier—does everything that it may govern have to have had its existence resolved in some way—and does the timeless analysis of future events proceed on the understanding that any future event is capable of being subjected to analysis from some sort of perspective from which its eventuality has been resolved? It is possible that the framework for the law of the excluded middles provides a structure in which these assumptions of modern logic can be examined.

[30] See, e.g., "On Determinism" in Jan Łukasiewicz, *Selected Works*, L Borkowski (ed.) (Amsterdam, North-Holland Publishing Company, 1970).

[31] *Ibid.* at 124.

three-valued logic is discussed by WV Quine.[32] Quine concludes that it is impossible to propose three truth values (1, 2, 3), and maintain classical negation. This conclusion arises from the attempt to arrange the three truth values of three-valued logic in a consistent linear form. However, we could locate 1, 2 and 3 in the three positions found in the framework for the law of the excluded middles, taking the different truth values to be represented within the three possible propositions:[33]

1 as Pp	[(1a)]
2 as P~p	[(2a)]
3 as (~Pp ∧ ~P~p)	[(3)]

As we have seen this upholds the law of the excluded middle, and is wholly faithful to classical negation, requiring only that we discern which combinations of possible negations of P and p we are dealing with. Acknowledging this does take us away from a simple linear progression among values to the more complex arrangement captured by the framework, but not at the expense of rejecting classical negation.

Another technical difficulty with Łukasiewicz's three-valued logic, that the framework analysis can provide a solution for, is the awkwardness of attributing to the disjunctive proposition, "Either there will or there will not be a sea battle tomorrow", not truth but indeterminate possibility. AN Prior has pointed out that this disjunctive proposition only has a value of ½ within the three-valued logic developed by Łukasiewicz, which departs from Aristotle's analysis under which it is true.[34] Within the framework analysis the corresponding proposition for this disjunctive proposition, (3), is in the form of the conjunction of two true negative propositions within bivalent logic and carries a truth value of 1, consistent with Aristotle's analysis.

VAGUENESS

The final application of the framework I wish to consider is the case of vagueness. Not only has this been put forward as a counter-example to the law of the excluded middle, but it seems the most obvious contender for reinstating (neither p nor ~p) as a meaningful expression. We may have concluded that

---

[32] *Philosophy of Logic* (Englewood Cliffs, NJ, Prentice-Hall, 1970; 2nd edn., Cambridge, MA, Harvard University Press, 1986) at 84.

[33] Quine's 1, 2 and 3 represent the values (e.g., truth, falsehood and possibility) and should not to be confused with the numerical strength that Łukasiewicz attaches to each value. That proposition (3) in seeking to represent 3 is capable of expressing the possibility of what is asserted at 1 and in addition the possibility of what is denied at 2 rather than treating the possibility of each separately, as does Łukasiewicz, can be justified on the ground that to regard something as possible is necessarily to regard its negation as possible. One pitfall of Łukasiewicz's strategy of separation is considered in the text that follows.

[34] Above n. 29, at 325–6.

there was no basis for saying that a contract is neither valid nor invalid unless it can be resolved as being one or the other, but surely the resolution of legal uncertainty or vagueness cannot be taken as a model for the treatment of vagueness in everyday speech? It seems absurd to claim that there is no point in saying that a man is neither bald nor not bald unless his status can be resolved as being one or the other. The apparent characteristic of such instances of vagueness is that it really is impossible to determine the issue one way or the other. Yet this concession to the colloquial raises the conundrum of how we can avoid the logical inference that the man is not bald if we find it impossible to say that he is bald, and vice versa.

The key to unlocking the conundrum is to clarify the different ways in which we can use the phrase "not bald". Part of the problem in Dworkin's illustration of the three categories of contract—"valid", "invalid", and "inchoate"—lay in the artificial use of terms so that "invalid" was not equal to ~valid. One possibility is that "not bald" may be understood as a definite state, not merely the negation of "bald", say synonymous with "having a good head of hair". This would then follow the analysis provided in the earlier case study of $(\sim p \wedge q) \vee (\sim p \wedge \sim q)$. There would be some cases of ~bald that involved having a good head of hair, and some that did not, so that if we take "not bald" as synonymous with "having a good head of hair" then we could have a case of something being neither bald nor (not bald in the restricted sense of having a good head of hair); i.e. a case of $\sim p \wedge \sim q$.

This, however, does not deal with the paradigm case of vagueness, where the problem is not linguistic infelicity which allows us to say at one and the same time that a person is neither bald nor not bald, but the problem of not being able to decide which of the two applies. What may lead to this indecision? One cause for the indecision is conflicting usage within the community, so that the speaker is unsure whether the person addressed would use the term "bald" to cover the subject under discussion. This could be overcome by indicating which variant usage was being followed: "*I* would call him bald." Or where the speaker is familiar with the other's usage: "*You* would say that he is not bald." If this were the only problem the law of the excluded middle would apply simply enough as soon as we had specified which of the variant usages we were employing.

A deeper problem arises when the vagueness is due to our being unable to decide the matter in accordance with any recognised usage of the terms "bald" and "not bald". However, if there really is no settled usage to determine the matter then we are confronted with a situation where we cannot regard the question as simply being whether the man is bald or not bald. The question is rather whether it is settled that a man such as this is to be regarded as bald or not. Seen like this the question readily falls to be analysed within the framework for the law of the excluded middles, taking P to refer to *it is settled by accepted usage*[35]

---

[35] I should stress that "settled by accepted usage" is a requirement that reaches no higher than the parties to the communication under consideration. It may be that these parties are members of a

and *p* to refer to *the subject is bald*. The indecisiveness we associate with the paradigm case of vagueness is seen in this light to be nothing more than an indication that our linguistic usage has not yet resolved how the term should be applied to such a case.[36] As such this does not offend the law of the excluded middle, but rather upholds it in precisely the ways that other instances of the law of the excluded middles were seen to do:

(1a) It is settled by accepted usage that *S* is bald.
(1b) It is not settled by accepted usage that *S* is bald.
(2a) It is settled by accepted usage that *S* is not bald.
(2b) It is not settled by accepted usage that *S* is not bald.

and where both (1b) and (2b) hold

(3) It is not settled by accepted usage that *S* is bald or not.

Of course the three forms of vagueness I have referred to in exploring the different ways in which we can use "not bald"—linguistic infelicity, conflicting usage, and unsettled usage—may intermingle. It may even be the case that unsettled usage ranges over conflicting usages of linguistic infelicity. However, regarded separately, the first case in itself is not a true case of vagueness that can be considered to fall under (neither *p* nor ~*p*), being more properly recognised as a case of $(\sim p \wedge q) \vee (\sim p \wedge \sim q)$. The second case, although properly treated as a form of vagueness in the sense that there may be uncertainty as to what exactly is meant by the term, does not in itself provide a case of (neither *p* nor ~*p*) but rather multiple cases of $p \vee \sim p$ across the range of conflicting usages. The third case, either in isolation or in combination with one or more of the other two, falls under the framework for the law of the excluded middles and also, accordingly, does not provide us with a case of (neither *p* nor ~*p*). We may then conclude that none of the types of colloquial vagueness we have considered provides a counter-example to the law of the excluded middle.[37]

---

community sharing a general usage of a word that settles its meaning in the context, but I do not make this assumption. It may equally be the case that the speaker is accepting a dialectical or even idiosyncratic usage employed by his audience.

[36] This takes a similar line to the semantic notion of vagueness found in Kit Fine, "Vagueness, Truth, and Logic" (1975) 30 *Synthèse* 265, without regarding the process of making a vague term more precise as being dependent upon existing established meaning. Strong argument against the plausibility of using an epistemic theory in order to resolve vagueness by reference to established use of a word is to be found in Endicott, above n. 7, ch. 6. Comparison may also be made with the approach considered by Michael Dummett, "Wang's Paradox" (1975) 30 *Synthèse* 301, also found in *Truth and Other Enigmas* (London, Duckworth, 1978) ch. 15, involving upholding the law of the excluded middle for vague terms by a process of "sharpening" the term (at 255–8).

[37] Dummett, *ibid.* at 265, eventually abandons his attempt to provide a logic of vague expressions, faced with the problems of observational predicates related to non-discriminable differences. However, the core of Dummett's problem relates to inconsistency arising through observing a range of, e.g., different shades of colour and being forced to consider in sequence each variation in colour when the variation occurs below the threshold of the observer's ability to discriminate difference in colour. This effectively creates an artificial usage for "red" such that the observer is forced to apply "red" to a colour that ordinarily he would describe as "blue", and so falls to be analysed as a case

We may now return to the question whether it is possible for a term, such as "bald", to remain vague—to persist in the unresolved condition represented by (3). The answer in general is that it can remain vague for as long as there may arise novel situations for which the application of the term can be considered, or situations over which conflicting usage has not conformed to an accepted usage. The answer changes as soon as we confront a particular situation in order to determine whether it is a case of "bald" or not. How could we speak of "bald" being vague in a particular context if we were not willing to determine whether to apply it? The residual effect of such a practice would be to restrict the usage of "bald" to past usage, so that in effect it would become a clear term.[38] This would, however, be a clear term of a stagnant language. And in this respect the practice of language is perhaps not so very different from the practice of the law. The court's resolution of vagueness in the instant case is an essential require-ment for the practice of law. Our determination of the applicability of terms to the situations we experience may equally be regarded as an essential precondi-tion of our ability to communicate about our experiences.

If three-valued logic and vagueness are accepted as falling within the frame-work for dealing with the law of the excluded middles, it might be worth recon-sidering whether other purported counter-examples to the law of the excluded middle can be treated similarly. I leave these issues to be pondered elsewhere. I hope at least to have succeeded in demonstrating here, in general that the law of the excluded middle merits a more rigorous analysis, and a more robust defence, than it has sometimes been granted; and with specific reference to more

---

of conflicting usages (artificial usage within the Dummett test, and ordinary usage)—or, even more carefully, artificial$_1$ usage when performing the test in the direction red-blue, and artificial$_2$ usage when performing the test in the direction blue-red.

This last point raises a more general problem for Endicott's use (above n. 7) of the sorites para-dox (each time a grain of sand is removed from a heap it is insufficient to prevent us calling what remains a heap, leading us to conclude that one grain of sand is a heap) as the basic model for vague-ness. The sorites paradox works both ways (starting with a single grain, each time a grain of sand is added it is insufficient to turn it into a heap, leading us to conclude that 100,000 grains of sand are not a heap) and cancels out the possibility of meaningful use of a term in either direction, and hence cannot be regarded as expressing the vagueness of a term that assumes some meaningful use in one direction. The sorites paradox is better regarded as expressing problems with our inability to per-ceive non-discriminable differences, which sets up an apparent problem for meaning only if we arti-ficially restrict subjects to take their meaning of terms from a paradigm followed by a succession of instances, each of which is separated by a non-discriminable difference. Although this may have some implications for our actual ability to use terms in particular circumstances (consider how we might see a colour differently if it were placed close to a series of adjoining colours with non-dis-criminable differences moving closer to blue, or moving closer to red), once we grasp that the sorites paradox runs in both directions it is impossible to use it as the basis for modelling how terms acquire meaning. A further point to note in this connection is that Endicott's attempt to fashion a stronger version of the sorites paradox, dealing with discriminable differences (above n. 7, at 128), cannot be regarded as tenable. A good cook, who can taste the difference that one eighth of a teaspoon of salt makes to the soup, will be able to judge which recipe is preferable (and even if the cook judges that a band of three possibilities are equally acceptable, will be able to say that the fourth, or fifth, etc, is not). Significantly, Endicott abandons the eighth of a teaspoon discriminable difference and slips back to a grain of salt by the top of the next page.

[38] Subject to any selection from conflicting usages that might be required.

immediate concerns, how a clearer understanding of this law of logic can assist in shedding light on some of the perplexing issues concerning legal reasoning. Within the studies found in the present and the preceding chapters, the fuller application of the law of the excluded middle that I have proposed demonstrates that it is possible for the law to be in an unresolved condition. This sets the scene for a deeper enquiry into the material condition of the law and the manner in which it is resolved.

Part II

Reasoning with Law

6

The Uses of Words

I F THE LAW is to be found in our books, the reason why our books will never complete our understanding of the law is because what is found in our books are words. Those learned in the law do not rely simply on the learning of their books but on their wit in using the words they find in them. The triumph of Portia is not that of a lay person who beats the law, but of "a learned judge" who draws from the books the words she is able to use so as to achieve her victory within the law. The dramatic marvel in *The Merchant of Venice* is not that a lay person could outwit the lawyers but that the heroine could so soon become a lawyer.

Lawyers are jealous of their learning and secretive about their wit. The inquisitive outsider who seeks to know what is required beyond the mastery of dry and dusty texts is left puzzled. Surely any intelligent person with sufficient time and determination could study the text of the law and reach as good an answer as any lawyer? Lawyers in response refer mysteriously to additional lawyerly skills that will turn an intelligent reading of the law into a good legal argument. Typically first year law students are informed that what will transform the base substance of their intellect into the sparkling skill of the lawyer is the acquisition of the ability to engage in legal reasoning—though, again, precisely what is required from legal reasoning beyond the general ability to reason from legal materials remains mysterious.

There is more at stake, as we probe the boundaries of learning and wit, or general reasoning and lawyers' reasoning, than professional vested interest. Beyond any self-interest of lawyers in keeping the secrets of legal reasoning to themselves there arise issues of far wider concern. First, there is the issue of citizens enjoying open and informed access to the law as opposed to being subjected to the esoteric practices of lawyers, an issue historically stronger than the issue of citizens enjoying participative rights in the democratic governance of society. Secondly, once we accept the appeal of democracy, a question has to be asked about the legitimacy of the part performed by an unelected judiciary in using the art of legal reasoning to determine the legal fate of citizens.

Confronting these questions may lead on to supplementary issues. If we find a residual discretion in the judicial role when we consider the manner in which judges reason with legal texts, we may raise the question of balancing that discretion by means of constitutional principle (such as in a Bill of Rights), or even attempt to strengthen it with requirements beyond the textual material itself found in a doctrine of the Rule of Law.

Wherever these questions lead us, the starting point is the lawyer's use of words. Words can restrain our choice and words can provide opportunity to choose. "Keep out." "Keep out of trouble." "Avoid all unreasonable risk." Perhaps we should be asking whether it is possible to clarify which uses of words restrain the hearer, and which uses of words offer opportunity to the hearer to choose how to use those words. If we could answer that question, then perhaps all the practical issues relating to the professional standing of lawyers, all of the ideological issues relating to the political standing of law, and all of the academic issues relating to the theory of law, would be reduced to so many variations on the themes of how we can use words to fix the conduct of others, and who gets to fix the words when the words don't fix the conduct.

Before we could write off the claims of law to recognition as an independent discipline, and relegate it to the status of an applied subdivision of the philosophy of language, we would have to acknowledge a range of characteristics that law possesses which seem to take it beyond the reaches of our burgeoning preoccupation with words. Law is coercive—not just words but words backed by threats. Law is authoritative—not just words but words backed by respect. Law is institutional—not just the words of a person but words from a person performing an institutional role. Law may be participative—not just somebody else's words but words that I have been given a part in influencing the form of. Law may be moral—not just words but words that promote the (public or individual) good.

Law as a discipline is also enriched by the versatility of its subject matter in lending itself to examination from the perspective of almost any other discipline within the humanities—historical, political, psychological, sociological, economic, literary, in addition to philosophical. The self-doubts of law as an academic discipline may be fed by its capacity for assimilation within so many other intellectual traditions, but surely this capacity for multi-faceted assimilation is one point that marks it off as distinctive.

We seem a long way away from leaving the issues that the practice or study of law raises as being satisfactorily answered by an enquiry into the uses of words. Yet there is a deep connection between this narrower enquiry and these broader issues because whatever (practical or theoretical) aspect of the rich nature of law we fix our interest on, our line of enquiry will sooner or later have to confront those elementary questions raised above, regarding which uses of words restrain the hearer, and which uses of words offer opportunity to the hearer to choose how to use those words. Whatever driving purpose or fundamental character is posited for the law (coercive, participative, moral, amoral, democratic, oppressive . . .); whichever perspective is taken on the law (historical, sociological, economic . . .); the purpose or character will be found exhibited only so far as the uses of legal words are capable of exhibiting it, and the perspective taken will similarly be upheld only so far as the uses of legal words are capable of transmitting it.

For example, suppose we take a Natural Law perspective and treat the nature of law as being bound up with a moral purpose. The moral purpose of the law will be conveyed by the words of the law, but in those cases where the use of legal words is unable to constrain, then there will be an opening for that moral purpose to falter (and a corresponding possibility of a failure to transmit the Natural Law perspective). In these circumstances, who has the opportunity to make use of the words used by the law, and how that opportunity is employed, will determine either whose moral purpose the law ends up supporting, or whether the law supports a moral purpose at all. Alternatively, take an economic perspective on law, and posit efficiency as the law's driving purpose. Still, where the words of the law do not constrain, the opportunity arises to defeat that purpose, or at least to deflect it to a particular partisan interpretation of efficiency which belies the existence of a *legal* pursuit of efficiency.

It is a truism of any intellectual discipline that it requires the use of words in an instrumental manner to convey its findings on the subject it enquires into. However, law has a deeper relationship with words. Like language itself, for law there would be no subject to study without words. Nevertheless, it might reasonably be objected that to focus on law as being affected by a difference between words that restrain and words that offer creative opportunity is arbitrary. If we explored such a difference it might equally impinge on the ability to state moral, or economic objectives. Imagine for the moment that we could derive a clear comprehensive system of morality which was capable of determining for each occasion of human conduct whether it was moral or immoral to engage in that conduct. If such a thing were possible, would it not follow that we must have achieved the means of using words so as to always restrain choice and never to allow opportunity to choose how to use the words expressing the morality of conduct? (Moreover, could not law then be harnessed to that moral purpose?)

There is a stage further we could go with this objection. The fact that we cannot imagine the system of morality required—or the system of economics, etc— says as much about our moral (economic, etc) understanding as it does about our use of words. The uncertainties of language may be regarded as a secondary reflection of our deficiencies of understanding. Even so, this is a reason for renewing our interest specifically in law.

Accepting that the uncertainties of our language relate to the deficiencies of our understanding, and that this state of affairs affects all the disciplines, it remains a peculiar characteristic of law that any uncertainties of language and deficiencies of understanding are capable of authoritative resolution in the practical judgment of a court. Law thus provides an unrivalled test-bed for examining the limits of the capacity our words have to restrain; for considering the choices that can be made when our understanding runs out; and for reflecting on how the necessity of reaching beyond our present limitations might affect our future capabilities.

The study of the uses of words that I propose to embark upon as a means of investigating wider concerns about legal reasoning is commenced with the presuppositions that if it has any repercussions for our understanding of law, it also has repercussions for the understanding sought of other human endeavours in other intellectual disciplines; that despite the restriction of my present interests to the narrow field of legal theory, any contribution to that field will not be self-contained; and that the most fruitful line of enquiry is likely to be that which is most open to the rudimentary features of general human experience. This takes us towards the entrance door of the domain of the philosophy of language, as offering reflection on the most basic issues concerning human uses of words and human understanding. Yet even a casual peep through the window will alert us to the recognition that this too is an intellectual discipline which is subject to those very limitations that it seeks to study. I hope that it is not too impudent to suggest that approaching this discipline with the hard practicalities of legal concerns may offer a robust and illuminating confrontation of these limitations.

If we come to the philosophy of language with eager expectation that it will offer us a more elementary grasp of the rudimentary features of human experience, it seems that only shock and disappointment await us. Instead of offering us a clearer insight into the common human experience of the uses of words, the practitioners of this intellectual discipline appear bent on transporting us to situations as far removed from common human experience as possible. The invitation to ponder the significance of non-existent states of affairs in this world ("The present King of France is bald.") are soon followed by journies to parallel earths where the parallel earthlings speak parallel English but due to their inability to distinguish unmixed water from a mixture of water and alcohol they use "water" to refer to both the substance we would refer to as "water" as well as to the substance we would refer to as a stiff drink. Yet stranger occurrences await us as we voyage around the imaginary universe of the philosophers of language, depending on who we entrust ourselves to as guide. We are introduced to earthlings with the same sensory faculties as ourselves, but whenever we see something that evokes the statement, "The cherry is on the tree", these earthlings state, "The cat is on the mat".

Given the perplexing and factious state of the philosophy of language, it would be naive to assume that we would meet with success, simply by entering this discipline to borrow insights so as to deal with the basic problems of legal theory regarding the uses of words. Despite the enormous impact of his work on philosophy in general and on the philosophy of language in particular, even the valiant efforts of Wittgenstein to deter philosophers from the perils of abstruse theory that confuses rather than clarifies the issues, seem to have led to greater outpouring of abstruse theory rather than to its abandonment. Nevertheless, following my presupposition that if there is any insight to be obtained for the concerns of legal theory over the uses of words it will be an insight that is gained from examining the most rudimentary features of general human experience, it seems sensible to at least consider the issues that have been identified within the discipline of the philosophy of language. The strategy I propose to employ is as follows.

Within this chapter I shall seek to construct an approach to some of the principal issues that have emerged in the philosophy of language. Informed by certain insights drawn from the literature of that discipline as well as motivated by the desire to avoid some of the apparently intractable disputes found within the literature, I shall be more concerned to find an approach that will assist with the narrower concerns of legal theory than to directly engage with the contributions to the philosophy of language. However, in the chapter following the present one I shall endeavour to go some way to supporting the presupposition that what may be of value to legal theory will not be self-contained within that field by relating the approach being developed here to some key themes of Wittgenstein. There are two reasons for making an effort to engage with Wittgenstein's work on language. The approach being developed has some affinities to Wittgenstein's philosophy, and secondly, Wittgenstein holds a growing attraction for legal theorists. In suggesting a defect in Wittgenstein's approach, I shall attempt to clarify further the approach being developed here, as well as preparing for a brief examination of a quite different approach to language which has been adopted by a number of legal theorists. Realism (metaphysical or otherwise) is treated in a further brief chapter, which is effectively an annex to the Wittgenstein chapter. The justification for this rather cursory treatment is found in the suggestion that what is found lacking in Wittgenstein's approach reemerges as a failing in realist approaches. In the chapter after that I return to the approach being developed here in more detail so as to reach some firm conclusions about the nature of legal reasoning.

COMMENCING AN ANALYSIS

One of the great difficulties facing any attempt to provide an analysis of our uses of words is to know at what stage in the development of our usage of words we should commence. The sophisticated state of our language potentially employs a number of distinct uses of words, which may be concealed in the complexity of linguistic exchanges we engage in. An obvious starting point is to see if it is possible to identify the most basic use of words and incrementally develop that into more sophisticated uses, and then to consider if in this way we have managed to capture all the facets of the uses of words that we are familiar with in our developed language. A comprehensive approach of this sort would be nothing less than a systematic philosophy of language. What follows is far less ambitious, but seeks to capture the salient points of such an approach that may prove helpful for our present concerns with legal reasoning.

Let us commence by reminding ourselves of some obvious points:

(1) We are investigating uses of words in the language of humans,
(2) as spoken by humans living in this world.

I accept that some of these humans have orbited the earth, and visited the moon, but assume they have continued to use their mother earth language during their extra-terrestrial experiences and that such language and their use of it has not been affected in any way by these experiences.

Let us add some further rather obvious points:

(3) The uses of words in the language we are investigating would not exist if there was no earth;

(4) they would not exist if there was an earth but no humans on it.

We can venture:

(5) The uses of words in the language we are investigating are dependent upon human experience of things in the world—no human experience of things existing in the world, no language.

This last point is not so obvious, and needs expanding. We need to recognise that humans living in this world are capable of two sorts of experience: an experience of things actually (i.e. existing independently of our experience of them) in the world; and an experience of the imagination. Imagination experiences may take different forms—day dreaming, literature, psychotic delusions—but in so far as we use words to deal with these works of the imagination, the use of words still relates to a human experience of things in the world—the day dream, the literary creation, the delusion, are all things experienced in the world. Until a human had experienced something of this kind in the world, there would be no call for the use of words to relate this subject matter. Until somebody had had the experience of imagining a unicorn, there would be no use of the word "unicorn". The letters constituting this word would be as much a word in our language as a random collection of letters—qwepfl. This further feature we have noted about human experience merits adding a point to qualify (5):

(6) Uses of words may relate to human experience of things actually in the world, or human experience of the imagination occurring in the world.

This takes us to a trickier point. It would be possible for a machine to generate a string of words which was meaningful, though it related to no human experience. We could suppose that the well used "The present King of France is bald" had arisen in this way. However, this sentence is meaningful (in the way that "the present qwepfl is bald" is not) precisely because each of its constituent words is related to human experience. We have experience of France as a country, of countries being ruled by kings, of kings being men, of men being bald, and of relating to the present member of a succession of holders of a particular office. The additional requirement for the sentence to be meaningful (in the way that "the present King of France is three o'clock" is not) is that each of these constituent words so relates to human experience that the total posited is capable of being experienced as an experience of an actual occurrence in the world or as an imagination experience.

This points to a more advanced use of words:

(7) Once a basic pool of words related to human experience is available, it is possible to construct different assemblies of those words depicting the subject of hypothetical human experiences, even though those experiences have never occurred.

(8) For these word assemblies to be meaningful, however, the constituent words used must relate together in such a way that the total posited is capable of being experienced as in (6) above.

We have spoken of experience of things in the world without worrying about the nature of the experience of the thing existing in the world, that the use of word is supposed to convey. Something enters the relationship between our experience and the thing in the world. We do not in having an experience of something experience the totality of that thing. We are limited by the faculties of human perception as to what we can experience of it. We are also limited by the extent of the particular experience as to what we might potentially experience of that thing through our human perceptions. What we acquire is an idea of that thing.

At a very low level we may have an idea of something we experience that does not transcend being able to give the coordinates of its existence so as to identify it as being separate from other things. This low-level idea may seem little more than a sense of how to find it without professing to know anything about it— "You can find the widget in the top drawer on the left but I've no idea what it is." Yet if pressed, we would probably be able to say more about it—it is small (it fits in the drawer). Our modesty in professing to have no idea, is born of the certainty that there is more to know about a widget that evades us.

This suggests a range of strengths in the ideas we may have about something, from a low-level idea that is limited to basics of identification (where it is to be found, what it looks like, etc) to a higher-level idea, which encompasses more and more understanding about the thing the higher we get. The word we use to refer to the thing in the world may accordingly relate not simply to that thing but to a range of ideas about it. Already we have introduced a degree of complexity in considering the relationships between: (a) things existing in the world, (b) our experience, (c) our ideas, (d) the words we use. The complexity and potential for confusion is indicated by the following analysis.

ELEMENTARY ANALYSIS OF A TERM

1 Let us use the term t to label something T that we have experienced in the world.

2 In our experience of T we will have perceived certain features of T that will provide us with a **loose idea** of T.

3 The term t serves two purposes: (i) t_i—to provide **identification** for T; (ii) t_u—to convey our **understanding** of T. We can say both "This is t" and "t is . . ." (filling out the statement with our loose idea of T).

4 At the initial point of experience (1), there will be no discrepancy between the two roles of t. However, for the purpose of identifying T we will not need to use all the features of T that we have perceived on that occasion which together go towards making up our loose idea of T, referred to as t_u. We will use one or more of those features (perhaps the physical location and shape will suffice: a nose is the pointed thing found in the middle of your face) for the purpose of identification of what we refer to as t_i.

5 However, our loose idea of t_u does not provide an exhaustive understanding of all the features of T for two reasons. First our experience and hence our perception of T is limited, and secondly in formulating our loose idea we are not simply cataloguing perceptions but using those perceptions (or drawing from those perceptions) to build our idea of T—we will emphasise one feature, neglect another, imaginatively fill in the gaps of our understanding with what seems to fit what we have already constructed, and so build up our idea. Two people with the same sensory perceptions and drawing on the same experience could nevertheless construct different ideas of T, and hence have different understandings of t_u, despite having t_i in common.

6 Assuming that the identification of T in our use of t_i remains constant, we may have varying ideas of t_u drawn from our different experiences of T, and the way we make use of our perceptions of T in those experiences. Hence there is the possibility of discrepancy arising between (i) t_i and t_{u1}, where further experience of T persuades us to abandon t_{u1} as no longer an accurate idea of what we call t_i in favour of t_{u2}; and between t_{uN} as held by N as an accurate idea of t_i and t_{uM} as held by M as an accurate idea of t_i.

7 As well as recognising *contradictions* in different ideas of t_u, which make them incompatible, we may also recognise a weaker form of discrepancy between t_{u1} and t_{u2}, or between t_{uN} and t_{uM} due to the incompleteness of our ideas of t_u (5) such that each is *incomplete but compatible* with the other.

8 The possibility of rational discussion with the aim of correcting or making more complete our idea of t_u is accordingly possible, given the assumption made above (6) of a constant t_i, and the further assumption that those engaging in the discussion are able to have the same experiences with the same faculties of perception—or, at least, in the use of their faculties are able to relate to the experiences of each other.

9 The impossibility of rational discussion arises not only (i) where the requirements above (8) are not met, but also (ii) where a person holds an idea of t_{u1} and is not prepared to consider the possibility of correcting it in the light of further experience of t_i; and (iii) where a person holds an idea of t_{uN} and falsely assumes that this provides an exhaustive idea such that nothing further can be learnt from other experience of t_i giving rise to a different idea of t_{uM}.

10 It should be stressed that confusion rages in practice over the matters discussed above (4–9) because we use the single term t to cover all those things that we have differentiated by means of different subscripts attached to t.

(To bring out the confusion try reading the above paragraphs ignoring the subscripts.)

So far we have spoken about words relating to *something* that is experienced in the world, or as conveying some sort of idea of something that is experienced in the world. To stop here would be an oversimplification in failing to account for our use of words to relate to *kinds of things* that we experience in the world. We use generic nouns as well as proper nouns; we use generic terms to refer to common sensations that we experience, and to refer to common qualities of what we experience.

The point to stress is that as our use of words moves from referring to particular things to referring to general kinds of things, including general sensations or general qualities, we are still as dependent on the ultimate role of human experience of things existing in the world, as we noted in the case of talking about a particular thing. If no human had ever experienced (actually in the world or in an imagination experience) a number of cats, a number of occasions of happiness, a number of things that were yellow, then the general terms, "cat", "happy", and "yellow" could not have arisen.

There does, however, seem to be an important difference in moving from the particular to the general. Whereas the shortcomings of our knowledge of the particular thing we had identified as t might have led to us employing the word t to convey different ideas of it, we were still able to direct discussion over our different ideas of what t was to further investigation of the thing we had called t. When we are dealing with a general term, because that general term has been used to refer to a number of things, each with a number of features, the general idea can now be based on different combinations of features among the different things that the term refers to. There is not (as there was in the case of a single thing) a stable source of features that we can use to discuss which idea is the most knowledgeable or accurate.

It would be possible to have a convention or authoritative determination of how we should restrict our use of the general term *if* there were some common feature(s) of all the things that we could employ the term for, e.g. the molecular structure H_2O for "water", or light within a strict frequency range for "yellow". In this way we would have for our general term the same sort of stable source of reference as we had for the particular term.

The recognition of general terms clearly requires us to expand our analysis in a number of ways. We may note a number of important points here:

(A) The stabilising of a general term is as much dependent on there being a distinctive feature of its instances that is accessible to human experience (including imagination experience), as is the possibility of a particular term arising being dependent on the thing conveyed by that particular term being accessible to human experience.

(B) General terms (unlike particular terms) may continue in an unstable form because of a failure to identify or agree upon a distinctive feature common to all instances.

(C) Where a general term continues in an unstable form this may give rise to a fragmentation of usage such that on different occasions the term is being used to convey, say, qualities 5–7, or 6–8, or 5&8–9, or 8–10, such that some instances are recognised as such for possessing features that are not present in other instances which are recognised for possessing other features.

(D) In the case mentioned in (C) we have different ideas related to the term, but not in the same way as we noted different ideas where the term referred to a particular thing in the world. In that case the different ideas were compatible or at least resolvable by reference to the thing that the term identified, but in this case the fragmentation in the usage of the term gives rise to a fragmentation of ideas, which are no longer parts of our knowledge of the single thing in the world.

(E) The tendency to identify kinds, or to generalise, is still dependent on human experience of things in the world. The particular generalisations or kinds that we recognise (as well as their stability or instability) are dependent on our experiencing and having the faculties of recollection and recognition of common features among different instances of our experience.

(F) The generalisations or kinds that we do in fact recognise will depend on our experience as it is affected by our characters, needs and aspirations. There is not a rigid relationship between the number of things that exist in the world and the different words we use in order to make our identifications of those things. The twenty-five words for snow in Arctic Quebec Inuktitut reflect the concerns of the Inuit. The vocabulary of the artist is likely to identify a more refined range of colours than the untrained eye can recognise. Where the member of the public will feel reasonably educated if able to distinguish between "uranium" and "plutonium", for the nuclear scientist there is a more refined distinction between different isotopes of uranium.

AN ILLUSTRATION OF PARTICULAR/GENERAL TERMS

Take "Mother" as referring to an identifiable person with three children, Tom, Sally, and Jane. Tom, Sally, and Jane will have different ideas of their Mother, as drawn from their different recollections of their experiences of her. These different ideas will possibly even clash: Tom has an idea of his Mother being very strict, Sally of her Mother being occasionally strict, whilst Jane has an idea of her Mother being easy-going. These differences do not contradict. They simply refer to different experiences that Tom, Sally and Jane had of their Mother, and each of these loose ideas need to be combined in order to bring us a full picture of Mother—who was strict with her first child, more lenient with her second child, and spoilt her youngest child. There is the possibility that Tom, Sally and Jane exaggerate, extrapolate from, or even distort their own recollections of their Mother so as to produce an inaccurate idea of Mother. There are then two possibilities: that each of their loose ideas might be accurate as far as it goes, but incomplete in the light of fuller information about Mother; or inaccurate, and needing modification in the light of better information about Mother. We can refer to these two possibilities as an **incomplete loose idea** and an **inaccurate loose idea**. In both cases there is no doubt as to what it is an idea of, and by gaining further information about the subject matter of the idea, the loose idea can be made more complete or more accurate.

Let us now take "mother" as a general term. A number of features may accompany our idea of a mother: having provided the egg which contributes to the genetic make-up of the child, having conceived, having carried the developing foetus in her womb, having given birth to a child, nurturing, caring for, bringing up a child. Although we may find all these features present in a particular instance to which we apply the term "mother", some instances will have different combinations of these features. Consider the different combinations of features in these instances of a mother: a biological mother who gives her child up for adoption, a surrogate mother providing her own egg, a surrogate mother with a donor egg, a step-mother where the natural mother has died, a step-mother where the natural mother is divorced and still has partial custody of the child, an adoptive mother.

Each of these instances of a "mother" has been the subject of human experience, and there has been some resemblance with some prior instance that has been given the term "mother" to warrant using the term "mother" for the next instance. However, it is not possible to state identifying features which are common to every instance of a mother. In this sense "mother" is a **fluid term** in contrast with a **fixed term** where there are identifying features of what the term is applied to so as to prevent the further usage of that term for something not possessing those features—as in the case of "water" being restricted to something with the molecular structure H_2O.

WHAT FIXES A GENERAL TERM?

An intriguing question to consider is whether a fixed general term can become a fluid term through subsequent usage. And if so, this raises the fundamental question whether *any* general term could become fluid, and under what circumstances? Depending on our answers to these questions we could end up with such potential flexibility in our use of words that the appearance of any stability that allows us to amplify and correct our understanding becomes virtually unattainable.

Consider the example we used above of a fluid term, "mother". At what point exactly does this become a fluid term rather than a fixed one? Could we not have stuck with just using the term for the birth mother? In part, the answer lies in again recognising the primacy of the point that all that we do use words to make identification of is bounded first by the existence of things in the world and secondly by our experience of them. If from the outset of human society it had been the practice for one woman to give birth to a child and another woman to bring it up, then our finding a word to refer to being the woman involved in the discrete practice of giving birth would have been a natural response to our experience of that aspect of human life in the world. Our experience of life in the world is of it being the normal practice for the woman who has given birth to the child to also care for that child, and so the role of a mother in our experience is richer, and the meaning of "mother" accordingly more complex. Because both the giving birth and the providing of care to the child can be associated with the primary experience that we use the term for, then it is an easy progression to continue to use the term when only one of the key features is present.

Consider next our example of a fixed general term, "water". We regarded this as fixed because there was a feature of it (its molecular structure) which was common to all recognised instances, by which we could restrict the use of the term. It is possible to conventionally fix a term in this way, but reflection on our actual use of "water" portrays a rather more complicated picture. The first thing to remind ourselves of is that fixing what the term can identity (whether by molecular structure or by a less formal means) does not fix the understanding that the term conveys. We may accept that "water" as a term used to identify something existing in the world has the same use for ourselves and for a primitive people living three thousand years ago—we and they both use it to refer to something in the world, a clear drinkable liquid, that falls from the sky in small drops as rain, and is found occurring naturally in streams, etc. However, "water" as a term used to label our idea of something existing in the world, to convey our understanding of it, may differ considerably: part of our idea of water is that it falls as rain from the sky in accordance with the principles of evaporation and condensation that go to produce the water cycle; part of their idea of water is that it falls as rain from the sky when the rain-god decides to urinate.

Secondly, even if it is possible to fix a general term as to what it may be used to identify, this in itself does not preclude further use of the term (what may be appropriately called extension of the term) for less rigid usage, nor even limitations upon the use of the term in particular contexts. So we use "water" for the salt solution that the sea is composed of, but "saline solution" for the salt solution dripped intravenously into a patient in hospital. The way in which we are prepared to allow the extension or contraction in the use of a term reflects the point made above at (F)—it will depend on our characters, needs and aspirations in a particular context that we experience. We are prepared to use "water" for the liquid found in the sea and the liquid coming out of a tap despite the fact that the taste is markedly different. We may on the grounds of taste alone notice no difference between the liquids in two containers. However, we do have grounds for declining to refer to the liquids in the containers as both being water, since the second contains a solution of a tasteless toxic substance which should more accurately and helpfully be labelled "poison".

Incidentally, the primacy of experience is illustrated here again. It is precisely because our further *experience* is capable of telling the difference between the two and alerting us to the dangers of regarding the two liquids in the same manner, that we can recognise the need to differentiate our use of words. (The parallel earthlings may not be able to tell the difference between water and a stiff drink, and so will never differentiate the two in their vocabulary. Visitors from our earth will do so on their arrival. The point is not what "water" can mean in all possible worlds, but what use people will have for "water" depending on their experience of life in those worlds.)

It seems that a number of different factors are at work in shaping the fluidity or rigidity of our terms. Perhaps a more helpful starting point would be to assume that all terms are potentially fluid and then to consider what, if anything, prevents them from flowing into other uses, so turning them into rigid terms. The following observations can be made regarding fluid terms:

(G) In the case of a fluid term, it is not possible to have a general idea of what the term applies to so as to cover all instances of the use of that term.

(H) It is possible for a particular person to have a loose idea of what a fluid term, such as mother, refers to, drawn from that person's own experiences of particular instance(s) of it, but it would not be possible to complete or rectify such a loose idea (in the way we could with Mother) because there is no recognised stable source of experience by which this could be done.

(I) If we wish to build a complete or accurate idea of a mother, we would first have to restrict our usage of the term, and talk of a complete or accurate idea of a mother in some restricted application of that term, e.g. the idea of a "birth-mother", or "adoptive mother".

(J) The use of a fluid term to cover a particular instance does not bring about the *existence* of that instance, whose existence in the world has been ascertained as a matter of human experience. Nor does the failure to use a fluid term to cover a particular instance prevent the existence of that instance.

(K) However, the use of the term, to cover what has been recognised as existing as a matter of human experience, may colour the way that we look upon it, and the way that it affects us. The use of the term may bring about emotional, legal or other social consequences which are associated with the other uses of the term. A child may need to know that her adoptive mother loves her as a mother; an adoptive mother will have legal responsibilities and rights as if a natural mother; a woman who adopts may feel the need to have the same social recognition as a natural mother enjoys.

(L)   The fluidity of a term does not open it up to limitless application—there is a connected flow between instances, though not a necessary connection between all instances to which the term has flowed. We could not start using the same term "mother" to cover an item of furniture.

(M)   Without this flow, the use of the same combination of letters in a word that possesses two meanings would have to be recognised not as two instances of a fluid term, but as a word being used for two distinct terms. Hence "savings bank" and "merchant bank" give two instances of the fluid term "bank"; but "savings bank" and "river bank" involve the same word being used as two separate terms.

(N)   How fluid a term might prove to be will depend on the variety of features associated with what it is initially applied to, the existence of other things open to human experience that share one or more of these features, and the ingenuity of the speaker in making the connection. It is not an exact science. All the instances of "mother" given above are precedented. What about a woman acting as an anonymous donor of an egg (who shares the first feature in our list) for a surrogacy undertaken by a second woman for an infertile third woman? Would this be enough for us to speak of the first woman as the "genetic *mother*" or should we simply refer to the "egg donor" or "genetic relation"?

(O)   We can only be sure that a fluid term will not have a further extension when all possible further extensions have been considered and rejected. The restriction associated with a particular term, for example, "Ben Nevis", is relatively straightforward. We do not have to range over many possible extensions in order to restrict our identification to the one thing: a mountain (exclusion of everything else in the world not fitting this class) with a particular geographical location (inclusion of only one possible mountain). Although there is some limit on the direction of flow (L)(M), there is no clear cut way of arriving at a restriction. It may be a matter of considering, then accepting or rejecting, possible extensions.

TALKING OF IDEAS

One possible objection to the analysis offered so far is that the emphasis on something experienced in the world seems to omit a common use of words that is of particular significance for law. Words are not used simply to identify and convey our understanding of *things* in the world. They are used to form and shape ideas in themselves—not just an *idea of something*, but an abstract or artificial idea that does not relate to something that had a prior existence in the world.

The response to this objection is to stress the previous emphasis (at (5) and (6)) on the possibility of imagination experience. Abstract or artificial ideas are a form of this sort of experience. In the same way that "unicorn" becomes a meaningful word only at the point of somebody having the experience in the world of imagining a unicorn, so too with abstract or artificial ideas.

An illustration of this point is provided by considering the idea of a "metre". Prior to a meeting of French scientists at the end of the eighteenth century, "metre" is as much a word as "qwepfl". The experience in the world at that meeting of a decision to provide a unit of measurement equivalent to one ten-millionth of the distance across the surface of the earth between the North Pole and the Equator to be called a "metre" is what turns the collection of letters into a meaningful word. Similarly, the idea of a metre was subsequently determined by the experience of deciding to have a standard one metre metal bar to be kept in the Louvre in Paris, as an authoritative representation of the unit of measurement. The crucial role of what we have experienced as a decision can be demonstrated if we imagine that the metal bar has been subjected to cleaning with an abrasive polish over the centuries. What was decided as the idea of a metre: whatever length of the bar remains in the Louvre, or the length of the bar as it was at the time it was called a metre? Only by reference to the actual experience can we decide what a "metre" means, and given the possibility of the experience here being an experience of a partial or unclear decision there is consequently the possibility of the idea conveyed by "metre" being incomplete or ambiguous.

The term used to convey an idea may of course be fluid, but there will still need to be some experience to which the term can flow in order to shape the idea with fresh contours. The proposal in 1960 to adopt the *Système International d'Unités* provided a different idea of a metre: the length of distance travelled by light in a vacuum during 1/299,792,458 of a second. The creation of ideas through our experiences in the world are sadly seldom so precise in their effects. Particularly when we turn to law there is an absence of a coherent path of experiences setting about refining the artificial ideas that enter our vocabulary, and the nature of the development of legal ideas will require further examination, which I shall undertake in chapter 9.

THE STAGE WE ARE AT

All this is well and good but rather tangential to our actual experience of the use of words, for we do not go around having experiences and making decisions as to what words to employ in relation to those experiences. Unless we are a pioneering scientist, explorer, writer of fantasy novels, or a theorist with a strange bent for neologisms like Bentham, it is unlikely that we shall ever be given the opportunity to actually decide upon a word in this way. We have experiences of things in the world but someone else usually teaches us what is the correct word to use for them.

Moreover, we also use words without worrying too much about what experiences (actual or imaginary) they might relate to—we engage in abstract discussion, seek rhetorical effect, use buzz words to make an impression, employ a conventional formula to have a desired effect, without thinking at all about the meaning (as apart from the effect) of the words we use.

In order to capture all the facets of the uses of words we are familiar with in our developed language, much more work would have to be undertaken. We would have to consider the development of metaphor, irony, slang, fictions and other forms of linguistic subterfuge. Nevertheless, however sophisticated our development of linguistic ploys, and however remote they seem from the basic analysis offered here, the connection can be maintained through observing that the explanation of such advanced uses of words assumes the use that has been analysed above, in relating the use of words to what can be experienced in the world. Metaphor depends upon our recognising an image of what is experienced in the world; irony affects to convey the opposite of the experience that the word(s) would normally convey so as to communicate our attitude; slang selects an alternative expression for the experience in order to express our familiarity with it and with others in a similar position; fiction pretends the experience; subterfuge transmits a deception of having the experience; and so on.

The real problem to face in utilising the analysis offered is that the multiplication of experiences, and the transmission of ideas of those experiences, in the uses of a particular word before it reaches our ears, may stretch the point of reference from something experienced in the world to a collection of things experienced, and a variety of ideas as to what is understood of those things. There is seldom likely to be a single thing in the world (actual or imagined) that acts as an authoritative reference point, experience of which can clarify and expand our understanding. And given the fluidity of terms, words may slide over a range of diverse experiences before our very eyes. Yet even in the advanced stage of the use of language we have reached, specifically in twenty-first century legal English, the rudimentary features of a less sophisticated and more accessible use of language may be employed to chart the extent to which the sophistication of our words and ideas has taken us beyond the capacity for coherent communication. I shall make an attempt to do this in chapter 9. Before doing so I wish to consider how the problems raised by our uses of words to relate to a diversity of human experiences have been addressed elsewhere.

ENDNOTE

Some of the key problems encountered in the philosophy of language (including other worlds, cherries and cats) are dealt with in a fairly approachable manner in Hilary Putnam, *Reason, Truth and History* (Cambridge, Cambridge University Press, 1981). Helpful introductions to the subject are provided by William Lycan, *Philosophy of Language: A contemporary introduction* (London, Routledge, 2000); and Martin Davies,

"Philosophy of Language" in Nicholas Bunnin and EP Tsui-James (eds.), *The Blackwell Companion to Philosophy* (Oxford, Blackwell, 1996).

References to some works on law and language, which draw on the philosophy of language, are provided in the Endnote to ch. 7 below. Other relevant references are to be found in the Endnote to ch. 2 (conceptual analysis and definition) and ch. 5 n. 36 (vagueness).

The device of other possible worlds has been exploited in an attempt to transform modal logic by providing a semantic reference point for what is *possibly true*: it *is true* in a possible world. An attempt to meet the objection, that this simply transfers the modality of the statement to the world in which it is held to be true, has been made by David Lewis, *On the Plurality of Worlds* (Oxford, Blackwell, 1986), by arguing that possible worlds exist in the same way as the actual world. This is a controversial claim. Less extreme employment of the device uses it as a tool to portray features of our actual world. For example, it can be argued that the use of possible worlds in Frank Jackson, *From Metaphysics to Ethics: A Defence of Conceptual Analysis* (Oxford, Clarendon Press, 1998) does nothing more than draw attention to the features of our world that are discoverable through collective, or "folk", experience.

My use of "extension" in relation to fluid terms should not be confused with the conventional technical use of the "extension" ("intension") of a term. The technical extension/intension distinction as applied to a term relates respectively to the range of things which a term denotes, and the qualities conveyed by a term. However, to talk of *the* extension or intension of a term can be misleading in failing to account for the differences between the things that a term can be used to denote, and the different qualities it can be used to convey on different occasions.

The different words for snow in Inuktitut are discussed by Louis-Jacques Dorais, "The Canadian Inuit and their Language" in Dirmid Collis (ed.), *Arctic Languages: An Awakening* (Paris, Unesco, 1990) at 205. Dorais also draws attention to the rich zoological vocabulary of the Inuit but by contrast their failure to have different words for grass and flowers.

7

Some Themes from Wittgenstein's Philosophical Investigations

INTRODUCTION

THERE IS UNDERSTANDABLY a certain amount of awe attached to Wittgenstein's philosophy. In part this amounts to the respect paid to something that is not understood but is perceived to be of a higher stature than the person paying the respect has attained—it is reported that the young Wittgenstein invoked this response from his teacher, Bertrand Russell.[1] In part it is the respect earned by something whose brilliance is comprehended as obvious in relation to all that lies before it—the acute observation which dispels previous approaches to an issue as hopeless muddle and confusion. There is thirdly an element of the sort of respect that we are prepared to pay to the scope of a person's ambition irrespective of whether that ambition is to be achieved—our admiration for the very willingness to broach such concerns that lesser mortals shrink from.[2]

If the feelings that Wittgenstein's philosophy arouses are complex, this reflects the character of his work. In parts it is not readily intelligible but invites the effort of further concentrated study. In parts it sheds instant illumination with an accessible familiarity. In other parts it sets out proposals for scaling great heights which remain unapproached. It is variously difficult to grasp, simply attainable, and merely inchoate. Wittgenstein himself had strong convictions about the great effort required by his work, the stark simplicity of some of his observations, and his own shortcomings in dealing with some of the issues which he had raised.[3] Anyone who wishes to engage with Wittgenstein's work faces the perils of confusing the complex and the simple, the perfected observation and the incomplete remark.

The course of scholarly debate on Wittgenstein's work has followed two related paths. The one takes some image or theme from Wittgenstein and seeks to work out what lies stored within it. The other seeks to draw out the implications of such an image or theme. So, for example, we can find intense discussion

---

[1] Ray Monk, *Ludwig Wittgenstein: The Duty of Genius* (London, Jonathan Cape, 1990).

[2] This is nicely illustrated in James Conant's discussion of Hilary Putnam's admiraton for Wittgenstein in his Introduction to Hilary Putnam, *Realism with a Human Face* (Cambridge, MA, Harvard University Press, 1990) xxxiv–xxxv.

[3] Noted in Monk, above n. 1.

over what Wittgenstein meant by following a rule, raising heated controversy over whether or not Wittgenstein took a sceptical position on the possibility of rule following.[4] In parallel we can find scholars attempting to draw out the implications of taking a sceptical (or non-sceptical) Wittgensteinian position on rule following in relation to law.[5]

What is perhaps surprising is that there is a tendency to take these themes as separate sources of illumination, both at the primary level of exegesis of Wittgenstein's texts and at the secondary level of applying his insights. It is as though Wittgenstein's images are so dazzling that each in turn blots out the consideration of anything else. This tendency is doubtless also fostered by Wittgenstein's epigrammatic style of writing, relying on a shower of sharp arrows to puncture the complacent errors of his reader so as to provoke the reader into thinking more clearly, without attempting to provide a comprehensive guide for the territory opened up by clear thought.

This tendency is apparent in the popular understanding of Wittgenstein. Those who have never read Wittgenstein are likely to associate him with his widely quoted marginal remark about a request to teach a game to the children not being intended to cover teaching them gambling with dice, as though the ambiguity illustrated by this is in isolation capable of summarising Wittgenstein's thinking. When we consider the application of Wittgenstein's insights to legal theory we similarly find much discussion of separate themes from Wittgenstein as though these in themselves are capable of delivering a Wittgensteinian position on law.[6] From Wittgenstein we are invited to learn that words and hence legal words have a complex usage, an inherent ambiguity; or, that rules and hence legal rules cannot be exhaustively followed; or, that words rely on a social practice for their meaning. Given the contentious nature of Wittgensteinian scholarship in general, it is not surprising that the attempts to construct a Wittgensteinian position on law have failed to earn widespread assent.

What seems to be less often attempted is pulling Wittgenstein's images and themes together. Even if doing this emphasises the incomplete nature of Wittgenstein's undertaking, I think that this may prove more illuminating (both for our grasp of Wittgenstein's thought and for its implications for legal theory) than the process of seeking understanding by gazing in turn at one or more

---

[4] The sceptical position is advanced and expanded by Saul Kripke, *Wittgenstein on Rules and Private Language: An Elementary Exposition* (Cambridge, MA, Harvard University Press, 1982). The anti-sceptical reading is defended by GP Baker and PMS Hacker, *Wittgenstein: Rules, Grammar and Necessity* (Oxford, Basil Blackwell, 1985). (See ch. 8 n. 2 for some further comment.) The view that Wittgenstein's approach to rule following must be mastered in order to provide cohesion to his thinking in *Philosophical Investigations* is advanced in Steven Holtzman and Christopher Leich (eds.), *Wittgenstein: to Follow a Rule* (London, Routledge & Kegan Paul, 1981). See, in particular, the contribution by Gordon Baker, "Following Wittgenstein: Some Signposts for *Philosophical Investigations* §§ 143–242".

[5] See Endnote for general bibliographical details on the application of Wittgenstein's ideas to law.

[6] For references on the following points, see Endnote.

dazzling spotlights. What I propose to do here is to provide a simplified model that seeks to capture the essential features of Wittgenstein's philosophy, without engaging in the controversies that have arisen over even some of the most basic aspects of Wittgenstein's thought.[7] By subjecting this model to scrutiny I hope to indicate serious shortcomings in Wittgenstein's approach without becoming embroiled in Wittgensteinian scholarship. I shall then seek to confirm the extent of these shortcomings through taking a close look at one of Wittgenstein's key texts. By adopting this strategy I hope to demonstrate how the central concerns of his work provide the impetus for reaching beyond the insights that Wittgenstein has himself provided.

Whatever their state of accomplishment and however significant their implications, three themes clearly surface in Wittgenstein's *Philosophical Investigations*.[8] The first is anti-theoretical in character, suggesting that philosophy or theory can obscure our understanding by setting up false problems which divert us from grasping what is really the case:[9]

> "And we may not advance any kind of theory. There must not be anything hypothetical in our considerations. We must do away with all *explanation*, and description alone must take its place. . . . The problems are solved, not by giving new information, but by arranging what we have always known. Philosophy is a battle against the bewitchment of our intelligence by means of language.
>
> When philosophers use a word—'knowledge', 'being', 'object', 'I', 'proposition', 'name'—and try to grasp the *essence* of the thing, one must always ask oneself: is the word ever actually used in this way in the language-game which is its original home?—
>
> What *we* do is to bring words back from their metaphysical to their everyday use."

The second theme places the emphasis on language, asserting that what pose as philosophical problems should be resolved by a study of "grammar", how words are appropriately used in expressing the way things actually are:[10]

> "A main source of our failure to understand is that we do not *command a clear view* of the use of our words.—Our grammar is lacking in this sort of perspicuity. . . .
>
> Philosophy may in no way interfere with the actual use of language; it can in the end only describe it.
>
> For it cannot give it any foundation either.
>
> It leaves everything as it is."

The third theme acknowledges diversity in human practices which is reflected in our use of words—we are mistaken to assume either that the same word is

---

[7] One of the most elementary controversies is the role of the interlocutor in *Philosophical Investigations*: whether it is the voice of the thinking that Wittgenstein is seeking to oppose or to espouse—raised by Frederick Schauer, "Rules and the Rule-Following Argument" in Dennis Patterson (ed.), *Wittgenstein and Legal Theory* (Boulder, CO, Westview Press, 1992) at 225.

[8] Ludwig Wittgenstein, *Philosophical Investigations*, 2nd edn. (GEM Anscombe transl) (Oxford, Basil Blackwell, 1958) hereinafter, PI, with § references to the numbered remarks of part I and bare numbers to the pages of part II.

[9] PI §§109, 116.

[10] PI §§122, 124.

always used in the same way, or that different words conform to general rules of usage in our language:[11]

> "There are *countless* kinds: countless different kinds of use of what we call 'symbols', 'words', 'sentences'. . . .
>
> It is interesting to compare the multiplicity of the tools in language and the ways they are used, the multiplicity of kinds of word and sentence, with what logicians have said about the structure of language. (Including the author of the *Tractatus Logico-Philosophicus*.)
>
> If you do not keep the multiplicity of language-games in view you will perhaps be inclined to ask questions like: 'What is a question?'. . ."

Alongside these three themes, three graphic images are prominent in Wittgenstein's *Investigations*: playing a game, following a rule, and family resemblance. These themes and images resonate throughout Wittgenstein's *Investigations*. The following model attempts to portray only some of their more elementary connections to each other.

A SIMPLE OVERVIEW

One cannot understand playing a game of chess apart from understanding it as playing a game of chess: to play it fully is to understand it fully; to understand it fully is to grasp the practice of playing it. Beyond this there is no room for a theory of chess.

Language can be likened to a game but as with other games it is only possible to play the game because the players are conversant with the rules. Language requires a degree of regularity which passes in the form of communication between speaker and audience. This regularity may be expressed as following a rule. *A* follows a rule in referring to a particular thing as "*x*", which *B* understands in accordance with the same rule as referring to the same thing. If we want to discover the rule we can only seek it in the practice of the "game" to which it applies. We understand what a word means by noting the proper practice of it within the language game of which its use forms a part. It is possible to follow a rule by being fluent in the practice which that rule expresses—as an adult native speaker of English one unconsciously adds an "s" to the third person verb form in the present tense. It is also possible to follow a rule by being trained in the correct usage so as to conform to the practice in question—as a learner of English as a foreign language one is trained to add the "s" to the third person verb.

Words acquire meaning outside the regular application of static rules. A word with one meaning may move to encompass another meaning which does not fall strictly under the rule governing the first meaning of the word. The applications of a word multiply by affinity rather than through the consistent application of

[11] PI §§23–4.

a rule. They display family resemblances amongst themselves rather than being cloned with exactly the same characteristics.

As a result of the diversity of word applications or meanings we may fail to grasp what rules are appropriate to govern the proper uses of a particular word. We may fail to see that the same word is being used in different applications governed by different rules of a language game, or even that one word is governed by the rules of different language games. This sort of problem is not simply the problem of ignorance (we do not know how to use a word—and so we ask for instruction) but is the problem of confusion (we think we are using a word correctly when we are not—and so make inappropriate responses or even pose inappropriate questions).

The role of philosophy is to set about repairing our understanding of the "grammar" of words. This involves understanding how words are properly used, discerning what rules express the appropriate use of a word in relation to a particular practice. So conceived philosophy is an enormous task, but without pursuing it in detail it is possible to provide insight into the skills involved which can then be adopted as required, to work through the details of everything that we have dealings with, all human practices that we use words to express.

If we imagine this mammoth task fulfilled we will have attained the understanding of everything in that we have grasped the appropriate way of speaking about everything that humans are capable of being involved in. It is as though we had fully understood chess by grasping the rules of the game to such an extent that we had covered the intricacies of every move that could possibly be made in every game that could possibly be played. This level of understanding would make any further questions about chess otiose. It would also be a type of understanding reached by accurately describing all that could exist *within* the game of chess. It would provide no metasystemic or higher theoretical insight into chess, but would simply provide with greater clarity than previously attained an expression of what things are within the game of chess—such level of description making further explanation uncalled for.

THE MODEL CONSIDERED

Let us suppose then that we can bring together in a coherent fashion Wittgenstein's observations on language games, family resemblances, rule following, and the point of philosophy. Let us take a particular word, W, whose use is found in a language game, G. There are in fact a variety of usages, U_{1-n}, reflecting family resemblances among a number of applications of the word W. These various usages as practised are precisely what constitutes the game G. It is possible for someone to be versed in these usages, and the proper use of W can be expressed as a number of rules, R_{1-n}, which a person can be trained to follow so as to reflect in their practice the different possible usages of W, i.e. play G properly.

The fact that the overall use of a word is in accordance with a game rather than in accordance with a single rule is one way of capturing the departure in Wittgenstein's *Investigations* from his *Tractatus.*[12] For in his earlier work Wittgenstein had set out to map the meanings of words into a logical system such that there was a simple linear relation between the meaning of elementary propositions and the atomic states of affairs that they could be taken to represent. The game allows for different "moves" or meanings to be appropriate in different circumstances, although if we are talking of the language game of a particular word[13] these different meanings may share family resemblances among themselves. The crucial point is that not all the usages of the word can be found to exhibit the same characteristics such that they can be regarded as conforming to a single rule.[14]

The word, game and variety of usages displaying family resemblances accordingly form a tripartite relationship which can be depicted as follows:

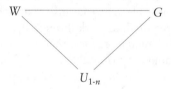

W is understood in accordance with G which consists of the practice of U_{1-n}, which reflect the meanings of W.

We can also detect a further tripartite relationship between the rules which reflect the different usages, which a person can be trained in following so as to properly play the game, depicted as follows:

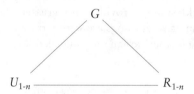

G consists of the practice of U_{1-n} which may be expressed by R_{1-n} which a person may be trained to follow so as to play G.

The two sets of tripartite relationships fit together thus, such that the meaning of W exists in parallel to the training in the proper use of the word:

---

[12] *Tractatus Logico-Philosophicus*, CK Ogden and FP Ramsey transl (London, Routledge, 1922) (subsequently translated by DF Pears and BF McGuinness (London, Routledge, 1961)).

[13] Wittgenstein's language games cover single words, groups of words, and phrases and also divide into different games with the same word.

[14] The diversity of usage in language game(s) is brought out by Wittgenstein in an explicit renunciation of his earlier work in PI §23, quoted at n. 11 above.

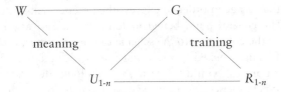

This illustrates diagrammatically the apparently closed system formed by Wittgenstein's approach to language, practice, and understanding. There is no phenomenological or ideal intermediary between our words and what we use them for, and nothing further to discover beyond what we are capable of expressing in our actual practice. Philosophy whose role it is to furnish us with the correct grammar for our use of words (which amounts to pointing out the rules of our language games) thus "leaves everything as it is".[15]

How does this integrated model of key Wittgensteinian themes stand up to scrutiny? A number of queries can be raised. First, a fundamental question to raise is why it is that this model does not collapse into the model that Wittgenstein was pursuing in the *Tractatus* and abandoned as incorrect in the *Investigations*. If each of the usages of W is expressible in the form of a single rule (usage$_1$ in accordance with rule$_1$, usage$_2$ in accordance with rule$_2$, ... usage$_n$ in accordance with rule$_n$), then it is possible to distinguish each usage of W in accordance with the distinct rule it conforms to, and we could then map the meaning of each distinct word usage (U_1, U_2, ... U_n) into a logical system as attempted in the *Tractatus*, such that there was a simple linear relationship between each word usage and the appropriate practice that it could be taken to express. The only refinement required is that instead of assuming that each elementary proposition relates to an atomic state of affairs in the world, we assume that each word usage relates to a particular practice in the world.

It is not a valid objection to this line of thinking to raise the point that Wittgenstein's language games are not restricted to the multiple usage of individual words displaying family resemblances (the example we have selected for the convenience of illustration of Wittgenstein's key themes). Wittgenstein allows for the development of new language games[16] and considers the possibility of the usage of a word within a language game not being governed by the rules of a language game—as the rules of tennis do not specify how high one must hit the ball.[17] Any usage of a word or phrase, however dynamic or innovative, inasmuch as it amounts to a usage that is capable of being recognized and understood, must be capable of being depicted in the form of a rule that permits

---

[15] Above at n. 10.

[16] PI §23, the text cited above at n. 11 where the limitations of the *Tractatus* are deprecated—cp 224.

[17] PI §68. Wittgenstein is failing to note the difference between and the relationship between mandatory and permissive rules. The rules of tennis permit one to hit the ball as high as one can so long as it lands in the required part of the court.

or requires that usage in order to express the practice being engaged in by the speaker.[18] The general point being made in the case of any language game, which secures the collapse into the schema of the *Tractatus*, is that if the game is capable of being depicted as a series of rules which relate to different usages (of words or phrases) within the game, we can logically relate those different usages to distinct practices in the world captured in following the different rules. If the different usages could not be related to such a series of rules then we would not be able to talk meaningfully of having a game.

If so simple an argument can be advanced for collapsing the language games of the *Investigations* into the attempted schema of the *Tractatus*, why was it not obvious to Wittgenstein that he was engaged in a similar enterprise, and more pointedly, why was he so willing in the *Investigations* to confess to the short-comings of the *Tractatus*? I think the answers to these highly pertinent questions lie in the unformed state of the language games in the *Investigations*. Although Wittgenstein succeeded in captivating the world of philosophy with his image of a language game, and employed facets of that image in discussing specific problems in the *Investigations*, nowhere did he provide a fully worked out example of an actual language game, nor even explore the implications of having a language game presented in its entirety.[19] The discussion of language games in the *Investigations* does not get beyond an inchoate stage of development.

The significance of this point is exhibited in two important ways. First, it allows Wittgenstein in discussing particular problems to locate the solution to the problem within a methodology, the discovery of the appropriate language game, without shouldering the burden of providing a detailed answer. The details seem too simple to discuss once we have taken the difficult step of seeing that they will be divulged by observation of the practice of the appropriate game.[20] Secondly, more generally, it permits the acknowledgment of the complex, if not untidy, state of our language (words are not used in accordance with strict rules but are played around with as if in a game), with the sense of accomplishment that all that needs to be philosophically done in relation to that state of affairs has been achieved *without having to tidy anything up*. The diversity and complexity we observe does not have to be reduced to a common or more elementary form, because it is in the observation of diversity and complexity that the language game is manifested. This then serves to conceal the limitations which Wittgenstein was ready to admit for the *Tractatus*. They are subsumed

---

[18] This is not to deny the existence of synonymous words or phrases in our language but there is a requirement to ascertain which usage of a word (or phrase) is synonymous with which usage of another word (or phrase). For example, we find $W_3 = X_6$, which is to say that the conditions for the usage of W in R_3 of the wordgame involving W are the same as the conditions for the usage of X in R_6 of the wordgame involving X.

[19] The "complete primitive language" imagined by Wittgenstein, PI §2, involving the movement of stones on a building site, is artificially constrained so that we do not reach the conditions of an actual language. See further, the discussion of Wittgenstein's language game of "game" below.

[20] Just "look and see", PI §66.

into the model of a language game. Because that game is never completed they are not allowed to resurface again.

Apart from the possible obscuring of the relationship between his *Tractatus* and *Investigations*, the failure to consider a fully worked out language game has other serious implications for an assessment of Wittgenstein's work. I want to consider some implications which counter the appearance of self-contained completeness depicted in the diagrammatic representation of the game above.

Let us try to imagine completing our observations of a language game. The game is constituted by the variety of usages of the word we are investigating. We observe the practice of that usage, and eventually recognise the rules which if followed allow us to participate in the game. However, we are assuming that the practice of usage though diverse is coherent, such that we can formulate rules that it accords with. Suppose that in our observations we come across some inconsistent usage which cannot be accommodated within a coherent body of rules. Wittgenstein allows for this possibility—we simply acknowledge that there are two different language games going on: the players of one game although they appear to be playing with the same word are in fact playing a different game to the players of the other game.[21]

This means that we cannot enter the game through the word, the W apex on our diagram, because that is capable of leading us to one or more different games—we could have a number of parallelograms rotating around the point W amounting to different language games with different usages and different rules ($WG_aR_aU_a$, $WG_bR_bU_b$, etc) for the word W. However, nor is it a solution to enter straight into the game, through the G apex, and come from that direction into the diverse usage so as to mark off the set of coherent usage that fits, say, WG_a—for what is to indicate that we should mark off that set rather than the set of coherent usage that fits WG_b? If the game is constituted by the usage, we cannot use the game to select the usage. Moreover, there is nothing to guarantee that we can find in practice from among the diversity of usage associated with a particular word a set of usages that amounts to coherent use of the word, even if we restrict ourselves to a single speaker. In some cases, a simple uniformity of coherent practice may be found but as soon as we broach the words that cause us particularly thorny problems, the probability diminishes fast.[22]

At this point we may acknowledge that the system of the language game is not completely linguistic but relies for its coherence on the practice not merely of what is said but of what is spoken about, the practice of using words in a particular context. The coherent use of the word emanates from the coherence of that practice, using words in moving stones on a building site, or whatever.[23] We can now enter the game not by picking on a word and tracing its usage but

---

[21] PI §§85–6, 239–42; 225–7—cp §64; 180.

[22] Such as the words considered at great length by judges and philosophers.

[23] Wittgenstein compresses the practice of using the word with the practice which that word expresses: "I shall also call the whole, consisting of language and the actions into which it is woven, the 'language game'." (PI §7)

by selecting from the practice of using that word in a particular context the coherent set of usages that fits that context.

Still we are faced with the problem of the possibility of discordant usage of a word within a particular context, now that context is recognised independently of the linguistic usage we are considering; and even the possibility of finding discordant usage entering the game itself—if we rely solely on practical context to demarcate the parameters of our language game. In this case we cannot rely on determining the grammar of the word (or the rules of the language game) to reveal to us the way things are. The confused state of the language game simply reveals our confusion over the way things are in that particular practical context.

There are other implications of trying to consider a complete language game even if we put to one side the problems of discordant usage. These relate to the problem of isolating a particular language game, or the practical context that gives rise to it. A remarkable characteristic of Wittgenstein's portrayal of language games is treating them as if they were played in complete isolation from each other. This is not only found in Wittgenstein's suggestion that people having inconsistent usages of a word are engaged in playing different language games. It also arises in his suggestion that there are different language games played by the same individual.[24]

Yet if we posit a practical context for a language game then there is a possibility that novel situations will occur not only within that practical context but also within the interface between that practical context and another. We cannot even contemplate the completion of a language game until we have completed our experience of all the practical situations that may be encountered by it. We cannot rely on the language game to provide us with the understanding of what is when we have not yet secured the experience of all the things that may be. It is in this respect that a language game differs crucially from a game of chess. A grasp of the rules of chess is sufficient to generate all the practical situations that may arise in playing the game, but in the case of a language game it is the response to those practical situations that generates the rules of the game. Wittgenstein treats the playing of each language game as though it were, like chess, a discrete response to a predefined portion of life and so ignores the shock of bumping into life at large.

There is in fact one place in the *Investigations* where Wittgenstein does appear to confront the problem of meeting a novel situation, but his brief response is to suggest that this will mean recognising another language game.[25] Wittgenstein's brevity here is revealing. It shows up his general unpreparedness to *engage* with the dynamic aspect of language. It also indicates the absence of a strategy for dealing with the chicken-and-egg conundrum over meaning and training. It is all very well to represent these as existing in parallel, as our diagram above does, but which came first: are we trained in what the words mean, or do the words mean what we are trained to understand by them?

---

[24] PI §77; 180.
[25] PI 224; cp §23.

This conundrum goes deep into the controversy surrounding how to interpret Wittgenstein's general approach to language, as sceptic or empiricist.[26] For if the training has to come first, every practical situation is a potential source of training and prior to that training being authoritatively delivered there is room for scepticism as to how it will determine proper usage for a word. Alternatively, if the words derive their meaning from their practice which comprises the proper usage, and that forms the basis of training, then we can take an empirical approach to finding the meaning of words by observing the practice. That this controversy within Wittgenstein's schema is at its core a chicken-and-egg conundrum becomes apparent as soon as we acknowledge, as Wittgenstein himself does,[27] that the past practice of using words is not in itself a secure indication of how those words are to be generally used: hence we need training, but if training is in relation to the meaning derived from their accepted use we first need established practice. This problem comes sharply into focus in considering how a language game meets a novel situation. Wittgenstein ducks the problem by suggesting that we simply need to move to a new language game but the problem would only reappear in the new game: do we first need training to deal with the novel situation now taken over by the new game, or do we first need to await the acceptance of a practice in the novel situation to form the basis of our training?[28]

Wittgenstein's remark on the novel situation underlines how he uses a language game as a device for cutting away problematic issues met in practice rather than as a means for portraying things as they are. The problematics of the novel situation are removed to another language game rather than being confronted, with the vague assumption that whatever the answer turns out to be will be detectable in the practices of that game (though the game is never played out for us).

If all the problematic issues of life, on which individuals disagree between themselves, or over which they cannot adopt coherent positions as individuals, are fragmented into separate areas of practice constituting isolated language games, then the language game does not serve to represent things as they are. It distorts our picture of reality by taking one of a number of conflicting strands of the reality we experience and are confounded by, and misrepresents it as a coherent whole.

The practical context of a language game provides us with a location in which a number of things can be seen, which together combine to provide a fuller picture of the reality of our experience, than the distorted view of an isolated language game. First we can see that the context can also form a context for another language game and hence the venue in which competing language

---

[26] Above n. 4.

[27] Most famously with the example of "+2", PI §§185–6.

[28] The importance to Wittgenstein of training in order to clarify meaning is evident (PI §§189–90, 692). Nevertheless, Wittgenstein appears nonchalant about the relationship between training and practice, "use" and "training" being treated as casual alternatives in §§189–90.

games can struggle for practical mastery of a context. Suppose we take Wittgenstein's building site as one such context. Different language games may arise for the naming of building materials but given a shared practical context it is possible that they will compete there—one language game may gain dominance because it is preferred by the biggest supplier of building materials when labelling its products.[29]

Secondly, since a practical context is a part of life, or, as I have described it in the previous chapter, part of our experience of the world, it amounts to the location of an interface with other practical contexts and a source of further experience of the world either occurring within that specific context or arriving there through its interface with other practical contexts. The practical context of game playing may interact with the practical context of child rearing, for example.

The more we probe the practical context of a language game, the more we see the impossibility of constructing a language game as a closed system and the artificiality of limiting a language game to its own practical context. For all these contexts are interrelated, since together they contribute to the world of which we have experience. And in that world in which we all live we cannot insulate competing viewpoints from one another, nor compartmentalise different life-experiences. The language we use to speak of our experiences in that world is the medium for expressing our bewilderment, our consternation, our conflicting views and disagreements, our ignorance—that we encounter in our experience of living in the world.

There is one other device which Wittgenstein employs, which may distract us from the impoverished resources of a language game to represent things as they are. This is his notion of a form of life.[30] Different forms of life may be identified with different language games at a point of conflict between how individuals view the world, and it would seem that a form of life is constituted by a number of language games.[31] However, Wittgenstein's use of the notion is allusive and the exact relationship between form of life and language game is never spelt out. The impact of this further notion lies in the suggestion that there is something beyond the isolated language game that provides coherence to an individual's response to the world. However, if the form of life is nothing more than a convenient shorthand for all the language games played by individuals during their respective lives it provides nothing by way of assistance to the depleted resources of those language games. On the other hand, if we were to read into a form of life some additional criterion which imposed a restriction on how a language game could be practised, or how one language game might be compatible with another for a particular individual, then the language game is inadequate on other grounds—the practice of the game does not furnish us with the opportunity to observe all that is, because that practice is itself determined

[29] As seen in the success of modern proprietary names like hoover.
[30] See Brian Bix, *Law, Language, and Legal Determinacy* (Oxford, Clarendon Press, 1993) 41–4, 55.
[31] PI §§ 19, 23, 241; 226.

by one or more external requirements which have to be understood by study of a form of life. Wittgenstein himself does not take this path, nor is it evident that taking it would resolve the problems encountered by relying on isolated language games to provide enlightenment. The form of life of an individual or group suffers from the same limitations as a language game on a grander scale. No form of life practised by humankind has yet attained a comprehensive and authoritative stock of responses to all issues that humans have to confront, and all theoretical attempts to refine the guiding principles of a form of life have brought controversy in their wake.[32]

If Wittgenstein's notion of a form of life cannot reinforce the depleted resources of his language game, this is not to suggest that either expression has no value. Our attempts to communicate through language often break down because of our drawing from our own limited experiences and the perspectives we take from them, assuming that our audience will understand our words by relating to those same experiences and perspectives whereas our audience is drawing on quite different experiences and/or perspectives. A form of life is a convenient expression to portray the manner in which individuals rely on their own blend of experiences and perspectives. A language game may well be a helpful image in representing our failed efforts at communication as people playing different language games. But it does not help to suggest that the way to further enlightenment is to clarify the games we play as though we can understand them in isolation from each other. The whole point that clamours for clarification is that people who are "playing different games" are trying to communicate with each other, and this calls for us first to consider the language as a whole (in which these different games are played) and beyond that to consider the world of which we try to speak, through the experience of which our language is formed.

Our attempts to see things truly as they are may involve seeing how little we know of what things are, and how much we speak from the limited extent of our partial perceptions of the world, though argue as though we knew and spoke much more.

THE GAME OF GAMES

I want to reinforce the argument made above for moving our focus of investigation from the language game to the language, and from the practical context of the language game to the wider experience of the world, by appealing to Wittgenstein's own most famous illustration of a language game.

---

[32] It is hard to believe that more intellectual resources have ever been poured into reflection over a form of life than those that have been expended over the centuries on the Talmud, yet the Talmud remains incomplete and retains its controversies. See Adin Steinsaltz, *The Essential Talmud* (New York, NY, Basic Books, 1976). Cp the discussion of liberalism as a form of life in ch. 9.

Wittgenstein uses the language game played with the word "game" as a paradigm for language games, but what do we observe on looking at this example of a language game? First, we can reiterate that it is presented in an incomplete state, with few comments on how it is actually played. Even so a number of pointers are present. One I have already alluded to above. The practical context of the game language game has an interface with the practical context of the child rearing language game—Wittgenstein's famous illustration of what it means to request someone to teach the children a game.[33] In the light of this illustration it is difficult to see how to maintain the pretense that we were dealing with a discrete language game.

Further revelation can be gleaned from the details of Wittgenstein's presentation of his illustration. The language game of "game" in §§66–71, 75–76 of *Philosophical Investigations* is discussed by Wittgenstein as a means of responding to his interlocutor's complaint that he has avoided the big question about the nature of language by breaking language down into language games and omitting to formulate a general explanation of what a language game is. Wittgenstein's example of a language game is provided as an attempt to show how language itself embraces the different language games by which it is constituted. The language game of "game" is meant to illustrate in microcosm the language game of "language".

How does Wittgenstein's explanation of the language game of "game" commence? It starts not with the word "game", nor with an idea of game, but with the various "proceedings" that the word "game" is attached to:

(A) "Consider, for example, the proceedings that we call 'games'." (§66)

And having taken us through a varied selection of these proceedings to make his point that they do not share a common core characteristic that makes them all games, Wittgenstein suggests that the games are bound together by "family resemblances":

(B) "And I shall say: 'games' form a family." (§67)

A brief comparison with the family of "numbers" leads Wittgenstein to make the point that the language game of "games" is open-ended:

(C) "I can also use [the word 'number'] so that the extension of the concept is *not* closed by a frontier. And this is how we do use the word 'game'. For how is the concept of a game bounded? What still counts as a game and what no longer does? Can you give the boundary? No. You can *draw* one; for none has so far been drawn. (But that never troubled you before when you used the word 'game'.)

'But then the use of the word is unregulated, the "game" we play with it is unregulated.'—It is not everywhere circumscribed by rules . . ." (§68)

The open-endedness raises the question how it is possible to explain to someone what a game is:

---

[33] PI marginal note at §70.

(D) " 'But if the concept "game" is uncircumscribed like that, you don't really know what you mean by a "game".' " (§70)

Wittgenstein's answer is not to seek out the elusive core characteristic that might provide a general definition, but rather:

(E) "One gives examples and intends them to be taken in a particular way. . . . Here giving examples is not an *indirect* means of explaining—in default of a better. For any general definition can be misunderstood too. The point is that *this* is how we play the game. (I mean the language-game with the word 'game'.)" (§71)

The examples used thus constitute the actual knowledge of "game":

(F) "What does it mean to know what a game is? . . . Isn't my knowledge, my concept of a game, completely expressed in the explanations that I could give? That is, in my describing examples of various kinds of game; shewing how all sorts of other games can be constructed on the analogy of these . . ." (§75)

And if someone persists in the effort to derive a clear concept of a game from the examples that Wittgenstein had provided, his concept would differ from Wittgenstein's:

(G) "If someone were to draw a sharp boundary I could not acknowledge it as the one that I too always wanted to draw, or had drawn in my mind. For I did not want to draw one at all. His concept can then be said to be not the same as mine, but akin to it." (§76)

It is illuminating to break down the elements of Wittgenstein's discussion. We have: (i) certain "proceedings" that humans experience (A); (ii) the term "game" used as a name or label for these proceedings (A); (iii) the recognition that the same label is used for a great variety of such proceedings (B); (iv) further use of this label for yet other proceedings is open-ended (C); (v) knowledge of the meaning of the label coming from its use (D, E, F); (vi) without a general definition (E); (vii) and without a clear concept (G).

The development of this language game—and since it is representative of the language game of "language", Wittgenstein's view of the development of language—can then be portrayed by the following sequence:

   (i)   experience of certain proceedings,
   (ii) use of word to label those proceedings,
   (iii) multiple use of word to label variety of proceedings,
   (iv) familiarity with multiple use provides for potential of further use,
   (v)   and amounts to knowledge of the meaning of the word,
   (vi) without acquiring a general definition,
  (vii) or a clear concept.

In order to present this as a general schema for the development of language, simply substitute for "certain proceedings", "some aspects of human experience in the world". It is worth considering how the view of the obstinate taxonomer whose suggestions Wittgenstein rejects at (G) departs from the above sequence. The insistence of a general definition and clear concept derived from the existing uses of the word, contrary to the positions at (vi) and (vii), will limit any further development of the word at (iv) beyond standard applications of recognised cases. The obstinate taxonomer lives uneasily with the dynamic character of language.

However, the real illumination that this sequence provides is on Wittgenstein's own view of language. For it is evident that in (i)–(iii) there is nothing beyond a report of current diverse usage of a word. It is unreconstituted raw linguistic practice. In this raw state we can recognise *terms*—words used as labels to identify different aspects of our experience of the world—but there is nothing here requiring us to derive a general *concept* for those aspects of our experience which fall to be labelled by the same term. Effective use of the word as a term for each of the aspects of human experience to which it was applied could be built on a fairly loose idea of each of those aspects sufficient to enable us to recognise another instance of it and employ the term appropriately. We would need a loose idea of football, of rugby, etc, or even at a more general level a loose idea of a ball-game, etc, in order to use the term "game" appropriately when we encountered a new instance. We would not need a general concept of game.

From our recognition of such loose ideas at a more general level, and our awareness that the term "game" had a history within our linguistic practice of being used as a term for a wide variety of "proceedings", we could even reach the stage (iv) of seeing the potential of the word to be employed as a term for further proceedings that we might encounter. Still there would be no requirement for a general concept of game.

Our understanding of the word "game" at (v) can accordingly be portrayed exactly as familiarity with current linguistic practice, including patterns within that practice that accommodate recognition of appropriate practice and further development of that practice. Still there is no requirement for a general concept of game.

This may seeem faithful to Wittgenstein's own account in that at (vi) and (vii) he eschews both a general definition of "game" and a clear concept of game, but it differs in a fundamental respect. For Wittgenstein introduces a concept of game early on as synonymous with the word "game", and in the end does not deny having a concept of game but only denies possessing a clear concept. The use of "game" as a term to label aspects of our experience is evident at (A): what we *call* these proceedings. The substitution of *concept* for label is introduced unheralded at (C): the extension of the concept of number is compared with the use of the word "game", before switching again to the concept of a game. It is the use of the word "game" that is not circumscribed by rules at (C) but by (D) Wittgenstein has switched to speaking of an uncircumscribed concept. The blurring of concept and term as label for proceedings is manifested at (D) in the typographical depiction of "the concept 'game' ". This differs from the (at least typographically) distinct "concept of a game" as appears in contrast to "the word 'game' " above at (C). And as we have remarked, by the end of his discusssion at (G) Wittgenstein does not berate the obstinate taxonomer for insisting on having a concept of game but only quarrels with him for insisting on a different, clearer concept to his own.

The point of importance is that Wittgenstein's own shadow concept of game is not substantiated by his representation of understanding of the word "game" as being purely a matter of familiarity with linguistic practice. To speak of a concept casts an additional feature of uniformity or coherence over that linguistic practice. Despite the fact that the practice is dynamic and cannot be pinned down by a general definition, howsoever it has developed and might develop in the future, by referring to a concept there is an indication of a coherent body of knowledge.

Expertise in this knowledge amounts in Wittgenstein's metaphor with skill in playing the language game. Wittgenstein's shadowy concept of game stands in apposition to the language game of "game". The vagueness or blurred boundary of the concept corresponds to the unregulated practices which are capable of extending the scope of the game, but whichever image is employed a connotation of coherence is introduced. Wittgenstein has offered nothing to demonstrate the existence of *a concept* or *a game*. There is nothing in his account beyond the actual practice of using the term "game" as a label for a variety of aspects of human experience which somehow or another between various subsets amongst themselves show a number of resemblances. Moreover, there is nothing in Wittgenstein's account to demonstrate that among all the resemblances detected in the practices of using the word "game", there is one concept or one language game. There may be a number of compatible concepts or language games. There may be a number of conflicting concepts or games. In short, concept or language game are redundant for Wittgenstein if he is only engaged in charting actual linguistic practice, and if they add something to a survey of practice they must do so in a way that mere linguistic practice alone can not inform us of.

This last point is illustrated in Wittgenstein's disagreement with the obstinate taxonomer at (G) above. The taxonomer imposes a sharp boundary upon linguistic practice in order to create a concept. Wittgenstein retains linguistic practice and claims to have a concept. If it is the act of drawing the boundary upon linguistic practice that creates a concept for the taxonomer, then Wittgenstein does not possess a concept of a game at all. If, on the other hand, the concept is associated with the linguistic practice, and it is arbitrary where the boundary is drawn, or whether no boundary is drawn at all, then we have no way of knowing whether in order to understand the word "game" we should refer to one or a number of concepts of game—and correspondingly whether we should be thinking in terms of one or a number of language games for the word "game". Significantly, Wittgenstein moves immediately without comment from examples of a single language game for "game" to examples drawn from a number of language games for the word "good".[34]

---

[34] PI §77.

Yet the act of imposing one or a number of concepts on our disparate linguistic practices relating to a particular term is precisely what amounts to changing our understanding of what the term refers to. The delineation of a particular concept, or the selection of a particular language game, is significant because it reflects a change in our understanding.

CONCLUSION

I have argued that Wittgenstein's central device of a language game proves to be inchoate on closer examination, and that instead of providing us with a clearer grasp of the way things are, the device operates to prevent us confronting the reality of the confusion that may beset us in the world. However, I have not sought to challenge some of Wittgenstein's wider concerns—to avoid abstruse theory, to acknowledge the significance of human experience and its diversity. Wittgenstein's view that the reality of our situation could be found through clarifying our use of language (which contributed to what came to be known as the linguistic turn in philosophy) stops short of facing the possibility that a closer examination of our language will reflect the problems we face in clarifying the situation we are in, and the controversies we enter in the midst of our confusion. How we might chart these controversies and also how we might endeavour to steer a route through them is of particular concern to any attempt to account for the path of the law. To this extent Wittgenstein's philosophy must be judged to have left the core concerns of legal theory unapproached. I shall seek to show in chapter 9 how the wider concerns that Wittgenstein embraced may provide the impetus for reaching further along that path.

ENDNOTE

The application of Wittgenstein's ideas to law can be traced as a pervasive or background influence as well as a principal focus in particular studies. The influence of Wittgenstein on Hart's approach to the understanding of general terms and rule following can be detected in the notes of *The Concept of Law* (Oxford, Clarendon Press, 1961) at 234, 249 in references to PI and indirectly through references to Peter Winch, *The Idea of a Social Science* (London, Routledge & Kegan Paul, 1958) relating to the internal aspect of rules and rule following at 242, 249. Winch's book takes an avowedly Wittgensteinian approach to developing a philosophical understanding of the nature of the social sciences, as distinct from that of the natural sciences, through a recognition of the need to embrace an internal appreciation of human practices in order to reach understanding of them. This rests on a view of language, expressed at 123 in a sentence which echoes PI §7: "To give an account of a meaning of a word is to describe how it is used; and to describe how it is used is to describe the social intercourse into which it enters."

Ronald Dworkin's Right Answer Thesis has an apparently Wittgensteinian influence, to be detected in "Pragmatism, Right Answers, and True Banality" in Michael Brint and

William Weaver (eds.), *Pragmatism in Law and Society* (Boulder, CO, Westview Press, 1991) at 360, 362 ("the key to meaning is use"), 380. This is discussed in Louis Wolcher, "Ronald Dworkin's Right Answers Thesis through the Lens of Wittgenstein" (1997) 29 *Rutgers Law Journal* 43, in which further references to Wittgenstein in Dworkin's work are provided at 48 n12. As previously mentioned in ch. 5, Wolcher is not convinced that Dworkin has rigorously responded to Wittgenstein's ideas, and he suggests at 48 that Dworkin's approach is "the fulfilment of Wittgenstein's sad prophecy that '[t]he seed I'm most likely to sow is a certain jargon.' "

Dennis Patterson (ed.), *Wittgenstein and Legal Theory* (Boulder, CO, Westview Press, 1992) is a useful anthology of essays on Wittgenstein and law, most of which were previously published in a special issue of (1990) 3 *Canadian Journal of Law and Jurisprudence*. The Proceedings of the 12th International Wittgenstein Symposium 1987 published as Ota Weinberger, Peter Koller and Alfred Schramm (eds.), *Philosophy of Law, Politics, and Society* (Vienna, Hölder-Pichler-Tempsky, 1988) contain a contribution by Enrico Pattaro, "On the Nature of Legal Science" at 202 and a number of contributions in part 3 on Wittgenstein's concept of a rule and the theory of meaning.

Books dealing with law and language and containing discussions of Wittgenstein include Andrei Marmor, *Interpretation and Legal Theory* (Oxford, Clarendon Press, 1992); Brian Bix, *Law, Language, and Legal Determinacy* (Oxford, Clarendon Press, 1993); Nicos Stavropoulos, *Objectivity in Law* (Oxford, Clarendon Press, 1996); and, Timothy Endicott, *Vagueness in Law* (Oxford, OUP, 2000). These authors seek to deal with Wittgenstein in their different ways but none develops a distinctively Wittgensteinian approach.

The collected essays of Thomas Morawetz, *Law's Premises, Law's Promise: Jurisprudence after Wittgenstein* (Aldershot, Ashgate, 2000), do embrace a Wittgensteinian approach. Morawetz sees a focus on the practice of the self-reflective insider as an antidote to false theoretical oppositions. Dennis Patterson, *Law and Truth* (New York, NY, OUP, 1996) also draws on Wittgenstein to detract established legal theory and to advance a jurisprudential concern for the truth of legal propositions based on the practice of legal argument. Patterson's views are clarified further in his contribution to a symposium on his book, "*Law and Truth*: Replies to Critics" (1997) 50 *SMU Law Review* 1563, and in "On Rhetoric and Truth: A Reply to Neil Duxbury" (2000) 13 *Ratio Juris* 216—responding to Neil Duxbury, "Truth as Rhetoric" (1999) 12 *Ratio Juris* 116. Patterson accepts much of the approach to US constitutional law found in Philip Bobbitt, *Constitutional Interpretation* (Oxford, Blackwell, 1991). This book is the subject of a symposium in (1994) 72 *Texas Law Review*. Among other contributions, the exchange between Steven Winter and Dennis Patterson (Steven Winter, "The Constitution of Conscience" at 1805; Dennis Patterson, "Wittgenstein and Constitutional Theory" at 1837; Steven Winter, "One Size Fits All" at 1857) and the response by Philip Bobbitt, "Reflections Inspired by My Critics" at 1869, demonstrate the colourful possibilities of bringing together Wittgenstein and the Constitution.

A Wittgensteinian approach to the doctrine of the Rule of Law is to be found in Margaret Jane Radin, "Reconsidering the Rule of Law" (1989) 69 *Boston University Law Review* 781 (also to be found in Patterson (ed.)). Radin attempts to reinterpret the doctrine by finding law in the practice of judges making moral choices for the good of society. Bruce Ackerman, "Four Questions for Legal Theory" in J Roland Pennock and John Chapman (eds.), *Nomos XXII: Property* (New York, NY, New York University Press, 1980), has acknowledged a Wittgensteininan influence on his analysis of the constitutional protection of property in terms of how lawyers use property talk. In proposing a distinction between different forms of property talk, Ackerman considers that Wittgensteinian methods are superior to those of ordinary language philosophy.

Charles Yablon, "Law and Metaphysics" (1987) 96 *Yale Law Journal* 613 provides a review of Kripke's book (above n. 4). This has been influential in setting out a sceptical Wittgensteinian position on rule following in law. Yablon in fact regards the implications of Kripke's argument for law to leave open the possibility of legal determinacy in certain cases but insists that such determinacy requires us to acknowledge the social, cooperative and political aspects of legal rule following, and in turn the significance of legal argument—how "lawyers can use language to change language" (at 635). In responding to Yablon's essay, Scott Landers, "Wittgenstein, Realism, and CLS" (1990) 9 *Law and Philosophy* 177, suggests that both Kripke and Yablon have erred in seeing Wittgenstein providing a solution to the sceptical problem. Landers considers that Wittgenstein saw the problem as a spurious one which indicated our misunderstanding of rules. At the heart of this misunderstanding, according to Landers, is seeing a rule as a form of words and hence relating rule indeterminacy to linguistic indeterminacy. Instead, legal indeterminacy should be viewed as caused by indeterminacy in social practices; and the task of clarifying the nature of legal rules should be approached by jettisoning assumptions that legal rules conform to a model of scientific rules.

More generally, Ahilan Arulanantham, "Breaking the Rules: Wittgenstein and Legal Realism" (1998) 107 *Yale Law Journal* 1853, surveys two groups of legal theorists taking a sceptical and non-sceptical approach respectively in understanding Wittgenstein on rule following (Yablon is among the former group). Employing the term as used in the tradition of American Legal Realism, Arulanantham dubs these groups the realists and anti-realists. He concludes that the anti-realists are correct in their interpretation of Wittgenstein in PI as adopting a position against the indeterminacy of rules. However, he regards Wittgenstein's position as being based on the features of rule following in everyday language and mathematics, and because these features are not present in the legal context Arulanantham considers that the anti-realists by winning an irrelevant battle have handed a surprise victory to the realists. The key differences are the existence of substantial disagreement in law, a different kind of certainty applying for the legal field, and the legal need for justification. In sketching how the anti-realists might regroup to provide a distinctively legal theory of decision making drawing on Wittgenstein's insights, Arulanantham significantly includes the requirement that such a theory should not rely on rules.

I offer three comments drawing on this survey of work on Wittgenstein and law. First, it confirms the centrality of Wittgenstein's position on rule following (above n. 4) as a means of developing a Wittgensteinian perspective on law.

Secondly, it raises the suspicion that the radical edge of some of Wittgenstein's insights have been blunted by partial representations of his ideas incorporated in the author's preferred theoretical model. This point is not restricted to those who take a more indirect approach to Wittgenstein's thinking (as in Wolcher's criticism of Dworkin). Patterson's concern to provide a full-blooded Wittgensteinian approach to law is still subsumed within his theoretical model of the truth of legal propositions. In his reply to Duxbury's suggestion that truth plays an unconvincing role in his model, Patterson relies on the distinction between the means for establishing the truth of legal propositions (the forms of legal argument) and the truth of the proposition. Yet Patterson does not demonstrate that from forms of argument that are successful we derive conclusions in terms of *truth*.

Indeed his emphasis in *Law and Truth* on the roles of persuasion and commendation in legal argument would suggest otherwise. (For broader discussion of this subject, see Anna Pintore, *Law without Truth* (Liverpool, Deborah Charles Publications, 2000).) Duxbury's criticism of Patterson's use of "truth" raises more obliquely Wolcher's criticism of Dworkin's use of "right answer" from a radically Wittgensteinian perspective that such terms are redundant theoretical baggage which obscures our proper description of, or participation in, the practice which we are seeking to understand. Of course, taking such a radical Wittgensteinian position might make life uncomfortable for theorists generally, as Paul Johnston has sought to show in relation to moral philosophy, *The Contradictions of Modern Moral Philosophy: Ethics after Wittgenstein* (London, Routledge, 1999).

Thirdly, there is a strong convergence among those taking Wittgenstein in different directions in relation to law on deriving from his insights an emphasis on the significance of law as a social practice. This is not to say that Wittgenstein has himself provided illumination on the particular significance of law as a social practice. The lack of a perspective from Wittgenstein on this substantive matter perhaps explains the continuing diversity of Wittgensteinian perspectives on law.

8

An Annex on Realism

THERE IS ANOTHER major influence affecting the way the role of language is considered in legal theory, which I want to briefly examine. Confusingly for those already acquainted with the realist movements in legal theory (American and Scandinavian) this is also referred to as realism. This form of realism, which we might distinguish as general philosophical realism, or as it is sometimes more narrowly found, metaphysical realism, differs from the two localised movements in legal theory which in their own ways espouse the realistic. In this respect, the observable conduct of the courts for the American Realists and the perceivable psychological phenomena for the Scandinavian Realists stand in juxtaposition to the subject matter of the realism I wish to consider here, particularly in its metaphysical form. For these two legal movements are anything but metaphysical in their approach, and they differ from even the less extreme versions of philosophical realism, which seek a reality that is not found in a realistic portrayal of human conduct, but one that lies beneath the surface of our daily business.[1]

In terms of an approach to language this realism takes words to be capable of referring to an underlying reality that we may not readily grasp. The confusion of language (and hence the confused state of our understanding) lies in the misrepresentation of reality through using words to portray our partial glimpses and skewed perspectives on a reality that our language could portray, if only we had properly comprehended it. Disagreement over the meaning of words is accordingly regarded not as arising out of differing expressions of subjective or relativistic viewpoints, but as based on errors (on one side at least) in comprehending the reality that those words should properly convey.

The contrast between realism in this sense and the Wittgensteinian approach considered in the previous chapter would at first sight seem absolute. If the approach of Wittgenstein is characterised as refining our understanding by seeking to clarify the meaning of words through a more acute grasp of the social practices which those words express, realism appears to stand this process on its head. We are supposed to refine our understanding of our social practices (and anything else besides) by clarifying our meaning of words in relation to a reality that may not be fully evident in the social practices we observe. However, I want to suggest that realism suffers from a defect it shares in common with the Wittgensteinian approach.

---

[1] For further discussion, see the material referred to in the Endnote.

The principal criticism I offered against Wittgenstein's approach to language was that his work was incomplete. Not simply that it was unfinished like a great symphony whose virtues could be detected in the parts that had been composed: my charge was that the incomplete nature of Wittgenstein's language games rendered them incapable of fulfilling the function he had given them. If we are to rely on language games to provide us with understanding then there must be some stability in the relationship between the practice of the game and the subject matter we hope to understand. If, however, as I argued, the incomplete nature of the language game rendered it arbitrary as to how it might be conducted in relation to its subject matter, then it would be incapable of providing us with illumination of the subject matter (though it might express one of a number of ways of regarding it). The essential incompleteness of Wittgenstein's language games was linked in my argument to the impossibility of treating a language game as discrete, as Wittgenstein purported to do. Any language game might bump up against practices which fell outside its own organised way of handling things. The possibility of a general remedy against this defect is ruled out by the recognition that the limitations of human experience render it impossible to devise either a comprehensive language game that could take in every possible aspect of human experience, or a limited language game whose potential interfaces could be secured against further aspects of human experience.

This criticism might seem to point the way towards realism. For if the basic failing we have identified is an attempt to construct understanding out of incomplete human experience, then are we not bound to recognise that such reality as exists must lie beyond the range of our immediate limited experience?

Unfortunately for the realists, the very spur to embracing realism inflicts a fatal gash upon their endeavours. For even if we acknowledge that there lies a reality beyond our immediate human experiences, the very limitations on our human experience as much as they suggest a reality beyond must equally signify our failure to fully grasp it. It is in this extremely simple acknowledgment of the limitations of human experience that the apparently diverse theories relying on empirical observation of social practice and the gaining of metaphysical insight are seen to share a common denominator. For any reality (metaphysical or otherwise) that might exist is only meaningful to humans insofar as they are capable of having some sort of experience of it. The reality of the argument on this page is meaningless for any earthworm wriggling its way across it, however you may wish to characterise the nature of the argument. The point about the limitations of human experience then is that this affects our capacity to grasp reality—whether we view that reality as empirical or metaphysical. (One might even suggest that we can only propose these conflicting models for reality because our grasp of reality is limited.) However, there is one further aspect of the limitations of human experience that we need to clarify in considering the way we depict our understanding in our use of language.

I criticised Wittgenstein's language games as incomplete rather than unfinished. This indicates that we can not regard the acquisition of understanding by playing language games as a cumulative enterprise, such that although our language game is not complete it could be relied upon to provide us with understanding as far as it went. But surely one can easily think of the cumulative gaining of understanding such that the incompleteness of our understanding does not invalidate the partial knowledge we have acquired? A child may master the two times table, and the child's acquisition of this understanding is not any the less sound because he or she has not yet progressed to the eight times table.

The problem in the case of Wittgenstein's language game was a vulnerability to bumping up against other aspects of human experience such that it could not be treated as a discrete game. But why should this be significant? The significance lies in the difference between isolating a particular section of human experience (what has conventionally been referred to as multiplying the numbers 1 to 12 by 2 in the base 10), and isolating the words that are used to identify it from any further experience.

Let us recall something observed in chapter 6, in our general survey of the uses of words. Even in the case of a word that could be used as a label to identify two different things, (e.g., "mother" for birth-mother and adoptive-mother), our experience of each of these two things could provide us respectively with some understanding of each. So long as we associated our understanding of each with a strict account of what we had so far experienced, we could regard our understanding as being cumulative in nature—the more we experienced, the more we understood. Error would only creep in, so that our prior understanding had to be revised in the light of understanding derived from our later experience, if instead of relying strictly on what we had experienced so far, we misunderstood our limited experience as the totality of possible experience, or added to what we had experienced an imaginary supplement to broaden our understanding. Such errors may be commonplace but the point is that where we are focusing our attention on a segment of *experience* there is no barrier in principle against isolating this experience and taking our understanding of it as complete *as far as it goes*. To understand the two times table in this sense is precisely to have such limited understanding as is possible from the experience of being able to multiply the numbers 1 to 12 by 2 in the base 10.

We can not, however, so isolate our words. The words may apply to different things, to different experiences of the same thing, and even to something we might experience in the future that through some sort of affinity with our earlier experience(s) we would be prepared to employ the words to label. So with "the two times table", it appears that the impact of decimilisation has led to "the two times table" nowadays sometimes being satisfied by multiplying the numbers 1 to 10 by 2.

The language game of "the two times table" can not then provide us with understanding precisely because it can not be isolated from other possible opportunities for the use of that phrase until the point is reached where all further human experience has been excluded or is catalogued and classified in a comprehensive set of language games. Short of this point any purported under-standing derived from the language game may be incomplete and misleading. On other hand, the experience of the two times table at a particular epoch in primary school education can be treated as discrete, and it is possible to acquire a sound understanding of that limited experience as far as it goes.

This validation of partial understanding by treating it as just an understand-ing circumscribed by the limitations of the experience we have gained is as awk-ward for the realist as it is for Wittgenstein. Wittgenstein's problem in relying on the language game rather than the experience is that the full significance of the words used in one language game can not be understood until the language games of other possible experiences have been played.[2] Similarly, if there lies a metaphysical reality of the two times table beyond our limited temporal experi-ence of a collection of mathematical propositions conveniently collected for the education of primary school children, then understanding of it must be different in kind from the modest understanding limited by that primary school experi-ence. It would amount to a reality that transcended and hence could be used to evaluate individuals' limited understanding gained from their own experiences of primary school education. Without the comprehensive experience of all pos-sible mathematical education, how could anybody be in a position to either assert their comprehension of the realist conception of the two times table, or to bring it to bear as a higher reality by which to judge an individual's partial understanding of the two times table as being in some way deficient?

The appeal of the realist position lies in the recognition that our understand-ing of a thing does sometimes increase with our increased experience of that thing—and the corollary—that understanding built upon a limited experience of something can be erroneous. However, the space for something more real if created in this way is a space which can not be filled without filling all spaces, i.e. being in a position to account for all human experience. This brings us back to exactly the position needed to be achieved by Wittgenstein's language games.

The point can be demonstrated by example. Take the idea of death, used by Michael Moore to argue for metaphysical realism in pointing out that more primitive conceptions of death were inadequate because the limited medical experience of that time was unable to account for modern methods of resusci-

---

[2] I think this point also underlies the competing sceptical and non-sceptical readings of Wittgenstein, referred to at n. 4 of ch. 7. The difference between "plus two" and Kripke's "quus two" as *experiences* is clear cut—in the former you carry on regularly adding two to provide a series of even numbers commencing with 2 and in the latter when you reach 1000 you change to adding four. You experience a different result in the respective series after 1000: 1002 or 1004. The problem is that if I am merely relying on the language game of "plus two" and I have not yet experienced counting beyond 1000, there is nothing to tell me what the correct number in the series beyond 1000 is, until both possible experiences have been classified in or out of the language game being played. The reason why Kripke's quus seems counterintuitive as a possiblity is, I suspect, because we are capable of extrapolating a series of potential experiences in a regular manner (and we are taught in a way that encourages this ability), and so this produces a presumptive classification for what experiences will be included in our language game of "plus two". Such an account relies on the significance of experience, and does not work in reliance on the use of words alone.

tation, which have effectively changed our understanding of death.[3] Moore argues that it is our understanding that has changed but all along there has been a constant reality of death, which has not altered through our changing levels of understanding and which can be employed to reveal the inadequacies of particular temporal stages of our understanding.

Two comments need to be made on this argument for metaphysical realism. First, the understanding at the primitive level is only erroneous to the extent that it indulges in one of the two errors noted above: either it falsely misrepresents the partial understanding as a totality; or, it supplements experience with imagination. Instead of deriving an authoritative conception of death from their limited experiences of it, our ancestors may have been content to assert an understanding bounded by their limited experience. If they had modestly claimed in such and such circumstances within our experience it is not possible to restore the patient to a living condition (regain a heart beat, restart breathing), their understanding could not have been faulted. Secondly, supposing that our medical understanding advances, if we wish to represent that as having a clear understanding of death, that itself will be misleading if it prevents us from recounting the experiences and level of understanding that applied in primitive times.[4]

These two points combine to require of any advance in understanding that it is capable not only of expressing the higher level of understanding reached but also from that position it is capable of accounting properly for the lower level of understanding (as well as the errors that may have accompanied it). The same point can be made more prosaically in relation to Plato's heavenly Idea of a chair.[5] Even if we acquire that level of enlightenment and from it are able to discern what amongst our temporal furniture should properly be graced with the title "chair", we still need words to apply to the rejected items that we have had the experience of actually sitting upon.

The requirement made of realism to account for all human experience is two-edged. Not only must it be capable of accommodating all past experience but also it must ensure that the purported realism of today is not itself rendered primitive by the advances in our experience tomorrow. Until we are capable of expressing all possible human experience, as humans we cannot invoke realism

[3] Michael Moore, "A Natural Law Theory of Interpretation" (1985) 58 *Southern California Law Review* 277 at 293–4, 297–300, 308–9, 322–8, 332, 382, discussed in Brian Bix, *Law, Language, and Legal Determinacy* (Oxford, Clarendon Press, 1993) 140–6.

[4] Significantly, Moore above n. 3 at 293–4, 297–8, 322, is concerned to prevent more primitive conventional notions of death hindering advances in medical knowledge, and so wishes to rule that the more primitive notions of death were wrong, but is not concerned to leave the primitives with an adequate language to account for their experiences.

[5] Despite there having been some controversy over whether Plato recognised Ideas of manufactured objects (see Sir David Ross, *Plato's Theory of Ideas* (Oxford, Clarendon Press, 1951) 171–5), there seems abundant evidence in favour, e.g. the Idea of bed is discussed in *Republic* X.i–ii, in distinguishing the work of the craftsman which resembles the Idea of bed, and the work of the artist which imitates the bed made by the craftsman.

to assist our understanding but rather need to admit the limitations on it.[6] Michael Moore might have selected a different example to support his case, though it is difficult to imagine a better example than death to bring home the point.

ENDNOTE

Hilary Putnam, *Realism with a Human Face* (Cambridge, MA, Harvard University Press, 1990), proposes a form of realism which is not metaphysical (loosely speaking, Putnam's "internal realism" replaces metaphysics with pragmatism) as a means of securing the values of objectivity and truth against philosophical scepticism. Susan Haack's "innocent realism", found in ch. 9 of her *Manifesto of a Passionate Moderate: Unfashionable Essays* (Chicago, University of Chicago Press, 1998), is discussed sympathetically in ch. 8 of William Twining, *Globalisation and Legal Theory* (London, Butterworths, 2000).

For helpful discussion of the difference between what I refer to as legal realism and philosophical realism, and what he refers to as Legal Realism and legal realism, see Michael Moore, "The Interpretive Turn in Modern Theory: A Turn for the Worse?" (1989) 41 *Stanford Law Review* 871, also found as ch. 10 of *Educating Oneself in Public* (New York, NY, OUP, 2000). For an early recognition of the distinction, see Roscoe Pound, "The Call for a Realist Jurisprudence" (1931) 44 *Harvard Law Review* 697 at 697.

Moore's book, which also includes his essay discussed in ch. 5 above, promotes in a spirited and sophisticated manner Moore's metaphysical realism. For a variety of examples of works adopting a realist position in legal theory, see: Robert George, *Making Men Moral: Civil Liberties and Public Morality* (Oxford, Clarendon Press, 1993); Bruce Anderson, *"Discovery" in Legal Decision-Making* (Dordrecht, Kluwer, 1996) (an illuminating discussion of the approach taken by Anderson is provided by Patrick Brennan, "Discovering the Archimedean Element in (Judicial) Judgment" (1998) 17 *Law and Philosophy* 177); Nicos Stavropoulos, *Objectivity in Law* (Oxford, Clarendon Press, 1996); James Penner, *The Idea of Property in Law* (Oxford, Clarendon Press, 1997). An ambitious form of realism drawing on particularism which seeks to bridge the gap with legal realism is to be found in David Jabbari, "Reason, Cause and Principle in Law: The Normativity of Context" (1999) 19 *Oxford Journal of Legal Studies* 203, and "Radical Particularism: A Natural Law of Context" (1999) 50 *Northern Ireland Legal Quarterly* 454.

Doubts about taking a realist position on statutory interpretation are expressed by Dennis Patterson in his exchange with David Brink: Dennis Patterson, "Realist Semantics and Legal Theory" (1989) 2 *Canadian Journal of Law and Jurisprudence* 175; David Brink, "Semantics and Legal Interpretation (Further Thoughts)" (1989) 2 *Canadian Journal of Law and Jurisprudence* 181; Dennis Patterson, "What Was Realism?: A Reply to David Brink" (1989) 2 *Canadian Journal of Law and Jurisprudence* 193.

---

[6] Moore, above n. 3 at 308, 332 n. 92, in talking of "temporary approximations" and avoiding definitions of "the basic concept of death", gives some indication of his awareness of these limitations.

Andrei Marmor, "An Essay on The Objectivity of Law" in Brian Bix (ed.), *Analyzing Law: New Essays in Legal Theory* (Oxford, Clarendon Press, 1998), argues for the possibility of recognising objectivity without embracing realism. Marmor takes a Wittgensteinian position on a pluralistic notion of truth played out in different language games, and in the course of his essay notes the modification that Putnam has made to his internal realism so making it more Wittgensteinian. Putnam's change of mind is recorded in his John Dewey Lectures, first published as "Sense, Nonsense and the Senses: An Inquiry into the Powers of the Human Mind" (1994) 91 *Journal of Philosophy* 445, and republished as part 1 of Hilary Putnam, *The Threefold Cord: Mind, Body, and World* (New York, NY, Columbia University Press, 1999). It is also related in Hilary Putnam, "Are Moral and Legal Values Made or Discovered?" (1995) 1 *Legal Theory* 1, and in his "Replies" (1995) 1 *Legal Theory* 69 responding to Brian Leiter, "The Middle Way" (1995) 1 *Legal Theory* 21, and Jules Coleman, "Truth and Objectivity in Law" (1995) 1 *Legal Theory* 33.

9

Words and Concepts

A BASIC ANALYSIS

THE PREOCCUPATION OF the previous three chapters has been with words, and our inability to rely on words to provide us with an understanding of the world in which we live. Words may be used to express our experience of the world but given the limitations of that experience and the absence of a systematic word coverage for all possible human experiences, we will be disappointed if we seek from the use of words either the expression of such understanding that might lie within human potential, or even the consistent expression of a flawed or incomplete human perspective on the world. We are not even capable of isolating in our language the variety of human perspectives. The underlying problem remains the same. The incompleteness of human experience means that the development of even a single perspective is always bound by words which are waiting to catch up with the next experience, rather than being capable of enunciating already the definitive manner in which each experience is expressed.

The fundamental problem caused by the limitations of human experience in the development of language expresses itself simply in the recognition that there are some things that may be encountered in the world which a particular word or phrase has not yet been determined as including or excluding. Alongside this obvious problem, we have come across three further problems besetting our use of language. The first relates to the use of a single term to identify more than one thing that we experience in the world. The cause of this may be the extension of the term from one thing to another where the second only contains a partial "family resemblance" to the first (Wittgenstein's "game"), or through the collectivisation by the one term of two things on the basis of what they do have in common without being concerned with other features that mark them apart (using "man" for male and female members of the human race). The particular problem arising here lies in the attempt to develop an idea of something to which that term relates. If we use the term "game" to refer to g_1, g_2, etc, we might through greater experience of it develop our understanding of g_1 but since we use "game" to refer to g_1 the slip is easily made into thinking that we are developing our understanding, or our idea, of a game. We noticed in chapter 7 that Wittgenstein himself made just this slippage between the term "game" and the idea (or concept) of a game.

A consistent development of our understanding would require us to separate our use of the term from the distinct understanding that we are acquiring of each of the things to which that term applies. Nevertheless, the tendency is often to speak as though we were acquiring a general idea of the term itself, which can only cause confusion since there is no constant subject of our experiences, from which our understanding is developing. The result is to produce a personal montage, of experiences of a selection of those things to which the term applies, and present this as our idea of. . . . As an exercise in word association this may be effective, but as an effort to communicate with any degree of precision or to acquire detailed understanding it is doomed. A more sinister outcome of this problem is when the increased understanding of one of the items to which the term applies is misrepresented as a general understanding of everything to which the term applies. The scope for this in misrepresenting understanding acquired through experience of the male human as an understanding of man, collectively applied to male and female members of the human race, has been pointed out often enough, but not too often to eradicate this source of error from legal reasoning.[1]

The second problem may arise even where there does exist a constant link between the term and the thing in the world to which it refers, so that there can be no confusion caused by taking our idea of x to be our idea of "x". It may also arise at a secondary level once we have distinguished which of a number of possible things we are taking our term to refer to. The problem arises when we mistake our partial understanding of x drawn from our limited experience of it, as the totality of understanding available, and so produce a rigid idea of x (or what "x" means) that prejudices us against developing our understanding of x through further experience of it. The third problem similarly arises when we supplement our partial understanding of x with an imaginary element to make good the defects in our understanding, which again precludes us from developing our understanding of it through further experience.

The potential for linguistic confusion sketched so far is enormous but should not be mistaken as a descent into total linguistic anarchy. The possibilities for confusion as analysed here are positioned on erroneous turns from the use of words to convey our understanding of things that we experience in the world. The analysis thus differs from Stanley Fish's turn off down the anti-formalist road, discussed in chapter 2. Communication may be effective just where these errors are avoided: where two parties are communicating on the basis of applying words to what they both have common experience of in the world. On a whole range of mundane matters this is easily accomplished, and given sufficient commonality of experience it may also be accomplished in a range of fairly sophisticated matters too. However, there is an additional layer of confusion that may beset our use of language which we have not directly confronted, and which is of particular significance to the practice (and theory) of law.

---

[1] See Caroline Forell and Donna Matthews, *A Law of Her Own: The Reasonable Woman as a Measure of Man* (New York, NY, New York University Press, 2000).

Our discussion so far has proceeded on the basis that our principal concern is to understand the world through an effective description of it. Certainly if this is not achievable then any attempt to legislate how the world is to be run is going to fall sooner or later at the initial hurdle: there will often be no clear understanding of what the legislator means. The additional layer of confusion occurs due to the fact that in our use of words we do not stop at our limited abilities to describe the world but blunder on regardless in attempts to decide how the world is to be run. In one sense this is not conceit on our part but necessity. Despite the fact that we may not know exactly what we are doing, the practicalities of life demand that something is decided, and that something is done.

If the fundamental problem in our attempts to use language to describe the world lies in the limitations imposed by the fact that we have not yet worked through all possible human experiences and generated an effective vocabulary to cover them, a parallel problem occurs with our attempts to use language to indicate how the world ought to be run, to work out how people should behave. We will use words to formulate our prescription of correct behaviour without yet having experienced and reached a decision on all the possible forms of conduct that we may wish to fall within or outside of that prescription. The root problem may be the same but it develops somewhat differently in the practical context of trying to issue instructions on how people should behave.

The basic difference arising out of the two practical contexts of using words, to describe the world or to run the world, can best be grasped by considering the relationships between words (terms), the subject matter to which they apply, and our ideas (concepts) of that subject matter which we use the same word to convey. This requires some concentration since we familiarly glide over the differences when we encounter, say, the letters b-o-o-k, between the word "book", the thing in the world that we call a book, and our idea of a book. I have considered elsewhere the problems this causes theorists in undertaking conceptual analysis.[2] My present concern is to show the practical difficulties arising in attempts to use words.

The underlying practical problems besetting someone who wishes to use words to communicate some description of the world is that misunderstanding may arise due to the fact that the words used have not been differentiated in their use to refer unequivocally to something or a limited group of things in the world, or it has not been clarified which of the possible things covered is being referred to, or it is not clear which aspects of the thing referred to as seen by the speaker are being conveyed. The solution to such misunderstandings is for greater communication by the speaker on the thing in the world he is attempting to describe. In principle, all these difficulties could be resolved, allowing for sufficient time and patience, and presuming that there is a commonality of

---

[2] "Concepts, Terms and Fields of Enquiry" (1998) 4 *Legal Theory* 187, which develops material from ch. I.3 of Andrew Halpin, *Rights and Law—Analysis and Theory* (Oxford, Hart Publishing, 1997).

experience between speaker and audience connecting to the thing being described. If this last condition is not satisfied then a second best type of communication may occur by finding as a channel of communication a common experience to which what the speaker is referring to can be compared. The extended dialogue may even result in the speaker acknowledging that he himself misunderstood what he was referring to.

All this is possible because as a starting point we take the thing in the world that the speaker is attempting to describe, and the speaker can return to this in the extended dialogue with his audience as a means of refining and clarifying his use of words through which he attempts to describe it.

The underlying practical problems besetting someone who wishes to use words to issue an instruction on some aspect of how the world is to be run do not arise solely from the problems of communication considered above. There is in addition to the need for communication of what the speaker may be describing, the need for the instruction to be carried out. In practical terms the second need may actually overtake the first. A common reason for issuing an instruction is to pass on the responsibility for getting something done. The opportunity for relaxed discussion with the speaker on this occasion may not be available. Moreover, the speaker may not have decided beforehand what the instruction is to refer to in terms of the result to be performed. Instead the speaker may have been conscious only of there being a need to do something about a particular issue with a vague sense of the sort of way it might be dealt with.

Consider an instruction from an employer to a cook to prepare dinner for four. It would of course be possible for the cook to return at each point of implementing the instruction to obtain further details of the employer's wishes. What vegetables? How are these vegetables to be prepared? What quantity should be provided? At some point the employer's exasperation is likely to surface in a pointed remark indicating that if she had wanted to sort out all the details of the dinner herself she would not have bothered employing a cook.

Suppose then that the cook goes ahead without bothering the employer for further instructions. The employer may be pleased with the cook's efforts or be displeased, but praise or criticism is not going to take the form of a discussion as to what the employer meant by "dinner". (I assume we are not dealing with a marginal case which would amount to misunderstanding the instruction because the cook is not addressing the issue that the instruction raises: for example, he provides courses of toast and marmalade and breakfast cereal for dinner.) It is going to take the form of an evaluation of how the cook's choice and its manner of execution is to be regarded from one or more external criteria of taste. The important point is that even if there were an extended debate on the merits of the dinner the cook had provided it would be impossible to conduct this argument on the basis of deciding what the employer had meant by her instruction. The cook and employer, or different diners at the table, would have to argue it out by supplying arguments for their own favoured standards of taste. The words used by the employer did not refer to something that existed in the world by reference to which these arguments could, even in principle, be settled. Rather, the words used by the employer referred to the idea of dinner, which the efforts of the cook had to render as something in the world which could be experienced.

I am not suggesting that every time an instruction is issued this characteristic is present. We could easily imagine a precise instruction, perhaps from the chef to the sous-chef stating what quantity of what vegetable was to be cooked in what manner for exactly what length of time. In this example, what the words can be taken to describe, as something existing in the world, is precisely what is required by the instruction. My point is that this further characteristic in our use of words may be present in situations involving the giving of an instruction, which is not present in the mere making of a description.

What label to give this further characteristic is problematic because at this stage I do not want to use any label with connotations that may narrow the characteristic to a particular sort of context. The context of an instruction we have just examined provides us with a characteristic of requiring the person addressed to decide what to do in order to get something done that is a way of satisfying the need raised by the issue to be found in the idea that the instruction contains. This participatory determination of what he is being required to do by the person addressed is something we have encountered before in chapter 4 when discussing the principles or standards on which judicial review is based. It was suggested there that, for example, the requirement that a power should be exercised in accordance with standards of reasonableness involves a deliberative endeavour rather than a mere communicative requirement.

Although the setting of an instruction, or some other requirement such as a legal norm, readily provides the impetus for the person addressed to sort out what he thinks is required in order to behave in compliance with the instruction or norm, I do not think that this characteristic of language is necessarily restricted to contexts where some requirement is made of the person responding to the words used. It might be possible for the need for, what we might in general call, a reflective participatory response, to arise in the word(s) used without there existing some further requirement to act. Some words express ideas that seem to invite a reflective participatory response, whether or not we are required to behave in accordance with that response. For example, the idea of justice may provoke such a response from us even if we wish only to enquire what justice is as a philosophical exercise. Words which deal with aesthetic appreciation also seem to have this characteristic. It would take us beyond our immediate concerns with legal reasoning to investigate this characteristic of language fully. However, in order to address those concerns, it may be helpful to provide a general analysis of the different relationships between words, the subject matter to which they apply, and ideas which words may convey, in the sort of situations we have been considering. I shall then examine in some detail the ways in which legal concepts may be recognised as possessing the characteristic we have been discussing.

If we take w to be a word (such as "book") which can be used both to identify something in the world (which we shall refer to as x, y, or z) and to express an idea of what is understood of that thing so identified, then the following relationships are possible.

where w identifies $x/y/z$
w –identify– x –understood as– w (idea of x)
w –identify– y –understood as– w (idea of y)
w –identify– z –understood as– w (idea of z)
note that an idea of $x/y/z$ referred to as w is possible but that a coherent idea of w is impossible

where w identifies x
w –identify– x –understood as– w (idea of x)$_1$
w –identify– x –understood as– w (idea of x)$_2$
w –identify– x –understood as– w (idea of x)$_3$
note that if w identifies x alone an idea of w becomes coherent though strictly speaking we are referring to an idea of what w means or identifies
note also if we talk loosely of an idea of w here that there may similarly be a number of such ideas as when we use the stricter expression w (idea of x)$_1$, etc

However, where w expresses an idea, we need to distinguish the following:

(1) w is an idea of $x/y/z$, as above
(2) w is an idea inviting a participatory response so as to identify $x/y/z$

CONCEPTS REQUIRING A PARTICIPATORY RESPONSE

In this section I want to reinforce the analysis offered above by briefly considering four ways in which it can be recognised that ideas, or concepts, are used in the law in a way which exhibits the characteristic we have been discusssing. The role of such concepts is not to identify by way of description something in the world that the law requires to be done, but requires a reflective participatory response in ascertaining what is required to be done. This provides a source of flexibility to certain legal concepts. A significant consequence of this flexibility in the legal context is that if such a concept appears in a law requiring behaviour by D, then there may be a material differences between how D responds to the invitation to consider how he should behave and the subsequent response by a particular judge in determining what behaviour is considered appropriate; as well as between the responses of different judges.

Determinationes of General Concepts

The first way of looking at this characteristic is found in Aquinas's notion of *determinatio*. The *determinatio* of a general concept amounts to a specific instantiation of it. Noting the variety of possible *determinationes* for a general concept has been used as an argument to support Natural Law against the criticism that the purported general principles of Natural Law are contradicted by the conflicting practices found in different cultures: despite the variety, each *determinatio* is seen as an outworking of the general concept found in the Natural Law principle.[3]

A clear explanation of Aquinas's notion is provided by John Finnis:[4]

> "*Determinatio* is best clarified by Aquinas' own analogy with architecture. The general idea or form of a dwelling-house (or a hospital), and the general ideas of a door and a doorknob (or a labour ward), must be made determinate as this particular design and house (or hospital), door, doorknob, etc.; otherwise nothing will be built. The specifications which the architect or designer decides upon are certainly derived from and shaped by the primary general idea, e.g. the commission to design a dwelling-house (or maternity hospital). But the specifications decided upon could reasonably have been rather different in many (even in every) dimension and aspect, and require of the designer a multitude of decisions which could reasonably have been more or less different."

It is evident from this explanation that a *determinatio* involves more than selecting something that is described by the general concept. Finnis makes it clear that the participation of the architect is required in working out what *determinatio* to provide. His explanation also reveals that the general idea is itself something more than an idea of something. It is used in a way that requires the person addressed to decide what to do in order to get something done, which is a way of satisfying the need raised by the issue to be found in the idea. In Finnis's words, the general idea amounts to a "commission to design a dwelling-house (or maternity hospital)".

If Aquinas's use of *determinatio* as part of an argument to support the credibility of general principles of Natural Law is sound, then each *determinatio* must express the value to be found in the general concept located in the natural law principle. The immutable natural law value is instantiated in each *determinatio*, whatever the variation due to local circumstances and the decisions made by those implementing the natural law principle in those circumstances. This notion of a *determinatio* provides a very weak scope to the reflective participatory response. The merits of the *determinatio* are to be judged not by external criteria (as was the cook's dinner) but by a standard found within the general idea itself. The plausibility of this argument is debatable. One would have to take a view on how to identify the immutable value, and how to recognise its instantiation in different *determinationes*. Most difficult of all would be the task of resolving a dispute between two contradictory opinions on what the general principle of Natural Law required on a specific occasion.

---

[3] See Thomas Aquinas, *Summa Theologiae* I–II q.95 a.2 ad 3; John Finnis, *Natural Law and Natural Rights* (Oxford, Clarendon Press, 1980) 284–9, 380.

[4] John Finnis, *Aquinas* (Oxford, Clarendon Press, 1998) 267.

A stronger scope to the reflective participatory response would be a weaker argument for Natural Law, for it would leave the general concepts of Natural Law as expressions of issues needing resolution (e.g., how to respect the dignity of each human being[5]) without providing the values with which a reflective participatory response could be made. The values would have to be sought elsewhere, and it may seem that this is a more realistic account of what has happened as a matter of historical record when the principles of Natural Law have been invoked to support contradictory positions.[6]

However, we need not enter the debate over Natural Law in order to deal with the broader matter that concerns us here. It is clear that a *determinatio* of a general concept with a strong reflective participatory response may be found in legal reasoning. Indeed Finnis himself acknowledges after introducing Aquinas's notion:[7]

> "True, the law is not to be regarded as unchangeable or irreformable; the reasoning supporting a *determinatio* will quite often prove to have been less than perfect; or circumstances may have changed; and in such cases the law should be altered by appropriate means."

The evaluation of the reasoning supporting the *determinatio* assumes one or more criteria that goes beyond the production of the *determinatio* merely in terms of what the general concept itself prescribes. In that case we would require not reform of or a change of *determinatio* but an acknowledgment that the purported *determinatio* was not a valid instantiation of the general concept. The argument over the merits of the *determinatio* as opposed to an argument over whether we have a valid *determinatio* is then dependent on the selection of some further standard by which the evaluation is to be conducted. We might, for example, consider the commission to design a maternity hospital and criticise the particular design produced, not on the grounds that it does not amount to a maternity hospital but on the grounds that it contains no wheelchair ramps. We apply as our evaluative standard equality of access for the disabled. Even if we focus our evaluation on aspects of the design that relate more directly to the general idea of a maternity hospital, and consider the presence or absence of particular facilities (e.g., a birthing pool) this can not be done by invoking the general idea. We need to summon further evaluative criteria from our favoured view of appropriate methods of delivery, freedom of choice, etc.

---

[5] For clarification of the issues here, see David Feldman, "Human Dignity as a Legal Value—Part I" [1999] *Public Law* 682; "Human Dignity as a Legal Value—Part II" [2000] *Public Law* 61.

[6] The view that the role of Natural Law is to raise questions is taken to the extreme by Costas Douzinas, *The End of Human Rights* (Oxford, Hart Publishing, 2000). The more conventional view that there is a set of Natural Law values whose instantiations can be determined for any situation arising in the world ineluctably embraces metaphysical realism, considered in ch. 8 above.

[7] Above n. 4, at 271.

Instantiation of Abstract Concepts

The second way of looking at the characteristic of requiring a reflective partici-patory response in legal concepts involves the recognition of abstract concepts and their instantiation. It may well be that the general concept of which a *deter-minatio* is made is expressed in the abstract, and I do not mean to suggest that the different ways of portraying this characteristic are mutually exclusive. Yet there is a feature of the use of abstract concepts which does deserve separate dis-cussion. Whereas different *determinationes* of a general concept can be regarded as competing with each other, there is a way of using an abstract concept where the competition is not between different possible instantiations of it but betweeen a potential instantiation and other factors that may oppose the recog-nition of the instantiation in a particular concrete situation.

This abstract quality of concepts is widely recognised in the more particular context of discussing rights. Human rights are notoriously abstract in this sense, even to the point that the factors that may oppose the instantiation of one right amount to factors that are regarded as supporting the instantiation of a differ-ent right, resulting in a balancing exercise between competing rights. Any abstract right may be regarded as containing an abstract concept. The right to free speech contains the concept of free speech. Since I have dealt with the nature and practice of abstract rights at length elsewhere,[8] I shall restrict myself here to drawing attention to the key features of abstract concepts and their instantia-tion.

One point that it is important to stress is the nature of the abstract quality we are considering, for it is possible to talk of abstract concepts in two quite differ-ent senses.[9] The crucial difference lies in the relationship between the abstract quality and concrete instantiations of it. In one sense of abstract, an abstract concept would distil in a pure form the quality that is to be found in all concrete instantiations of that concept. The argument for Natural Law considered above relied on general concepts having an abstract quality in this sense. In the other sense of abstract, the abstract quality of the concept divorces it from practical considerations that are relevant to determining whether a concrete instantiation will occur. It is in this latter sense that the law commonly recognises abstract rights, or concepts, without yet determining whether a potential concrete instantiation will be given legal recognition.

That the process of determining whether a particular concrete instantiation of an abstract legal concept will be recognised requires a reflective participatory response should be evident once we have grasped the nature of these abstract concepts. The enunciation of the abstract concept in itself does not determine which behaviour will be required. It does present an issue which must be taken into consideration by the person addressed (or the tribunal judging that person's

[8] *Rights and Law* above n. 2, chs. V & VI. See in particular 120–3, 159–74.
[9] See *Oxford English Dictionary* entries A.4 and B.3 for "abstract".

conduct) alongside competing factors, in deciding how exactly to behave in a way which gives such respect to that issue as is regarded appropriate in the circumstances. The concepts of free speech, or duty of care,[10] pose questions which require us to identify exactly what respect we need to pay to the speech of others, what care we owe our neighbour. They do not themselves identify what conduct is required.

Of course, within a particular culture there may be conventionally accepted instantiations of such abstract concepts.[11] Some may wish to argue that there are some instantiations which should be universally accepted as applicable to the whole human race. Even allowing for some reclaiming of the abstract territory of these concepts by generally accepted instantiations of them, the residual abstract quality can be seen in areas that are still contested. Moreover, the underlying abstract nature of these concepts may surge back over territory once considered reclaimed to open up the issue that the concept requires to be addressed. Commentators on the English law of negligence,[12] or recklessness in the English criminal law,[13] in recent years have frequently had their understanding washed away by the force of this incoming tide.

The argument over the merits of a particular instantiation of an abstract concept, as with an argument over a *determinatio*, is then dependent on the selection of some further standard by which the evaluation of the issue raised by the abstract concept together with competing factors is to be conducted. The need to involve criteria external to the concept itself is particularly evident in consideration of abstract concepts in the ECHR which are subjected to a margin of appreciation,[14] or the abstract concepts of EU law subjected to a principle of proportionality.[15]

Resolution of Essentially Contestable Concepts

A third way of looking at the characteristic of requiring a reflective participatory response in legal concepts is to utilise WB Gallie's notion of an essentially

---

[10] *Rights and Law* above n. 2, ch. VI.2–3.

[11] This may mark off an area of general concrete application for the abstract concept—see the discussion of abstract and general concrete rights, *ibid.*, chs. V.2(5)–VI.

[12] See *ibid.*, ch. VI.2.

[13] See Andrew Halpin, "Definitions and Directions: Recklessness Unheeded" (1998) 18 *Legal Studies* 294.

[14] See the extensive discussion in (1998) 19(1) *Human Rights Law Journal*; in particular, Paul Mahoney, "Marvelous Richness of Diversity or Invidious Cultural Relativism?" at 1, and Jeroen Schokkenbroeck, "The Basis, Nature and Application of the Margin-of-Appreciation Doctrine in the Case-Law of the European Court of Human Rights" at 30.

[15] Illuminating discussion of the ways in which the principle of proportionality is used to weigh conflicting interests is provided by Francis Jacobs, "Recent Developments in the Principle of Proportionality in European Community Law", and Walter van Gerven, "The Effect of Proportionality on the Actions of Member States of the European Community: National Viewpoints from Continental Europe", both in Evelyn Ellis (ed.), *The Principle of Proportionality in the Laws of Europe* (Oxford, Hart Publishing, 1999).

contested concept.[16] Gallie's suggestion that certain concepts are doomed to be the subject of irresolvable conflict has made a wide impact in a number of fields, though the exact nature of an essentially contested concept is itself contestable.[17] The concept of democracy is one of Gallie's paradigms for an essentially contested concept, and one way of regarding this is to view it as so complex in detail that any selection of details will necessarily conjur up a different view of what democracy amounts to. If this is so then Gallie's observations might better be couched under the heading of essentially contested terms, and the underlying problem be recognised as the possibility of the same term applying to different ideas, each adopting, with varying emphases, different combinations from a complex range of features associated with democracy. This would accord with the analysis provided above where w identifies x but x is understood variously as w (idea of x)$_1$ / w (idea of x)$_2$ / w (idea of x)$_3$. However, this assumes that there is a recognised source providing us with the features of democracy, and it would seem historically more accurate to suggest that we have an essentially contested term due to the diversity of instances that the fluid term democracy has been extended to cover, from direct Athenian democracy to representative Westminster democracy, and beyond. This would now accord with the alternative analysis provided above, where w identifies $x/y/z$ and variously expresses w (idea of x) / w (idea of y) / w (idea of z).

A different way of regarding Gallie's illustration[18] is to see the concept of democracy as incomplete because it contains an evaluative element that requires completing by drawing on a standard external to the concept itself. Thus regarded, to talk of democracy is to raise the question as to what idea of democracy is required, rather than to describe a state of affairs that has already been expressed in the idea itself. Seen in this light the contestable concept also displays the characteristic of requiring a reflective participatory response in order to ascertain what is appropriately regarded as falling under the concept.

This reading of Gallie gains some support from the text of his article. At one point he regards clarification of such a concept as being a process of fulfilling "recognized standards".[19] Elsewhere, he considers the possibility of the concept of democracy not being essentially contestable if there is general acceptance of "actual political conditions or actions" or "certain political aspirations".[20] This would relate the contestability of the concept of democracy to the background of a pluralist moral environment from which different standards might be selected in order to fill out the evaluative element that the concept contains. In

---

[16] WB Gallie, "Essentially Contested Concepts" (1956) 56 *Proceedings of the Aristotelian Society* 167.

[17] For further bibliographical detail, see *Rights and Law* above n. 2, at 21 n48 (which considers the relevance of essentially contestable concepts to rights); and for further discussion, see Andrew Mason, "On Explaining Political Disagreement: The Notion of an Essentially Contested Concept" (1990) 33 *Inquiry* 81; and the works cited below n. 24.

[18] The discussion that follows draws from "Concepts, Terms" above n. 2, at 203–4.

[19] Above n. 16, at 197.

[20] *Ibid.* at 183*ff*.

respect to democracy this possible reading of contestability is captured by noting Aristotle's observation on the criterion for a democratic assignment of resources: "democrats make the criterion free birth".[21] Aristotle's simple concept of democracy clearly illustrates how the concept contains an evaluative element, contestable due to the plurality of values relating to who should be considered free,[22] and how the filling out of the evaluative element is subject to considerations that are not provided within the concept itself.

Whether or not this reading of Gallie is persuasive, any legal concept containing an evaluative element may be essentially contestable in the manner suggested. This will occur where the legal concept is operating within a moral environment which is pluralist in the sense of containing competing sets of moral standards, or even where the environment contains a recognised set of standards but these standards are only accepted in an abstract form and it remains contestable as to which concrete instantiations of these standards should be accepted.[23]

Conceptions of a Concept

The final way of looking at the characteristic is more suggestive, in providing the reflective participatory response with an intellectual aura. The device of "conceptions of a concept" has enjoyed a fairly wide appeal.[24] Legal theorists

---

[21] *Nichomachean Ethics* V.v.7.

[22] That this should be limited to adult male Athenian citizens was evidently contestable even at the time of Aristotle, see *Politics* I.ii.3 regarding the position of slaves; and Aristophanes' *Lysistrata* is some indication of the position of women not being beyond question.

Taking a historical continuum as the moral environment can sharpen the contestability of democracy, but such contestability can also be found within contemporary societies. In the UK, residence rather than property holding did not become the basis for enfranchisement until the Representation of the People Act 1918, which also enfranchised women over the age of thirty. The Good Friday Agreement 1998 declares a "total and absolute commitment to exclusively democratic and peaceful means", but the proposals for the Assembly in Northern Ireland with their distinctive power sharing arrangements ("safeguards to ensure that all sections of the community can participate and work together successfully") provide a concept of democracy by which the practices of the Westminster Parliament would have to be regarded as significantly undemocratic. For the full text of the Agreement and detailed discussion, see Colin Harvey (ed.), *Human Rights, Equality and Democratic Renewal in Northern Ireland* (Oxford, Hart Publishing, 2001). For an impressive historical survey of democracy and what he refers to as the contemporary "fact-versus-value tensions", see Giovanni Sartori, *The Theory of Democracy Revisited* (Chatham, NJ, Chatham House Publishers, 1987).

[23] It is arguable that the Criminal Law Revision Committee in making their proposals for the definition of theft enacted in the Theft Act 1968 made exactly the mistake of assuming a uniform standard of dishonesty in society where in fact a plurality of standards existed, and so unwittingly provided a contestable concept of dishonesty in the definition of theft, see further "The Test for Dishonesty" [1996] *Criminal Law Review* 283.

[24] For example, Michael Naish, "Education and Essential Contestability Revisited" (1984) 18 *Journal of Philosophy of Education* 141, employs the device for the concept of education; Fred D'Agostino, *Free Public Reason: Making It Up As We Go* (New York, NY, OUP, 1996) ch. 2, uses it for the concept of public justification. Interestingly, both these authors (in different ways) relate the device to essential contestablility.

are most likely to have encountered it in the works of Ronald Dworkin and John Rawls.[25] There is presumed to exist a singular concept, such as justice or fairness, and different viewpoints or different theorists' attempts at conceptual analysis are portrayed as conceptions of that concept.

That the "concept" poses a question is acknowledged explicitly by Dworkin, and obliquely by Rawls. Dworkin in considering the example of fairness states that, "When I appeal to fairness I pose a moral issue; when I lay down my conception of fairness I try to answer it."[26] Considering his instruction to his children not to treat others unfairly, he remarks: "my children, in my example, can do what I said only by making up their own minds about what is fair."[27]

Rawls in his discussion of conceptions of a concept of justice considers that the concept itself expresses "the need for. . . principles for assigning basic rights and duties and for determining . . . the proper distribution of the benefits and burdens of social cooperation."[28] In taking this view of justice Rawls states he is following HLA Hart, who in his depiction of justice as involving "a central element" of treating like cases alike analyses this element as incomplete until it is supplemented by "criteria of relevant resemblances and differences [which] may often vary with the fundamental moral outlook of a given person or society."[29]

The problem with characterising the response to the question posed in the concept as a conception of it is that it suggests the process of reaching the answer is essentially a process of intellectual reflection upon the question. Hart, who avoids the device, cannot be regarded as making this suggestion for he openly acknowledges the incompleteness of the central element ("concept") which requires completion by the selection of external criteria.

There is nothing to prevent one concept forming the subject matter of another concept, and sensibly talking of a concept of a concept. We could, for example, in the analysis provided above, where w identifies x, take x to be the concept of a legal power in the work of HLA Hart and ask a number of students to write about what they understood Hart's concept of a legal power to be. This might provide us with x –understood as– w (idea of x)$_1$, –understood as– w (idea of x)$_2$, –understood as– w (idea of x)$_3$. We could refer to all of these as concepts, or conceptions, of Hart's concept of a legal power. This would make sense because their subject matter is uniformly identifiable as something that exists in the world—the concept of a legal power in the writings of Hart.

We could similarly take a question that has been posed in a particular context and ask our students to give us their views of what they understood by the

---

[25] See John Rawls, *A Theory of Justice* (Oxford, Oxford University Press, 1972) 5–6 and Ronald Dworkin, *Taking Rights Seriously* (London, Duckworth, 1977) 134–6, 226, *Law's Empire* (London, Collins, 1986) 70–1, 74. The comments here build on "Concepts, Terms" above n. 2, at 193 n21.

[26] *Taking Rights Seriously* above n. 25, at 135.

[27] *Ibid*. 136.

[28] *A Theory of Justice* above n. 25, at 5.

[29] *The Concept of Law*, 1st edn. (Oxford, Clarendon Press, 1961) 155, 158. Hart himself does not employ the device of conceptions of a concept.

question. For example, we could ask them what they think the question of justice in Western thought since the time of Aristotle has been about. The responses might vary. One student might answer that it raises the question what principles govern fair relations or conduct between people. Another student following Rawls might answer that it raises the question what are the principles for assigning basic rights and duties and for determining the proper distribution of the benefits and burdens of social cooperation. A third student might prefer the suggestion of Hart that it is a question of what distributions and compensations are fair.[30] Again we could follow the analysis suggested above, and sensibly speak of these as conceptions of the the concept of justice in Western thought, given that the question of justice can be presented as a concept of justice, and given that the subject matter of our students' conceptions is identifiable as something existing in the world—the extant thinking on the question of justice in the Western world since the time of Aristotle.

In terms of the analysis provided above, it follows then that where w expresses an idea of the form (2) (w is an idea inviting a participatory response so as to identify $x/y/z$), it is possible for that idea, as a question which can be identified as something that exists in the world to be understood in the same way as anything else that exists in the world: i.e. there may be different conceptions of it (w (idea of x)$_1$, etc). However, we now need to distinguish the thing in the world that exists as a question, and the thing in the world that arises as an answer to that question. To avoid error, we should more accurately speak of w (idea of q)$_1$, etc as being the conceptions of the concept, and the participatory responses to that question (in whichever conception) as identifying $x/y/z$.

In simple terms the problem is this. If I ask you a question with a number of possible answers depending on your personal viewpoint (e.g., Who would you vote for in the next election?), you may be able to rephrase my question to represent what you understood my question to mean (Who do I think should run the country? Who do I want to form the next government? Which party do I support?), but you would not for a moment imagine that by rephrasing the question you were answering it. Admittedly, your rephrasing the question might in some circumstances colour the sort of answer you would give, but even so it would not of itself amount to the answer. There is a danger that using the device of conceptions of a concept will cause us to confuse our answer with our understanding of the question.

In the two examples of conceptions of a concept we have considered—conceptions of Hart's concept of a legal power, conceptions of the concept of justice in Western thought—the conceptions provide understanding of the concept. In the second example, even if we take the concept to involve a question, the conceptions provide understanding of the *question*. The problem arises when we take the *answers* to be conceptions of the concept in the same way. This is particularly easy to do where the same word is employed for the question (con-

---

[30] *The Concept of Law*, 1st edn. 154–5.

cept) and for the answers to it, as it is when we raise "justice" as a general issue and then also label different views as to what justice amounts to as "justice".

The device of conceptions of a concept here is misleading. There simply has never existed such a concept of justice which has had such a relationship with all the "conceptions". There has been thinking about justice which encompasses a number of ideas,[31] some varying slightly, some utterly contradictory; some transparently coherent, others muddled or inconsistent. To suggest that all these attempts to provide an idea of justice are conceptions of the one concept, as though that concept or some aspect of it were present in each of these attempts, is to repeat on a far grander scale the natural law presumption that all *determinationes* can be regarded as reflecting the immutable value contained in the general concept of Natural Law.

The danger is not merely a matter of terminological confusion. If we misrepresent the relationship in this way, it is a simple matter to foist upon someone a particular reflective participatory response to the issue that the general concept poses, on the basis that he has accepted the general concept. The favoured response, as a "conception of the concept", is equated with the concept itself that our victim has accepted, despite the fact that he may feel a different response ("conception") is more appropriate. Dworkin himself employs this ruse in his discussion of reverse discrimination, notwithstanding that he refers back to the way of regarding a conception of a concept mentioned above. Having stated that the Constitution "makes the concept of equality a test of legislation, but it does not stipulate any particular conception of that concept", Dworkin proceeds to provide a particular conception of equality that endorses reverse discrimination, loses the distinction between concept and conception, and within two pages is concluding that the person suffering from reverse discrimination must accept it because it is "a consequence of the meritocratic standards he approves."[32]

THE SIGNIFICANCE OF EXPERIENCE

The acknowledgment one way or another that concepts we employ pose questions rather than convey understanding raises the problem where the answers are to come from, in order to provide the understanding we currently lack. If we reject viewing the process of reaching an answer as being essentially a matter of intellectual reflection upon the question (in the way that treating the answer as a conception of the concept appears to suggest), an alternative way of dealing with this quandary is to regard the acquisition of further knowledge as primarily an experiential endeavour.

---

[31] In "Concepts, Terms" above n. 2, I suggest that the ideas/conceptions should better be described as "concepts" responding to a "field of enquiry", thus avoiding the confusing "conceptions of a concept" altogether.

[32] *Taking Rights Seriously* above n. 25, at 226–8.

An emphasis on experience as the key to making an appropriate reflective participatory response to the issues contained in the sort of concepts we have been discussing actually commands support from a great diversity of sources. In contemporary legal theory it would be difficult to imagine a sharper contrast than that between those supporting Natural Law and Critical Theory perspectives. Yet a central concern with experience can be seen to be common to both.[33]

Contemporary Critical Theory can be traced back to the hermeneutical approach of the early eighteenth Italian philosopher Vico, via the role of *Verstehen* in the nineteenth century works of Dilthey and Weber. The approach emphasises forming a reflective understanding from within in contrast to adopting a "scientific" method of understanding external objective data. Raymond Geuss, in his illuminating investigation of Critical Theory, spells out this contrast:[34]

> "Critical and scientific theories are alike in a trivial and uninteresting sense in that both are forms of 'empirical' knowledge—both are *based on and can be confirmed only by experience*. However, the 'experience' on which a critical theory is based includes not only observation but also the 'Erfahrung der Reflexion.' Whatever differences in epistemic status or cognitive structure exist between scientific and critical theories are to be attributed to the role 'reflection' plays in the confirmation of critical theories."

Although the concern of Geuss is to point out the contrast, his statement of Critical Theory, in the words that I have emphasised, also draws attention to the fundamental role that experience plays in the development of Critical Theory.

This very same concern with experience can be found in the exposition of Natural Law. Aristotle raised the warning:[35]

> "Again, each man judges correctly those matters with which he is acquainted; it is of these that he is a competent critic. To criticize a particular subject, therefore, a man must have been trained in that subject; to be a good critic generally, he must have had an all-round education. Hence the young are not fit to be students of Political Science. For they have no *experience of life and conduct*, and it is these that *supply the premises and subject matter of this branch of philosophy*."

John Finnis has drawn attention to the need for the person skilled in Aristotle's "practical reason" (which is similarly contrasted with scientific or inferential

---

[33] For another illustration of the concern with experience, see Frank Jackson's reliance on folk experience in his approach to conceptual analysis, mentioned in the Endnote to ch. 6. Here the concern is not so explicit. In his book, Jackson's folk theory seems at first to rely upon intuition (e.g., at 31). However, it becomes apparent that intuition is itself dependent upon experience—what the folk are "acquainted with" (at 39). Ultimately, Jackson takes us to the notion of a mature folk morality which is dependent upon sufficient critical reflection (133, 151). Jackson's invocation of maturity and sufficient experience brings him to a similar position as that described by John Finnis (below, text at n. 36) as being occupied by Aristotle's *ho spoudaios*.

[34] Raymond Geuss, *The Idea of a Critical Theory: Habermas and the Frankfurt School* (Cambridge, Cambridge University Press, 1981) 91 (footnote omitted, emphasis added).

[35] Aristotle, *Nicomachean Ethics* I.iii.5–7 (emphasis added).

reason by its call for reflection and thinking from the inside) to be a person of maturity (Aristotle's *ho spoudaios*) with "enough experience".[36]

The wide recognition for the role of experience in developing our understanding of the social world, does not in itself indicate how we should proceed to live within the social world. More particularly it does not assist us in developing a particular legal response. In broader social or political theory the acknowledgment that human experience is limited can be linked to an exploration of the role of ideology. Ideology may be regarded as oppressive: it inculcates a false consciousness in the minds of the oppressed to deter them from reflecting appropriately on their own experiences.[37] However, it may also be seen as a necessary requirement for engaging in the social world, in that we need to act before waiting for the full understanding that our limited human experience denies us.[38] Michael Freeden has effectively portrayed this positive aspect of ideology:[39]

> "The analysis of political concepts is not, on this understanding, most usefully pursued by projecting their logical permutations and ethical possibilities in the abstract, often attached to universalizable models—currently the most common method of exploring them—but through locating them within the patterns in which they actually appear. Such patterns are most conveniently known as ideologies, those systems of political thinking, loose or rigid, deliberate or unintended, through which individuals and groups construct an understanding of the political world they, or those who preoccupy their thoughts, inhabit, and then act on that understanding."

The danger of one person's ideology providing a liberating engagement with the social world for that person, whilst amounting to another person's psychological and social confinement should be too obvious to need stressing here. Nevertheless, it is worth reiterating a point that has been made earlier in our discussion of forms of life in chapter 7, that even within the tradition of a particular ideology there exists dissent and controversy over how the broad approach that characterises the ideology should grapple with actual issues in the world.[40] Even if we take Freeden's point about the practical necessity of embracing some ideology, this does not so much deal with the fundamental problem as provide an approach to coping with it.

If the significance of human experience is conceded, and the limitations of human experience are acknowledged, it takes a tremendous amount of optimism to propose a way forward beyond the tainted partisan ideologies of

---

[36] Finnis, above n. 3, at 30–4.

[37] See further, Geuss, above n. 34, at 12–22.

[38] Cp the discussion in the opening section of this chapter regarding the practical need of responding to an instruction or legal norm.

[39] Michael Freeden, *Ideologies and Political Theory: A Conceptual Approach* (Oxford, Clarendon Press, 1996) 3.

[40] See Freeden himself, *ibid.* part II, for a survey of some of the fragmentations of liberalism. For a provocative and illuminating discussion of different liberal approaches in a setting that draws out the issues to which liberalism responds, see Oren Ben-Dor, *Constitutional Limits and the Public Sphere: A Critical Study of Bentham's Constitutionalism* (Oxford, Hart, 2000) ch. 8.

political or social life that rely only in part on the garnering of experience, which is then fully supplemented by the imagination of convenience. Nevertheless, there are those whose optimism outruns their imaginations, in assuming that we are capable of reaching a point of non-partisan consensus fully cognisant of each person's experience, despite the fact that we cannot collectively yet imagine what that position will be. Such optimism is evident in the discourse ethics propounded by Jürgen Habermas:[41]

> "Discourse ethics rests on the intuition that the application of the principle of universalization, properly understood, calls for a joint process of 'ideal role taking'. . . . Under the pragmatic presuppositions of an inclusive and noncoercive rational discourse among free and equal participants, everyone is required to take the perspective of everyone else, and thus project herself into the understandings of self and world of all others; from this interlocking of perspectives there emerges an ideally extended we-perspective from which all can test in common whether they wish to make a controversial norm the basis of their shared practice . . ."

The fissure between such optimism and the realities of human decision making in the social world is disclosed in Habermas's representation of the subject matter to be decided from the "we-perspective" as a "controversial norm".[42] My concern in the next section is to consider how legal reasoning proceeds in circumstances where individual human experience remains limited; the collective experience lies beyond our imagination; and our imagination is harnessed instead to permit the flourishing of a number of conflicting perspectives, each capable of endorsing a particular view of how the interest of one individual should be regarded alongside others' interests.

CONCEPTUAL DEVELOPMENT OR CONCEPTUAL DISLOCATION

The construction of a detached viewpoint in the law which is capable of rising above the subjective or partisan perspectives on how competing interests in society should be balanced holds an obvious attraction. Even if sceptics question how detached the legal viewpoint can be, and the legal viewpoint is seen as one chosen to favour a particular way of life or vision of society, nevertheless the sense that the legal viewpoint offers a coherent or principled approach to resolving the conflicting interests within society is somehow reassuring. At least we know where we stand under the law, and if we are open to the benefits of democ-

---

[41] Jürgen Habermas, "Reconciliation through the Public Use of Reason: Remarks on John Rawls' Political Liberalism" (1995) 42 *Journal of Philosophy* 111 at 117.

[42] The underlying problem can also be unpicked by relating the perspectives to the issue to be decided. The element of controversy arises due to the perspectives being in conflict. Being prepared to take the perspective of the other will not resolve the conflict but merely exchange positions to the conflict. The "we-perspective" as a common perspective accordingly requires something further than the requirement to take the other's perspective. It would require nothing less than a shift from the experiences on which the conflicting perspectives proceed.

racy we can further see the possibility of affecting which viewpoint the law favours through the mechanisms of constitutional change to the law.

Still this reassurance is posited on there being a legal viewpoint, and it is the flimsiness of this presupposition that we are now in a position to question. I want to do this not by engaging in the anti-formalist techniques of deconstruction,[43] nor by making the conventional compromise offered by positivism in acknowledging the gaps remaining in the legal viewpoint,[44] but by stressing the human element in the legal enterprise and demonstrating how human limitations technically impose limitations on law. The analytical shift I propose transports us from reasoning from a legal viewpoint to reasoning with law. The transfer of law from source to object of reasoning has a number of serious implications for the practice and theory of law, which I will broach in the final chapter. My aim in the concluding section of this chapter is to draw on the observations collected in this chapter in order to provide an analysis of a feature at the core of legal reasoning. This feature exhibits an inherent incoherence rather than contributing to a coherent development of legal reasoning.

The conventional treatment of legal reasoning, as a process of working from general principles to particular instances or from particular instances to general principles, tends to neglect the medium through which the process of reasoning takes place. If the legal medium combines both the general imprecision of language due to the incompleteness of human experience, and more particularly the occurrence of concepts requiring a participatory reflective response, then what is conventionally portrayed as a process of legal reasoning must include opportunities of making responses to the existing material in both respects: in determining more precisely how existing language will be used in the law; and in determining an appropriate response to those concepts which necessarily invite one.[45]

---

[43] The process of deconstruction is problematic in seemingly providing no brake against extreme scepticism or nihilism. The problem is discussed by Martha Nussbaum, "Skepticism about Practical Reason in Literature and the Law" (1994) 107 *Harvard Law Review* 714, who sees the remedy in an Aristotelian account of immersed ethical reasoning. However, the more earnest exponents of deconstruction dismiss the purely negative excesses undertaken as deconstruction as unrepresentative of the ethical aspect of deconstruction, see Christopher Norris, *Deconstruction and the Interests of Theory* (London, Pinter Publishers, 1988), particularly ch. 5 "Law, deconstruction and the resistance to theory"; and Raimo Siltala, *A Theory of Precedent* (Oxford, Hart Publishing, 2000) 22–9. Nevertheless, to reap the ethical insights of deconstruction without abandoning deconstruction seems insoluble (see Timothy Endicott, *Vagueness in Law* (Oxford, OUP, 2000) 15–17 for a concise presentation of the problem). The beneficial prospects of deconstruction possibly require one to kick away the ladder that one has used to climb up. The image, borrowed by Wittgenstein, is derived from Sextus Empiricus, identified by Nussbaum as Derrida's classical counterpart (Nussbaum at 721). If so, this assumes that we have some way of identifying the place we wish to rest, apart from the process of climbing an endless ladder. More specifically, this suggests that the underlying defect of deconstruction is its lack of any correspondence with the world.

[44] For example, Hart, above n. 29, at 124–5; Joseph Raz, *The Authority of Law* (Oxford, Clarendon Press, 1979) 49–50.

[45] Edward Levi's influential, *An Introduction to Legal Reasoning* (Chicago, IL, University of Chicago Press, 1949) attempted to show how legal reasoning by example provided an opportunity to respond to the ambiguity of legal materials, but nevertheless considered that the law provided a

The first, more general, task of determining how particular words shall be used can be broadly regarded as simply getting on with the job of developing language in a legal context. As I pointed out in chapters 5 and 6, there is nothing peculiarly legal about the requirement of resolving vague language. In the legal context words may take on a technical legal meaning, so that this general feature of our use of language may be employed for a specialist outcome: the development of legal doctrine rather than colloquial understanding. Even so, legal doctrine is itself composed of words that are still subject to the general imprecision of language, as well as the more particular problem—the occurrence of concepts requiring a participatory response. Legal doctrines have yet to provide a systematic word coverage for all possible human experiences.[46]

The more particular task of responding to those concepts which require a reflective participatory response has been linked above to the same fundamental problem of the limitations of human experience. Accordingly, the opportunities of making responses to the existing legal materials in performing either the more general or the more particular task can be analysed in a similar manner. The common opportunity is to determine how the law is to dispose of the instant case, given that no comprehensive legal viewpoint embracing the case has yet been produced—and will not be produced—after the disposition of the instant case. The comprehensive legal viewpoint is not formed either side of the legal disposition of the case, and yet the case is decided against the backdrop of

coherent "moving classification system", dynamically adjusting to changes in society. OC Jensen, *The Nature of Legal Argument* (Oxford, Blackwell, 1957) attempted a more rigorous challenge to the assumption that legal reasoning could be standardly regarded as a process of inference from legal materials, suggesting that the deductive process in legal reasoning is subordinate to the initial process of classification. Jensen's efforts were not particularly well received. Tony Honoré in his review of Jensen's book ((1958) 74 *Law Quarterly Review* 296) concluded that it was "both stimulating and disappointing". Both Levi and Jensen are at pains to point out that lawyers frequently conceal the true nature of legal reasoning under the pretence of its being a deductive process. This is a theme also taken up by Julius Stone, *Legal System and Lawyers' Reasonings* (Stanford, CA, Stanford University Press, 1964), expanding part of his earlier *The Province and Function of Law: Law as Logic, Justice and Social Control* (Sydney, Maitland Publications, 1946; London, Stevens, 1947). Stone continues to track down "legal categories of illusory reference" in *Precedent and Law: Dynamics of Common Law Growth* (Sydney, Butterworths, 1985).

[46] The incompleteness of doctrinal coverage may be seen in the generation of competing doctrinal precepts in arguing for different dispositions of a concrete case, and also in argument over whether a particular line of doctrine should extend to the case at issue. As an example of the first phenomenon, note the switch from the rule of non-recovery for mistake of law to the principle of unjust enrichment in *Kleinwort Benson* v. *Lincoln City Council* [1998] 3 WLR 1095 at 1113–14 (*per* Lord Goff). [This is the case referred to in ch. 2 n. 63.] A recent example of the latter phenomenon is provided by the House of Lords recognising a "tenancy" in the absence of a proprietary interest, where the landlord had no estate in land: *Bruton* v. *London & Quadrant Housing Trust* [2000] AC 406. Whichever way the material of legal doctrine is portrayed (e.g., as rules or principles), the underlying problem is precisely the general problem of the incompleteness of language in that there has been a failure to account for the particular experience arising in the concrete case (whether this omission is couched as a problem with the scope of a rule or the weight of a principle). That doctrinal coverage remains incomplete *after* these two decisions is evident in their respective discussion by Peter Birks, "Mistakes of Law" (2000) 53 *Current Legal Problems* 205, and by Martin Dixon, "The Non-Proprietary Lease: The Rise of the Feudal Phoenix" (2000) 59 *Cambridge Law Journal* 25.

existing legal material and is regarded as itself contributing to our understanding of legal material. How do we capture the development of the law in these cases?

The clue lies in acknowledging that the legal material that may appear constant in such cases is constant only at a superficial level of being formulated by the same word(s). Beneath the legal term, or beyond the legal idea requiring a participatory response, there is more going on than the legal materials alone can account for. Let us first represent the apparently coherent development of the law, by the application of a legal term to two cases, A and B, which are disposed of on the basis that the legal term does or does not apply on their facts. The term may be a single word (e.g., "consideration" in the law of contract) or a complex phrase (e.g., "no man may benefit from his own wrongdoing"). For our purposes it does not matter whether the case is disposed of by holding that the term applies or not. Either way the cases seem to be disposed of by applying the term, *w*:

Even if case B is regarded as novel within the legal community, we can apparently speak of the coherent development of *w* as a legal idea so as to embrace B.

The picture is utterly transformed when we place *w* within the different positions that might be available in the analysis provided in the first section of this chapter. The disposition of A or B is now determined not by *w* but by the view of *w* that is taken. This is obvious where *w* is regarded as an idea requiring a participatory response, for we could in response end up with *w* with a participatory response *x*, *w* with a participatory response *y*, *w* with a participatory response *z*, etc. In fact, the view as to how *w* should be approached may become significant at an earlier stage in deciding whether to approach the legal idea as an idea of this kind.[47]

Even if the view is not that the legal idea under consideration is of the sort requiring a participatory response, within the existing legal materials it is likely that the legal term can be found to be related to a variety of things existing in the world such that it would be possible to select as the operative idea: *w* (idea of *x*), *w* (idea of *y*), *w* (idea of *z*), etc. These "things in the world" may themselves be abstract ideas, or general ideas covering a number of concrete instances, which the existing case law is capable of throwing up. Similarly, where the legal idea is regarded as covering a uniform idea, or a uniform class of instances, there

---

[47] For example, the idea of fraud in the pre-Theft Act English criminal law was regarded as not requiring a participatory response, in contrast (according to some opinion at least) to the idea of dishonesty in the Act.

will still be the possibility of selecting as the operative idea something which places the emphasis in a particular place: w (idea of x)$_1$, w (idea of x)$_2$, w (idea of x)$_3$, etc. These manoeuvres will be particularly important where the operative idea selected is intended to cover the instant case by way of analogy to decisions found in the existing legal materials.

Having taken a view of w, it may be that the disposition of the case then follows as a matter of simple inference, but it is the view taken of w that determines the outcome. The case is not disposed of by simply applying the legal term. The particular view taken, say V_1 or V_2, is not discernible on the face of w, nor is it determined by the law. It is the view taken of which idea of w should form the appropriate response to A or B. The full analysis must acknowledge that it will be a view *of w* that comes into play in disposing of the case, but it must allow for the determinative factor being the view that is taken:

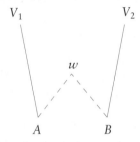

The criteria for selecting V_1 as opposed to V_2 are external to the law itself, but the difference in criteria may produce only an imperceptible wobble in the legal concept between cases A and B, hidden beneath the apparent constancy in the legal term. On other occasions the conceptual dislocation arising by the selection of V_2 rather than V_1 may effect a radical change in the law.

The criteria used in taking a view as to how a particular case is to be determined are unlikely to isolate that case from the view as to how other cases are to be regarded, and may sensibly be treated as forming part of a wider way of life, or vision of society. That is the tendency we have as humans in general and judges in particular.[48] However, once recognised, this feature of "legal reasoning" introduces incoherence in the law precisely because of the partial attempts made at different times to introduce different visions of society as the legal viewpoint. The incompleteness of any one of these attempts leaves legal material in a state where the same process (potentially introducing further incoherence) of selecting a view of w may be attempted again in the future by those adopting an alternative vision of society. Even if we relied on a dominant vision of society as

---

[48] This tendency perhaps accounts for the respect accorded by one eminent judge to Dworkin's theoretical model which treats judicial decisions as being made as part of an integrated legal vision of society. See LH Hoffmann, Review of Simon Lee's *Judging Judges* (1989) 105 *Law Quarterly Review* 140. What is lacking in this enthusiasm is the recognition of the diverse attempts at various times to construct competing visions of society.

having gained judicial support at a particular time, the incompleteness of human experience means that no way of life or vision of society has attained a comprehensive and coherent form.

I do not want to overemphasise this feature of reasoning with law. I am not suggesting that it should be regarded as the standard case of legal reasoning. I accept there are cases where we cannot assume the possibility of different readings of the existing legal material containing *w* and there is no opportunity for taking a view of *w*, in the same way that outside of the law there are many contexts where the meaning of words is clear. I do suggest that the assumptions I make at the end of the previous section as the basis for considering it are a fair assessment of the contemporary human condition. That opportunities for taking a view of *w* will necessarily arise on a frequent basis in any modern system of law.[49] And that reasoning with law in the manner described here is a commonplace in the arguments and decisions found recorded in the reports of the appellate courts.

If these suggestions are convincing there is reason to consider the implications of recognising this incoherence at the heart of legal reasoning.

---

[49] The phenomenon of necessary and legitimate judicial view-taking may encourage judicial activism elsewhere where it is not legitimate, as suggested in ch. 3, n. 54 and text thereat.

10

Implications

M Y SUGGESTION AT the end of the last chapter was that it would be worthwhile to explore the incoherence that lay at the heart of legal reasoning.
The route taken to reach this conclusion may seem to many to be unnecessarily
arduous. First year law students are capable of reaching the conclusion that
legal reasoning is incoherent from their attempts at digesting far fewer and far
less demanding materials than the reader of this book has been subjected to.
And those familiar with the more elevated reaches of legal study will not consider it novel fare to be offered a statement of this incoherence. I suffer no illusion that I can convince the reader that the route selected was the most scenic
possible but I hope in this concluding chapter to give some grounds for thinking
that it might have been of some value.

The particular route taken in this book was motivated by a curiosity over
what it is about law that makes it possible for such vehement disagreement to
persist among those who are concerned with the discipline of law (both in its
study and its practice) not simply over what the law is on a particular point but
over what the law is. It is not simply that the debate is contested but the nature
of the debate is itself a contest. At this point sympathies naturally emerge for
those practitioners who are happier to get on with the business of seeking to win
the debate rather than to engage in reflection on the nature of the debate—and
for those theorists who are prepared to move the deeper debate over to another
arena altogether. I have tried in chapter two to suggest that although it is possible to practice law within the theory proofed confines of limited areas of practice, it is not possible to insulate practice from theory altogether—that
ultimately practitioners' interests will catch up with the concerns of theorists
(whether or not they gain benefit from the work of any particular theorist). As
to those theorists who give up on a specific theory of law and capitulate to a view
of law as politics (in the extreme sense of law-is-politics), my response emerges
most fully in this final chapter.

One of the most striking features of those concerned with the law outside the
two groups just mentioned is that alongside the disagreement at both the specific practical (what is the law on this point) and the wider theoretical (what is
the law) levels, there exists a solid commitment to providing *legal* answers. I am
far from suggesting here that practitioners and theorists who become involved
with the law develop an obsessive compulsion to think only in terms of the law.
In both camps there are copious examples of open-minded, broad minded,
roundly educated, and enlightened viewpoints, taking in the connections and

influences between law and other aspects of society, and other disciplines in the academy. My point is the narrower one that however eclectic the viewpoint the tendency is to find in diverse ways an explanation for law that preserves an area of purely legal influence.

This tendency has been illustrated in this book in chapter 4 in looking closely at the opposing views on the basis for judicial review, and I suggested in that chapter that the disagreement between the parties to the debate could possibly be explained by the striving to furnish a discrete legal answer to an issue that demanded resources that the law alone could not provide. Further illustration can be seen in the wholly different theoretical approaches of Joseph Raz, considered in chapter 3, and Ronald Dworkin, considered in chapter 5.[1] In completely different ways each seeks to preserve discrete legal territory: Raz in a more subtle manner in his attempt to mark off an area of reasoning that can merit a legal epithet whilst retaining a moral input; Dworkin in a more aggressive manner by asserting (despite the accommodation within law of principles of a society's background political morality) that the law can always come up with the right answer (theoretically, at least).

The nature of legal reasoning seems an obvious place to locate an enquiry which encompasses both the specific practical and wider theoretical issues, and certainly the outpouring of academic treatises indicates that it is a fertile subject. The area has also benefited from the deliberations of practitioners over the years, some of which have been referred to in this book. The problem is that the prospects for contributing a novel or stimulating perspective within this controversial field seem far greater than the chance of engaging with the principal curiosity over what it is in the nature of law that provides such opportunity for controversy in the first place.

The peculiar route travelled here has been chosen in an attempt not to lose sight of this quest. The proposal for a recognition of reasoning with law as an integral element of the conventional depiction of legal reasoning, with due emphasis on the phenomenon of conceptual dislocation (or wobble), is made in the view that it contributes to wider issues in our understanding of the practice and theory of law. In putting forward this analysis I have admitted to the presumptions that our circumstances are such that individual human experience remains limited; the collective experience lies beyond our imagination; and our imagination is harnessed instead to permit the flourishing of a number of conflicting perspectives, each capable of endorsing a particular view of how the interest of one individual should be regarded alongside others' interests. These assumptions may seem a fair reflection of contemporary Western societies, though I have suggested them as pertaining to the human condition in general, to a greater or lesser extent. More significantly, I have sought to demonstrate

---

[1] For further illustrations of this tendency, see the illuminating discussion of "Republican Constitutionalism" in Emilios Christodoulidis, *Law and Reflexive Politics* (Dordrecht, Kluwer, 1998).

how these conditions are not secondary to our understanding of law but are seen to impact upon the elementary techniques on which legal reasoning and hence "the law" relies. In emphasising in my analysis the nature of the medium in which law is practised, I have found it necessary to stress the inadequacies that this brings to the law, and hence the inadequacies of legal resources.

I have consistently departed from the tendency remarked on above of finding a peculiarly legal territory, but in so doing I have sought to bring to light the peculiar characteristic of law, lending itself so easily to controversy whilst at the same time enjoying the unrivalled opportunity to make authoritative resolution of controversy. In the remaining part of this chapter I want to briefly consider the implications of the proposed analysis of reasoning with law, which surface in the consideration of some key concerns for the theory and practice of law. I shall do so by commencing in slightly more detail with the institutional nature of law as a means of leading into the other issues.

Recognition of the institutional nature of law might be thought to be the obvious antidote to the matrix of uncertainties that can be found in the legal medium. The idea that the gaps or other uncertainties in legal materials can be remedied by an appropriate institutional legal response seeems an obvious way of maintaining a distinct legal territory. Although there exists a variety of theoretical perspectives under an institutional approach to law, they can be collectively represented as adopting a common strategy in an emphasis on the nature of law as a normative institution, combining norms affecting general conduct as well as norms providing authorisation to officials.[2] If we were to imagine that the government of society could be arranged merely by having a hierarchy of officials, each authorised to deal with the conduct of those citizens or officials below, and we were then to suggest that this system of government set up a discrete system of authority to determine the acceptable behaviour of citizens, there would be two immediate intuitive objections to the characterisation of this arrangement as a distinct state of affairs.

First, it would be objected that the authority system depended upon the historical, political, and other features of society (and its members) that permitted it to emerge, to develop, and to thrive. Secondly, it would be objected that the system itself only catered for identifying who got to determine appropriate conduct of whom—it did not deal with what that conduct would be determined to be. This objection would draw attention to the need to recognise influences beyond the authority system in determining the acceptable behaviour of citizens.

More rigorously than these intuitive objections, it can be shown that a hierarchical system of authorising norms is essentially incomplete.[3] Combined with

---

[2] The best known institutional approach to law is Neil MacCormick and Ota Weinberger, *An Institutional Theory of Law: New Approaches to Legal Positivism* (Dordrecht, D Reidel Publishing, 1986). MacCormick and Weinberger, as representatives of an institutional theory of law, are subjected to critical scrutiny by Sean Coyle, "Our Knowledge of the Legal Order" (1999) 5 *Legal Theory* 389.

[3] I offer a demonstration of this through an application of Gödel's Theorem in "The Limitations of a Legal System" [1981] *Juridical Review* 29.

one of the major implications of the analysis provided in this book, that to view the norms applied to determine appropriate conduct as composing a complete systemic coverage of human conduct within a society is unsustainable, this suggests that there is no basis for securing a discrete territory for the authority system. Accordingly, any attempt at an institutional theory of law will be forcing the problem of legal incoherence deeper within the theory—characteristically losing it in the mysterious nature of norms.[4]

The split between formal and substantive authority for law emerged in considering the competing theories for judicial review in chapter 4. Beyond the specific concerns of dealing with the theoretical basis for judicial review, this debate can be viewed as being concerned about legal legitimacy. The tendency recently has perhaps been to look more for a substantive basis for the legitimacy of law as opposed to a formal basis relying ultimately on sovereignty.[5] However, the implications of the analysis proposed here have an equally devastating effect on this venture as upon the substantive aspect of an institutional analysis of law. More specifically, the proposed analysis reinforces the question mark tangentially raised against a doctrine of the rule of law in chapter 4, and has an even more specific impact on the employment of democratic ideals as a basis for legal legitimacy. It is not only that the concept of democracy is itself contestable, as indicated in chapter 9,[6] but also that the view of democracy entertained in a particular society's laws will be fragmented by the dislocations that it has undergone, so that no stable or coherent concept of democracy is available to be invoked as a source of legitimacy.

An obvious place to consider some of the practical implications of the analysis of reasoning with law that has been provided is the scope and role of legal definitions. Since it is standard for legal definitions to contain general ideas, the analysis proposed here may assist in clarifying the potential response to a definition in terms of recognising the particular kind of idea it may contain. Although I have suggested there may be room for contestability over just what kind of idea it is that we are dealing with, in some contexts it may be clear that one kind of idea rather than another is under consideration. For example, it may be clear from the nature of the evaluative term contained in the definition, together with a recognition of the background moral environment, that a concept requiring a participatory reflective response is at issue. At the very least our awareness of

---

[4] See the opening remarks of Neil MacCormick's "The Legal Framework: Institutional Normative Order" in his *Questioning Sovereignty: Law, State, and Nation in the European Commonwealth* (Oxford, OUP, 1999), referring to Kelsen's "great mystery". Cp Coyle, above n. 2, at 391: "The 'fundamental problem' is normativity." Coyle's attempt to rescue an institutional theory of law by means of a Fregean strategy itself depends upon a recognition of coherent legal entities.

[5] Significantly, the doctrine of parliamentary sovereignty has proved unhelpful in working through the constitutional implications of the Good Friday Agreement 1998. For discussion see Colin Harvey (ed.), *Human Rights, Equality and Democratic Renewal in Northern Ireland* (Oxford, Hart Publishing, 2001).

[6] See ch. 9, n. 22.

the range of different possibilities that might be under consideration should alert us to different kinds of argument that may be appropriate. Inappropriate arguments may win cases or round off judgments. However, if our concern is with the coherent development of the law then it will be important to recognise the nature of the concept involved, and hence the sort of response that will assist in the development or the dislocation of that concept.

In general, the recognition that different kinds of argument are appropriate for different kinds of ideas should avoid the simplistic representation of legal reasoning as being a straightforward syllogism from the general legal definition to a recognition of a particular instance so as to conclude the legal outcome. In terms of the discussion in chapter three, we may now venture to suggest in more detail what lurks behind the facade of Syllogism 4. A process of reasoning with law may be required so as to provide the general premise, captured by the parenthetical clause {the court will find that}, before the apparently straightforward legal reasoning can proceed. This parenthetical clause was linked in the final section of chapter three to a range of possible judicial activities. In the light of the analysis of legal concepts in chapter nine, we can see how some of these activities can be regarded as taking steps that are necessary in order to develop the law; some as teasing out favoured outcomes from the incoherent condition of the law; and some as dislocating, or even defying the law. Apart from the judicial role, the responses of lawyers arguing in favour of a particular reading of the law may similarly be taking up positions which vary not only in relation to the legal materials, but also in relation to the respect paid to the law itself.

One particularly suggestive piece of evidence for the broader view of reasoning with law proposed in this book is to be found in the explicit recognition within legal materials that the legal idea involved in the determination of a case can not be made the subject of straightforward inferential reasoning, but raises the need to consider a number of criteria. These criteria must then be taken into acccount in different ways in different circumstances in order to dispose of particular cases. Such criteria are to be found in the legislative concerns with the welfare of the child, in the judicial "definition" of ethnic group, and in many other places.[7] However, this phenomenon has not always received a welcome response. It may be met by a reaction that seeks to retain within the province of law a process of strict inferential reasoning.[8] The implication of the analysis proposed here is that such a reaction can not be sustained

---

[7] See Children Act 1989, s 1(3); *Mandla* v. *Dowell Lee* [1983] 1 All ER 1062 HL; and for a stimulating suggestion on harnessing "the criteria for determining unconscionability", see Michael Spence, *Protecting Reliance: The Emergent Doctrine of Equitable Estoppel* (Oxford, Hart Publishing, 1999).

[8] This reaction is apparent in Peter Birks' review, (1999) 115 *Law Quarterly Review* 681, of David Wright, *The Remedial Constructive Trust* (Sydney, Butterworths, 1998). Birks castigates Wright for offering "free-spinning criteria" where the aspiration of the jurist should be to provide "a rigid skeleton" (despite acknowledging that the law lacks one). A more receptive review of Wright's book is provided by Kit Barker in (1999) 13 *Trust Law International* 204.

successfully on the grounds that a particular form of legal concept is a necessary feature of law.

Further related practical implications obviously flow in considering issues concerned with law reform, and the practices of following precedent and legal interpretation (of statute or precedent[9]). The key points to be reiterated are that the variety of kinds of legal concepts, the possible and appropriate responses that can be made to them, and the necessary limitations of legal materials, all have to be given due attention in our understanding of any of these practices. A subsidiary issue to be considered is a clarification of the roles of first instance and appellate courts, which can vary according to the nature of the legal concept in question. In particular, where the relevant legal concept is one requiring a reflective participatory response, the question needs to be raised as to whether an appeal (or a further appeal) is simply providing another set of judges the opportunity of offering their reflections on the issue to be determined. The fundamental question to be broached is whether judicial responses to such concepts are best undertaken by the court closest to the presentation of the facts, or by a court charged with the final determination of the law. It is difficult to find a rationale for having the job done twice.

Practical implications will in turn spill over into theoretical considerations of the practice of law. The analysis reached in chapter 9 confirms the suspicion earlier aired in chapter 3 of the presence of instability as an inherent feature of law. It similarly confirms the disappointments awaiting attempts to provide a model of law where those models are purporting to identify a discrete legal territory. This will have a particular bearing on the use of rules as a theoretical device: neither can models of law be constructed as systems of rules;[10] nor can propositions of law be contained within rules.[11]

Finally, I want to consider the implications for the nature of law's critical aperture. Recognition of reasoning with law and of law's incoherent core brings within the legal enterprise the opportunity to practice that critical reflective attitude that has so often been exercised as an external device and associated with a dimunition in the standing of law as a discipline. I would go further in suggesting that an implication of the analysis offered in this book is that the opportunity is a necessity. Moreover, it follows that the failure to openly recognise

---

[9] Neil MacCormick and Robert Summers (eds.), *Interpreting Precedents* (Aldershot, Dartmouth, 1997) bears an instructive title in this respect.

[10] A suspicion also raised in ch. 3, at n. 75.

[11] Criticism made of the "semantic autonomy" of rules proposed in Frederick Schauer, *Playing by the Rules: A Philosophical Examination of Rule-Based Decision Making in Law and in Life* (Oxford, Clarendon Press, 1991) by Timothy Endicott, *Vagueness in Law* (Oxford, OUP, 2000) 18–19 ("a speaker and an 'understander' cannot share a language, and share nothing else", at 19), or by Mark Tushnet, Review of Schauer's *Playing with the Rules* (1992) 90 *Michigan Law Review* 1560 ("for 'playing by the rules' to be a coherent practice, Sylvester must be different from Susan, but for rules to constrain because of their semantic autonomy, Sylvester must be part of the same linguistic community as Susan", at 1567) are reinforced by chs. 6, 7 and 9 of the present book. Schauer's proposal requires more than a common linguistic community. It requires a linguistic community sharing a univocal determination of the rule.

this opportunity will lead to a dulling of its exercise in practice; a promotion of distorted theory, which sucks intellectual energy from consideration of the practice of law into introspection on artificial theoretical concerns; and, in general, a failure to portray "everything as it is".

Bibliography

Bruce Ackerman, "Four Questions for Legal Theory" in Pennock and Chapman (eds.) (1980)

T.R.S. Allan, "Comment: The Rule of Law as the Foundation of Judicial Review" in Forsyth (ed.) (2000)

Bruce Anderson, *"Discovery" in Legal Decision-Making* (Dordrecht, Kluwer, 1996)

Arthur Applbaum, "Are Lawyers Liars?" (1998) 4 *Legal Theory* 63

Thomas Aquinas, *Summa Theologiae*, with English translation (London, Blackfriars/Eyre & Spottiswoode, 1966)

Aristophanes, *Lysistrata* in the Loeb edition, *Aristophanes* III, with translation by Benjamin Bickley Rogers (London, William Heinemann, 1924)

Aristotle, *Nichomachean Ethics*, Loeb edition with translation by H Rackham (Cambridge, MA, Harvard University Press, 1934)

—— *On Interpretation* in *The Organon* I, Loeb edition with translation by Harold Cooke (Cambridge, MA, Harvard University Press, 1938)

—— *Politics*, Loeb edition with translation by H Rackham (Cambridge, MA, Harvard University Press, 1932)

Ahilan Arulanantham, "Breaking the Rules: Wittgenstein and Legal Realism" (1998) 107 *Yale Law Journal* 1853

John Austin, *The Province of Jurisprudence Determined*, Wilfrid Rumble (ed.) (Cambridge, Cambridge University Press, 1995)

Stephen Bailey, "Comment: Judicial Review in a Modern Context" in Forsyth (ed.) (2000)

Gordon Baker, "Following Wittgenstein: Some Signposts for *Philosophical Investigations* §§ 143–242" in Holtzman and Leich (eds.) (1981)

G.P. Baker and P.M.S. Hacker, *Wittgenstein: Rules, Grammar and Necessity* (Oxford, Basil Blackwell, 1985)

J.M. Balkin and Sanford Levinson, "Getting Serious About 'Taking Legal Reasoning Seriously' " (1999) 74 *Chicago-Kent Law Review* 543

N.W. Barber, "Sovereignty Re-examined: The Courts, Parliament, and Statutes" (2000) 20 *Oxford Journal of Legal Studies* 131

Kit Barker, Review of David Wright's *The Remedial Constructive Trust* (1999) 13 *Trust Law International* 204

John Bell, *Policy Arguments in Judicial Decisions* (Oxford, Clarendon Press, 1983)

Oren Ben-Dor, *Constitutional Limits and the Public Sphere: A Critical Study of Bentham's Constitutionalism* (Oxford, Hart Publishing, 2000)

Peter Birks, "Historical Context" in Birks (ed.) (1994)

—— (ed.), *Reviewing Legal Education* (Oxford, Oxford University Press, 1994)

—— Editor's Preface in Birks (ed.) (1996)

—— (ed.), *Pressing Problems in the Law, vol. 2, What are Law Schools for?* (Oxford, Oxford University Press, 1996)

—— "The Academic and the Practitioner" (1998) 18 *Legal Studies* 397

Peter Birks, Review of David Wright's *The Remedial Constructive Trust* (1999) 115 *Law Quarterly Review* 681

—— "Mistakes of Law" (2000) 53 *Current Legal Problems* 205

Brian Bix, *Law, Language, and Legal Determinacy* (Oxford, Clarendon Press, 1993)

—— "Conceptual Questions and Jurisprudence" (1995) 1 *Legal Theory* 465

—— (ed.), *Analyzing Law: New Essays in Legal Theory* (Oxford, Clarendon Press, 1998)

—— "Conceptual Jurisprudence and Socio-Legal Studies" (2000) 32 *Rutgers Law Journal* 227

Simon Blackburn, *The Oxford Dictionary of Philosophy* (Oxford, Oxford University Press, 1994)

Philip Bobbitt, *Constitutional Interpretation* (Oxford, Blackwell, 1991)

—— "Reflections Inspired by My Critics" (1994) 72 *Texas Law Review* 1869

Anthony Bradney, "An educational ambition for 'law and literature' " (2000) 7 *International Journal of the Legal Profession* 343

Patrick Brennan, "Discovering the Archimedean Element in (Judicial) Judgment" (1998) 17 *Law and Philosophy* 177

Scott Brewer, "Exemplary Reasoning: Semantics, Pragmatics, and the Rational Force of Legal Argument by Analogy" (1996) 109 *Harvard Law Review* 923

David Brink, "Semantics and Legal Interpretation (Further Thoughts)" (1989) 2 *Canadian Journal of Law and Jurisprudence* 181

Michael Brint and William Weaver (eds.), *Pragmatism in Law and Society* (Boulder, CO, Westview Press, 1991)

Harold Brown, "Why Do Conceptual Analysts Disagree?" (1999) 30 *Metaphilosophy* 33

W.W. Buckland, *A Text-book of Roman Law*, Peter Stein (ed.), rev 3ed (Cambridge, Cambridge University Press, 1975)

Nicholas Bunnin and E.P. Tsui-James (eds.), *The Blackwell Companion to Philosophy* (Oxford, Blackwell, 1996)

Ronald Butler, "Aristotle's Sea Fight and Three-Valued Logic" (1955) 64 *Philosophical Review* 264

Emilios Christodoulidis, *Law and Reflexive Politics* (Dordrecht, Kluwer, 1998)

Morris Cohen, "Jurisprudence as a Philosophical Discipline" (1913) 10 *Journal of Philosophy Psychology and Scientific Methods* 225

Jules Coleman, "Truth and Objectivity in Law" (1995) 1 *Legal Theory* 33

Dirmid Collis (ed.), *Arctic Languages: An Awakening* (Paris, Unesco, 1990)

James Conant, Introduction to Putnam (1990)

Roger Cotterrell, "Pandora's box: jurisprudence in legal education" (2000) 7 *International Journal of the Legal Profession* 179

Sean Coyle, "Our Knowledge of the Legal Order" (1999) 5 *Legal Theory* 389

Paul Craig, "Formal and Substantive Conceptions of the Rule of Law: An Analytical Framework" [1997] *Public Law* 466

—— "*Ultra Vires* and the Foundations of Judicial Review" (1998) 57 *Cambridge Law Journal* 63 (also in Forsyth (ed.) (2000))

—— "Competing Models of Judicial Review" [1999] *Public Law* 428 (also in Forsyth (ed.) (2000))

—— "Public Law, Political Theory and Legal Theory" [2000] *Public Law* 211

Fred D'Agostino, *Free Public Reason: Making It Up As We Go* (New York, NY, Oxford University Press, 1996)

Donald Davidson, "On the Very Idea of a Conceptual Scheme" (1974) 47 *Proceedings and Addresses of the American Philosophical Association* 5

Martin Davies, "Philosophy of Language" in Nicholas Bunnin and E.P. Tsui-James (eds.) (1996)

Martin Dixon, "The Non-Proprietary Lease: The Rise of the Feudal Phoenix" (2000) 59 *Cambridge Law Journal* 25

Louis-Jacques Dorais, "The Canadian Inuit and their Language" in Collis (ed.) (1990)

Costas Douzinas, *The End of Human Rights* (Oxford, Hart Publishing, 2000)

Antony Duff (ed.), *Philosophy and the Criminal Law* (Cambridge, Cambridge University Press, 1998)

Michael Dummett, "Wang's Paradox" (1975) 30 *Synthèse* 301 (also published as ch. 15 of *Truth and Other Enigmas*)

—— *Truth and Other Enigmas* (London, Duckworth, 1978)

Neil Duxbury, "Truth as Rhetoric" (1999) 12 *Ratio Juris* 116

—— *Jurists and Judges: An Essay on Influence* (Oxford, Hart Publishing, 2001)

Ronald Dworkin, "Judicial Discretion" (1963) 60 *Journal of Philosophy* 624

—— *Taking Rights Seriously* (London, Duckworth, 1977)

—— "No Right Answer?" in Hacker and Raz (eds.) (1977), revised in (1978) 53 *New York University Law Review* 1, reproduced as "Is There Really No Right Answer in Hard Cases?" in *A Matter of Principle* ch. 5

—— *A Matter of Principle* (Cambridge, MA, Harvard University Press, 1985)

—— *Law's Empire* (London, Collins, 1986)

—— "Pragmatism, Right Answers, and True Banality" in Brint and Weaver (eds.) (1991)

—— *Freedom's Law: The Moral Reading of the American Constitution* (Cambridge, MA, Harvard University Press, 1996)

David Dyzenhaus (ed.), *Recrafting the Rule of Law: The Limits of Legal Order* (Oxford, Hart Publishing, 1999)

—— "Form and Substance in the Rule of Law: A Democratic Justification for Judicial Review" in Forsyth (ed.) (2000)

Harry Edwards, "The Growing Disjunction between Legal Education and the Legal Profession" (1992) 91 *Michigan Law Review* 34

—— "The Growing Disjunction between Legal Education and the Legal Profession: A Postscript" (1993) 91 *Michigan Law Review* 2191

—— "Collegiality and Decision Making on the D.C. Circuit" (1998) 84 *Virginia Law Review* 1335

Louis Eisenstein, "Some Iconoclastic Reflections on Tax Administration" (1945) 58 *Harvard Law Review* 477

Mark Elliott, "The *Ultra Vires* Doctrine in a Constitutional Setting: Still the Central Principle of Administrative Law" (1999) 58 *Cambridge Law Journal* 129 (also in Forsyth (ed.) (2000))

—— "The Demise of Parliamentary Sovereignty? The Implications for Justifying Judicial Review" (1999) 115 *Law Quarterly Review* 119

—— "Fundamental Rights as Interpretative Constructs: The Constitutional Logic of the Human Rights Act 1998" in Forsyth (ed.) (2000)

—— "Legislative Intention Versus Judicial Creativity? Administrative Law as a Co-operative Endeavour" in Forsyth (ed.) (2000)

Evelyn Ellis (ed.), *The Principle of Proportionality in the Laws of Europe* (Oxford, Hart Publishing, 1999)

Timothy Endicott, "Linguistic Indeterminacy" (1996) 16 *Oxford Journal of Legal Studies* 667

—— *Vagueness in Law* (Oxford, Oxford University Press, 2000)

Joel Feinberg, *Rights, Justice and the Bounds of Liberty* (Princeton, NJ, Princeton University Press, 1980)

David Feldman, "Human Dignity as a Legal Value—Part I" [1999] *Public Law* 682

—— "Human Dignity as a Legal Value—Part II" [2000] *Public Law* 61

—— "Convention Rights and Substantive *Ultra Vires*" in Forsyth (ed.) (2000)

Helen Fenwick, "The Right to Protest, the Human Rights Act and the Margin of Appreciation" (1999) 62 *Modern Law Review* 491

Kit Fine, "Vagueness, Truth, and Logic" (1975) 30 *Synthèse* 265

John Finnis, *Natural Law and Natural Rights* (Oxford, Clarendon Press, 1980)

—— *Aquinas* (Oxford, Clarendon Press, 1998)

Stanley Fish, "Dennis Martinez and the Uses of Theory" (1987) 96 *Yale Law Journal* 1773

—— *Doing What Comes Naturally: Change, Rhetoric, and the Practice of Theory in Literary and Legal Studies* (Oxford, Clarendon Press, 1989)

—— "How Come You Do Me Like You Do? A Reply to Dennis Patterson" (1993) 72 *Texas Law Review* 57

—— *The Trouble with Principle* (Cambridge, MA, Harvard University Press, 1999)

George Fletcher, "The Fall and Rise of Criminal Theory" (1998) 1 *Buffalo Criminal Law Review* 275

Caroline Forell and Donna Matthews, *A Law of Her Own: The Reasonable Woman as a Measure of Man* (New York, NY, New York University Press, 2000)

Christopher Forsyth, "Of Fig Leaves and Fairy Tales: The *Ultra Vires* Doctrine, the Sovereignty of Parliament and Judicial Review" (1996) 55 *Cambridge Law Journal* 122 (also in Forsyth (ed.) (2000))

—— "Heat and Light: A Plea for Reconciliation" in Forsyth (ed.) (2000)

—— (ed.), *Judicial Review and the Constitution* (Oxford, Hart Publishing, 2000)

Andrew Fraser, "Beyond the Charter Debate: Republicanism, Rights and Civic Virtue in the Civil Constitution of Canadian Society" (1993) 1 *Review of Constitutional Studies* 27

Sandra Fredman, "Judging Democracy: The Role of the Judiciary Under the Human Rights Act 1998" (2000) 53 *Current Legal Problems* 99

Michael Freeden, *Ideologies and Political Theory: A Conceptual Approach* (Oxford, Clarendon Press, 1996)

W.B. Gallie, "Essentially Contested Concepts" (1956) 56 *Proceedings of the Aristotelian Society* 167

John Gardner, "Criminal Law and the Uses of Theory: A Reply to Laing" (1994) 14 *Oxford Journal of Legal Studies* 217

Robert George, *Making Men Moral: Civil Liberties and Public Morality* (Oxford, Clarendon Press, 1993)

—— (ed.), *The Autonomy of Law* (Oxford, Clarendon Press, 1996)

Raymond Geuss, *The Idea of a Critical Theory: Habermas and the Frankfurt School* (Cambridge, Cambridge University Press, 1981)

Robert Goff, "The Maccabean Lecture: The Search for Principle" (1983) 69 *Proceedings of the British Academy* 169

—— "The Mental Element in the Crime of Murder" (1988) 104 *Law Quarterly Review* 30

Jeffrey Goldsworthy, *The Sovereignty of Parliament: History and Philosophy* (Oxford, Clarendon Press, 1999)

Kent Greenawalt, "Discretion and Judicial Decision: The Elusive Quest for the Fetters that Bind Judges" (1975) 75 *Columbia Law Review* 359

John Griffith, "Judges and the Constitution" in Rawlings (ed.) (1997)

——— "The Brave New World of Sir John Laws" (2000) 63 *Modern Law Review* 159

Susan Haack, *Manifesto of a Passionate Moderate: Unfashionable Essays* (Chicago, University of Chicago Press, 1998)

Jürgen Habermas, "Reconciliation through the Public Use of Reason: Remarks on John Rawls' Political Liberalism" (1995) 42 *Journal of Philosophy* 111

P.M.S. Hacker and J Raz (eds.), *Law, Morality and Society* (Oxford, Clarendon Press, 1977)

Andrew Halpin, "The Limitations of a Legal System" [1981] *Juridical Review* 29

——— "The Test for Dishonesty" [1996] *Criminal Law Review* 283

——— "Law, Libel and the English Court of Appeal" (1996) 4 *Tort Law Review* 139

——— *Rights and Law—Analysis and Theory* (Oxford, Hart Publishing, 1997)

——— "Definitions and directions: recklessness unheeded" (1998) 18 *Legal Studies* 294

——— "Concepts, Terms, and Fields of Enquiry" (1998) 4 *Legal Theory* 187

Learned Hand, "Chief Justice Stone's Conception of the Judicial Function" (1946) 46 *Columbia Law Review* 696

Alon Harel, "The Rule of Law and Judicial Review: Reflections on the Israeli Constitutional Revolution" in Dyzenhaus (ed.) (1999)

J.W. Harris, "Unger's Critique of Formalism in Legal Reasoning: Hero, Hercules, and Humdrum" (1989) 52 *Modern Law Review* 42

H.L.A. Hart, *The Concept of Law* 1ed (Oxford, Clarendon Press, 1961)

Colin Harvey (ed.), *Human Rights, Equality and Democratic Renewal in Northern Ireland* (Oxford, Hart Publishing, 2001)

R.F.V. Heuston, *Essays in Constitutional Law* 2ed (London, Stevens & Sons, 1964)

L.H. Hoffman, Review of Simon Lee's *Judging Judges* (1989) 105 *Law Quarterly Review* 140

Steven Holtzman and Christopher Leich (eds.), *Wittgenstein: to Follow a Rule* (London, Routledge & Kegan Paul, 1981)

Ted Honderich (ed.), *The Oxford Companion to Philosophy* (Oxford, Oxford University Press, 1995)

Tony Honoré, Review of Jensen's *The Nature of Legal Argument* (1958) 74 *Law Quarterly Review* 296

Alan Hunt, "Jurisprudence, philosophy and legal education—against foundationalism" (1986) 6 *Legal Studies* 292

Lord Irvine, "Judges and Decision-Makers: The Theory and Practice of *Wednesbury* Review" [1996] *Public Law* 59

David Jabbari, "Reason, Cause and Principle in Law: The Normativity of Context" (1999) 19 *Oxford Journal of Legal Studies* 203

——— "Radical Particularism: A Natural Law of Context" (1999) 50 *Northern Ireland Legal Quarterly* 454

Frank Jackson, *From Metaphysics to Ethics: A Defence of Conceptual Analysis* (Oxford, Clarendon Press, 1998)

Francis Jacobs, "Recent Developments in the Principle of Proportionality in European Community Law" in Ellis (ed.) (1999)

Louis Jaffe, *Judicial Control of Administrative Action* (Boston, MA, Little, Brown & Co, 1965)

Jacob Janzen, "Some Formal Aspects of Ronald Dworkin's Right Answer Thesis" (1981) 11 *Manitoba Law Journal* 191

O.C. Jensen, *The Nature of Legal Argument* (Oxford, Blackwell, 1957)

Paul Johnston, *The Contradictions of Modern Moral Philosophy: Ethics after Wittgenstein* (London, Routledge, 1999)

Jeffrey Jowell, "Of *Vires* and Vacuums: The Constitutional Context of Judicial Review" [1999] *Public Law* 448 (also in Forsyth (ed.) (2000))

Justinian, *Institutes*, J.B. Moyle (ed.) 5ed (Oxford, Clarendon Press, 1912)

Matthew Kramer, "Coming to Grips With the Law: In Defense of Positive Legal Positivism" (1999) 5 *Legal Theory* 171

Saul Kripke, *Wittgenstein on Rules and Private Language: An Elementary Exposition* (Cambridge, MA, Harvard University Press, 1982)

Nicola Lacey, *Unspeakable Subjects: Feminist Essays in Legal and Social Theory* (Oxford, Hart Publishing, 1998)

—— "Philosophy, History and Criminal Law Theory" (1998) 1 *Buffalo Criminal Law Review* 295

—— Review of Michael Moore's *Placing Blame: A General Theory of the Criminal Law* (2000) 63 *Modern Law Review* 141

J.A. Laing, "The Prospects of a Theory of Criminal Culpability: Mens Rea and Methodological Doubt" (1994) 14 *Oxford Journal of Legal Studies* 57

Scott Landers, "Wittgenstein, Realism, and CLS" (1990) 9 *Law and Philosophy* 177

Sir John Laws, "Law and Democracy" [1995] *Public Law* 72

—— "The Problem of Jurisdiction" (from Supperstone and Goudie (eds.) (1997)) in Forsyth (ed.) (2000)

—— "The Limitations of Human Rights" [1998] *Public Law* 254

—— "Judicial Review and the Meaning of Law" in Forsyth (ed.) (2000)

Brian Leiter, "The Middle Way" (1995) 1 *Legal Theory* 21

Edward Levi, *An Introduction to Legal Reasoning* (Chicago, IL, University of Chicago Press, 1949)

David Lewis, "How to Define Theoretical Terms" (1970) 67 *Journal of Philosophy* 427

—— *On the Plurality of Worlds* (Oxford, Blackwell, 1986)

Martin Loughlin, "Comment: Whither the Constitution?" in Forsyth (ed.) (2000)

—— *Sword and Scales: An Examination of the Relationship between Law and Politics* (Oxford, Hart Publishing, 2000)

David Luban, "Reason and Passion in Legal Ethics" (1999) 51 *Stanford Law Review* 873

Jan Łukasiewicz, *Selected Works*, L Borkowski (ed.) (Amsterdam, North-Holland Publishing Company, 1970)

William Lycan, *Philosophy of Language: A contemporary introduction* (London, Routledge, 2000)

David Lyon, *Postmodernity* 2ed (Buckingham, Open University Press, 1999)

Gerald MacCallum, "Dworkin on Judicial Discretion" (1963) 60 *Journal of Philosophy* 638

Neil MacCormick, "The Democratic Intellect and the law" (1985) 5 *Legal Studies* 172

—— "The Legal Framework: Institutional Normative Order" in *Questioning Sovereignty*

—— *Questioning Sovereignty: Law, State, and Nation in the European Commonwealth* (Oxford, Oxford University Press, 1999)

Neil MacCormick and William Twining, "Theory in the Law Curriculum" in Twining (1997) (previously published in Twining (ed.) (1986))

—— and Ota Weinberger, *An Institutional Theory of Law: New Approaches to Legal Positivism* (Dordrecht, D Reidel Publishing, 1986)

—— and Robert Summers (eds.), *Interpreting Precedents* (Aldershot, Dartmouth, 1997)

Paul Mahoney, "Marvelous Richness of Diversity or Invidious Cultural Relativism?" (1998) 19 *Human Rights Law Journal* 1

Kate Malleson, *The New Judiciary: The Effects of Expansion and Activism* (Aldershot, Ashgate, 1999)

Richard Markovits, "Legitimate Legal Argument and Internally-Right Answers to Legal-Rights Questions" (1999) 74 *Chicago-Kent Law Review* 415

—— " 'You Cannot Be Serious!': A Reply to Professors Balkin and Levinson" (1999) 74 *Chicago-Kent Law Review* 559

Andrei Marmor, *Interpretation and Legal Theory* (Oxford, Clarendon Press, 1992)

—— "An Essay on The Objectivity of Law" in Bix (ed.) (1998)

Andrew Mason, "On Explaining Political Disagreement: The Notion of an Essentially Contested Concept" (1990) 33 *Inquiry* 81

Robert Merton, *Social Theory and Social Structure* (New York, NY, The Free Press, 1968)

Eleni Mitrophanous, "Soft Positivism" (1997) 17 *Oxford Journal of Legal Studies* 621

Ray Monk, *Ludwig Wittgenstein: The Duty of Genius* (London, Jonathan Cape, 1990)

Michael Moore, "A Natural Law Theory of Interpretation" (1985) 58 *Southern California Law Review* 277

—— "Metaphysics, Epistemology and Legal Theory" (1987) 60 *Southern California Law Review* 453

—— "The Interpretive Turn in Modern Theory: A Turn for the Worse?" (1989) 41 *Stanford Law Review* 871 (also published as ch. 10 of *Educating Oneself in Public*)

—— *Placing Blame: A General Theory of the Criminal Law* (Oxford, Clarendon Press, 1997)

—— *Educating Oneself in Public* (New York, NY, Oxford University Press, 2000)

Thomas Morawetz, *Law's Premises, Law's Promise: Jurisprudence after Wittgenstein* (Aldershot, Ashgate, 2000)

Michael Naish, "Education and Essential Contestability Revisited" (1984) 18 *Journal of Philosophy of Education* 141

Alan Norrie, *Punishment, Responsibility, and Justice: A Relational Critique* (Oxford, Oxford University Press, 2000)

Christopher Norris, *Deconstruction and the Interests of Theory* (London, Pinter Publishers, 1988)

Martha Nussbaum, "Skepticism about Practical Reason in Literature and the Law" (1994) 107 *Harvard Law Review* 714

Dawn Oliver, "Is the *Ultra Vires* Rule the Basis of Judicial Review?" [1987] *Public Law* 543 (also in Forsyth (ed.) (2000))

—— "The Underlying Values of Public and Private Law" in Taggart (ed.) (1997)

—— *Common Values and the Public-Private Divide* (London, Butterworths, 1999)

—— "Review of (Non-Statutory) Discretions" in Forsyth (ed.) (2000)

Henrik Palmer Olsen and Stuart Toddington, *Law in Its Own Right* (Oxford, Hart Publishing, 1999)

Oxford English Dictionary, 2ed prepared by J.A. Simpson and E.C.S. Weiner (Oxford, Clarendon Press, 1989)

Stephanie Palmer, "Human Rights: Implications for Labour Law" (2000) 59 *Cambridge Law Journal* 168

Enrico Pattaro, "On the Nature of Legal Science" in Weinberger, Koller and Schramm (eds.) (1988)

Dennis Patterson, "Realist Semantics and Legal Theory" (1989) 2 *Canadian Journal of Law and Jurisprudence* 175

—— "What Was Realism?: A Reply to David Brink" (1989) 2 *Canadian Journal of Law and Jurisprudence* 193

—— (ed.), *Wittgenstein and Legal Theory* (Boulder, CO, Westview Press, 1992)

—— "You Made Me Do It: My Reply to Stanley Fish" (1993) 72 *Texas Law Review* 67

—— "Wittgenstein and Constitutional Theory" (1994) 72 *Texas Law Review* 1837

—— *Law and Truth* (New York, NY, Oxford University Press, 1996)

—— "*Law and Truth*: Replies to Critics" (1997) 50 *SMU Law Review* 1563

—— "On Rhetoric and Truth: A Reply to Neil Duxbury" (2000) 13 *Ratio Juris* 216

Christopher Peacocke, *A Study of Concepts* (Cambridge, MA, MIT Press, 1992)

James Penner, *The Idea of Property in Law* (Oxford, Clarendon Press, 1997)

J Roland Pennock and John Chapman (eds.), *Nomos XXII: Property* (New York, NY, New York University Press, 1980)

Terri Peretti, *In Defense of a Political Court* (Princeton, NJ, Princeton University Press, 1999)

Gavin Phillipson, "The Human Rights Act, 'Horizontal Effect' and the Common Law: a Bang or a Whimper?" (1999) 62 *Modern Law Review* 824

Anna Pintore, *Law without Truth* (Liverpool, Deborah Charles Publications, 2000)

Plato, *Republic*, Loeb edition with translation by Paul Shorey (London, William Heinemann, 1935)

Richard Posner, *Overcoming Law* (Cambridge, MA, Harvard University Press, 1995)

Gerald Postema, "Law's Autonomy and Public Practical Reason" in George (ed.) (1996)

Roscoe Pound, "The Decadence of Equity" (1905) 5 *Columbia Law Review* 20

—— "Do We Need a Philosophy of Law?" (1905) 5 *Columbia Law Review* 339

—— "The Call for a Realist Jurisprudence" (1931) 44 *Harvard Law Review* 697

A.N. Prior, "Three-Valued Logic and Future Contingents" (1953) 3 *Philosophical Quarterly* 317

Hilary Putnam, *Reason, Truth and History* (Cambridge, Cambridge University Press, 1981)

—— *Realism with a Human Face* (Cambridge, MA, Harvard University Press, 1990)

—— *Renewing Philosophy* (Cambridge, MA, Harvard University Press, 1992)

—— "Sense, Nonsense and the Senses: An Inquiry into the Powers of the Human Mind" (1994) 91 *Journal of Philosophy* 445 (also published as part 1 of *The Threefold Cord*)

—— "Are Moral and Legal Values Made or Discovered?" (1995) 1 *Legal Theory* 1

—— "Replies" (1995) 1 *Legal Theory* 69

—— *The Threefold Cord: Mind, Body, and World* (New York, NY, Columbia University Press, 1999)

W.V. Quine, *Philosophy of Logic* (Englewood Cliffs, NJ, Prentice-Hall, 1970; 2ed, Cambridge, MA, Harvard University Press, 1986)

Michael Quinn, "Argument and Authority in Common Law Advocacy and Adjudication: An Irreducible Pluralism of Values" (1999) 74 *Chicago-Kent Law Review* 655

Margaret Jane Radin, "Reconsidering the Rule of Law" (1989) 69 *Boston University Law Review* 781 (also in Patterson (ed.) (1992)

Joseph Rauh, "Lawyers and the Legislation of the Early New Deal" (1983) 96 *Harvard Law Review* 947

Richard Rawlings (ed.), *Law, Society, and Economy* (Oxford, Clarendon Press, 1997)

John Rawls, *A Theory of Justice* (Oxford, Oxford University Press, 1972)

Joseph Raz, "Legal Reasons, Sources, and Gaps" (1979) *Archiv für Rechts- und Sozialphilosophie, Beiheft* 11, 197 (also published as ch. 4 of *The Authority of Law*)

—— *The Authority of Law* (Oxford, Clarendon Press, 1979)

—— *The Concept of a Legal System* 2ed (Oxford, Clarendon Press, 1980)

—— *The Morality of Freedom* (Oxford, Clarendon Press, 1986)

—— "Facing Up" (1989) 62 *Southern California Law Review* 1153

—— *Ethics in the Public Domain* (Oxford, Clarendon Press, 1994)

—— "Postema on Law's Autonomy and Public Practical Reasons: A Critical Comment" (1998) 4 *Legal Theory* 1

—— "Two Views of the Nature of the Theory of Law: A Partial Comparison" (1998) 4 *Legal Theory* 249

Richard Revesz, "Environmental Regulation, Ideology, and the D.C. Circuit" (1997) 83 *Virginia Law Review* 1717

—— "Ideology, Collegiality, and the D.C. Circuit: A Reply to Chief Judge Harry T. Edwards" (1999) 85 *Virginia Law Review* 805

Richard Robinson, *Definition* (Oxford, Clarendon Press, 1954)

Sir David Ross, *Plato's Theory of Ideas* (Oxford, Clarendon Press, 1951)

Charles Sampford, "Rethinking the Core Curiculum" (1989) 12 *Adelaide Law Review* 38

—— and David Wood, " 'Theoretical Dimensions' of Legal Education—A Response to the Pearce Report" (1988) 62 *Australian Law Journal* 32

Giovanni Sartori, *The Theory of Democracy Revisited* (Chatham, NJ, Chatham House Publishers, 1987)

Kevin Saunders, "What Logic Can and Cannot Tell Us About Law" (1998) 73 *Notre Dame Law Review* 667

Frederick Schauer, *Playing by the Rules: A Philosophical Examination of Rule-Based Decision Making in Law and in Life* (Oxford, Clarendon Press, 1991)

Frederick Schauer, "Rules and the Rule-Following Argument" in Patterson (ed.) (1992)

Jeroen Schokkenbroeck, "The Basis, Nature and Application of the Margin-of-Appreciation Doctrine in the Case-Law of the European Court of Human Rights" (1998) 19 *Human Rights Law Journal* 30

Alfred Schutz, "Concept and Theory Formation in the Social Sciences" (1954) 51 *Journal of Philosophy* 257

Sir Stephen Sedley, "Human Rights: a Twenty-First Century Agenda" [1995] *Public Law* 386

—— *Freedom, Law and Justice*, 1999 Hamlyn Lectures (London, Sweet & Maxwell, 1999)

—— "Public Power and Private Power" (from Sedley (1999)) in Forsyth (ed.) (2000)

Sextus Empiricus, *Against the Logicians* in the Loeb edition, *Sextus Empiricus* II, with translation by R.G. Bury (London, William Heinemann, 1935)

Raimo Siltala, *A Theory of Precedent* (Oxford, Hart Publishing, 2000)

Quentin Skinner, Introduction to Skinner (ed.) (1985)

Quentin Skinner, (ed.), *The Return of Grand Theory in the Human Sciences* (Cambridge, Cambridge University Press, 1985)

Keith Smith, *Lawyers, Legislators and Theorists* (Oxford, Clarendon Press, 1998)

Michael Spence, *Protecting Reliance: The Emergent Doctrine of Equitable Estoppel* (Oxford, Hart Publishing, 1999)

Nicos Stavropoulos, *Objectivity in Law* (Oxford, Clarendon Press, 1996)

Adin Steinsaltz, *The Essential Talmud* (New York, NY, Basic Books, 1976)

Julius Stone, *The Province and Function of Law: Law as Logic, Justice and Social Control* (Sydney, Maitland Publications, 1946; London, Stevens, 1947)

—— *Legal System and Lawyers' Reasonings* (Stanford, CA, Stanford University Press, 1964)

—— *Precedent and Law: Dynamics of Common Law Growth* (Sydney, Butterworths, 1985)

Robert Summers (ed.), *Essays in Legal Philosophy* (Oxford, Basil Blackwell, 1968)

Michael Supperstone and James Goudie (eds.), *Judicial Review* 2ed (London, Butterworths, 1997)

The Supreme Court Practice 1997 (London, Sweet & Maxwell, 1996)

Michael Taggart (ed.), *The Province of Administrative Law* (Oxford, Hart Publishing, 1997)

—— "*Ultra Vires* as Distraction" in Forsyth (ed.) (2000)

Brian Tamanaha, *Realistic Socio-Legal Theory: Pragmatism and a Social Theory of Law* (Oxford, Clarendon Press, 1997)

—— "Conceptual Analysis, Continental Social Theory, and CLS: A Response to Bix, Rubin and Livingston" (2000) 32 *Rutgers Law Journal* 281

Philip Thomas (ed.), *Legal Frontiers* (Aldershot, Dartmouth, 1996)

Dennis Töllborg, "Law as Value" (1998) 84 *Archiv für Rechts- und Sozialphilosophie* 489

Mark Tushnet, Review of Frederick Schauer's *Playing with the Rules* (1992) 90 *Michigan Law Review* 1560

William Twining (ed.), *Legal Theory and Common Law* (Oxford, Basil Blackwell, 1986)

—— *Blackstone's Tower* (London, Sweet & Maxwell, 1994)

—— *Law in Context: Enlarging a Discipline* (Oxford, Clarendon Press, 1997)

—— *Globalisation and Legal Theory* (London, Butterworths, 2000)

R.C. Van Caenegem, *Judges, Legislators and Professors: Chapters in European Legal History* (Cambridge, Cambridge University Press, 1987)

Walter van Gerven, "The Effect of Proportionality on the Actions of Member States of the European Community: National Viewpoints from Continental Europe" in Ellis (ed.) (1999)

Adrian Vermeule and Ernest Young, "Hercules, Herbert, and Amar: The Trouble with *Intratextualism*" (2000) 113 *Harvard Law Review* 730

Sir William Wade, "Comment: Constitutional Realities and Judicial Prudence" in Forsyth (ed.) (2000)

Neil Walker, "Setting English Judges to Rights" (1999) 19 *Oxford Journal of Legal Studies* 133

W.J. Waluchow, *Inclusive Legal Positivism* (Oxford, Clarendon Press, 1994)

Max Weber, "Value-judgments in Social Science" in W.G. Runciman (ed.), *Max Weber* (Cambridge, Cambridge University Press, 1978)

Ota Weinberger, Peter Koller and Alfred Schramm (eds.), *Philosophy of Law, Politics, and Society* (Vienna, Hölder-Pichler-Tempsky, 1988)

Glanville Williams, "The Concept of Legal Liberty" (1956) 56 *Columbia Law Review* 1129 (also in Summers (ed.) (1968))

—— "The Lords and Impossible Attempts, or *Quis Custodiet Ipsos Custodes?*" (1986) 45 *Cambridge Law Journal* 33

Peter Winch, *The Idea of a Social Science* (London, Routledge & Kegan Paul, 1958)

Steven Winter, "Bull Durham and the Uses of Theory" (1990) 42 *Stanford Law Review* 639

—— "The Constitution of Conscience" (1994) 72 *Texas Law Review* 1805

—— "One Size Fits All" (1994) 72 *Texas Law Review* 1857

Ludwig Wittgenstein, *Tractatus Logico-Philosophicus*, C.K. Ogden and F.P. Ramsey transl (London, Routledge, 1922) (subsequently translated by D.F. Pears and B.F. McGuinness (London, Routledge, 1961))

—— *Philosophical Investigations*, G.E.M. Anscombe transl, 2ed (Oxford, Basil Blackwell, 1958)

Louis Wolcher, "Ronald Dworkin's Right Answer Thesis through the Lens of Wittgenstein" (1997) 29 *Rutgers Law Journal* 43

Lord Woolf, "Droit Public—English Style" [1995] *Public Law* 57

—— "The Legal Education the Justice System Requires Today" (2000) 34 *The Law Teacher* 263

David Wright, *The Remedial Constructive Trust* (Sydney, Butterworths, 1998)

Charles Yablon, "Law and Metaphysics" (1987) 96 *Yale Law Journal* 613

—— "Justifying the Judge's Hunch: An Essay on Discretion" (1990) 41 *Hastings Law Journal* 231

David Yalof, *Pursuit of Justices: Presidential Politics and the Selection of Supreme Court Nominees* (Chicago, IL, Chicago University Press, 1999)

John Yoo, "Choosing Justices: a Political Appointments Process and the Wages of Judicial Supremacy" (2000) 98 *Michigan Law Review* 1436

Index